Hawai'i Wetland Field Guide

*an ecological and identification guide
to wetlands and wetland plants
of the Hawaiian Islands*

TERRELL A. ERICKSON
CHRISTOPHER F. PUTTOCK

photographer
LAURA M. CRAGO

Funded by
Environmental Protection Agency
grant CD-96911601-0 to
Hawai'i Department of Land and Natural Resources/
Division of Forestry and Wildlife

Honolulu

This field guide was made possible by a U.S. Environmental Protection Agency grant CD - 96911601-0 to the Hawai'i Department of Land and Natural Resources/Division of Forestry and Wildlife. The views and opinions expressed in this publication do not necessarily represent those of the agencies that provided support for this project. The first printing of this field guide was made possible by generous support from the Cooke and Engelhardt Foundations.

Printed in China
First edition. First printing

Library of Congress Cataloging-in-Publication Data
Erickson, Terrell A. (Terrell Ann), 1962–
  Hawai'i wetland field guide : an ecological and identification guide to wetlands and wetland plants of the Hawaiian Islands / Terrell A. Erickson and Christopher F. Puttock.
    p.   cm.
  Includes bibliographical references.
  ISBN 1–57306–268–5 (pbk. alk. paper)
  1. Wetland plants – Hawaii – Identification.   2. Wetland ecology – Hawaii.
  3. Wetlands – Hawaii.   4. Wetland plants – Hawaii.   5. Phytogeography – Hawaii.
  I. Puttock, Christopher F. 1954– II. Title.
  QK938.M3.E75 2006   581.9794–dc21

Designed by Christopher F. Puttock
Photography by Laura M. Crago (unless otherwise indicated)
Illustrations by Christopher F. Puttock (unless otherwise indicated)

Distributed by Bess Press Books, Honolulu, Hawai'i

All proceeds from the sale of this publication go to the "Hawai'i Wetlands Research and Restoration Fund" managed by the Hawai'i Conservation Alliance.

This book is dedicated to the conservation of Hawaii's wetlands

— and the one that brought the editors together —
— Waipiʻo Valley, Hawaiʻi —

— and to —

— R. Lani Stemmermann —
— (1953–1995) —

CONTENTS

PREFACE

This field guide is for those who love wetlands and recognize wetlands as being an integral and vital part of all tropical ecosystems. We also designed it for those who are fortunate enough to have wetlands as part of their work, particularly those involved in wetland delineations, assessments, monitoring and planning. The plant descriptions, keys, photographs and notes will be useful for all plant and wildlife naturalists who would like to learn about wetland ecosystems in Hawai'i. Some knowledge of wetland identification procedures, wetland ecology and botany is assumed. This field guide is intended to be used in the field. It is not intended to replace wetland textbooks, agency manuals or other plant and animal guides.

One must be a sleuth to recognize a wetland — to determine its boundaries, to interpret hydrology and hydric soils, to identify the plants, and to understand its ecological complexities. This field guide provides a major piece of the puzzle. It illustrates 208 wetland plants commonly found in Hawaii's lowlands. It describes wetland soils and hydrology, and restoration and mitigation concepts relevant to the islands. It also includes some of Hawaii's unique wetland animals: endangered birds, native fish and shellfish, and rare and declining native insects.

We also present a new analysis protocol for wetlands. It recognizes five basic wetland types in Hawai'i: coastal flat, anchialine pool, estuarine wetland, palustrine wetland and bog. This protocol was developed to better describe the underlying abiotic factors and cycles that coalesce to form a particular wetland type. Understanding the underlying processes of a wetland, such as its geomorphology and flow regime, can ensure greater success in mitigation and restoration projects, and ensure wetland survival and sustainability in the next millennia.

The selection of the 208 plants in this field guide was based upon the wetland status as determined for the revised *Wetland Status List for Hawaiian Plants* (Puttock & Imada 2004), and whether the plants are commonly encountered in lowland wetlands, those places most readily accessible and most likely to be impacted by developmental pressure. Several uncommon species were included because they may have been previously overlooked, or could be anticipated, at lower elevations.

Wetlands in Hawai'i are captivating places. Take the time to identify the plants and get dirty in the muck and colorful soils. Watch for aquatic animals dependent on wetlands. Travel around the islands and note the diversity of wetland habitats. Be passionate, for wetlands' sake, as are the authors of this field guide.

Terrell Erickson and Christopher Puttock
February 24, 2006

ACKNOWLEDGMENTS

More than a decade ago in wetlands of East Moloka'i, *Adam Asquith* suggested that I write a wetlands field guide; thank you, Adam. Until now, the only field resource for wetland plants in the Pacific region was Lani Stemmermann's 1981 "*A Guide to Pacific Wetland Plants*". This well-used and repeatedly photocopied booklet has been THE handbook of every student that wandered into these amazing places. With gratitude, this field guide is dedicated to Lani.

This field guide would not have been produced over the past 15 months without the collaboration, cooperation and assistance of many people, and without significant financial support. Special kudos to *Wendy Wiltse* and *Kathy Dadey* for recognizing the need for this work and encouraging Chris and me to apply for an Environmental Protection Agency (EPA) grant, and to *Mary Butterwick* of EPA (Region 9 Office) for her foresight, oversight and evaluation once this project got underway.

The "Hawai'i Wetland Field Guide" project was funded by EPA through Hawaii's Department of Land and Natural Resources (DLNR) in October 2004. *Mahalo nui loa* to the folks at DLNR for their support and drive for restoration and research of wetlands in the state: *Paul Conry*, for his support of aquatic programs and this project; we're all glad you are supervisor and head of Division of Forestry and Wildlife (DOFAW); *David Smith*, for his extraordinary talents, bringing wetland proponents together every year, restoring wetlands in the state, and agreeing to oversee this grant for us; and *Christina McGuire*, for her administration of this grant.

To all of the contributors of the ecology section: *Kim Uyehara*, private consultant, for her dedication to Hawaii's waterbirds, and her research on *Koloa* and on Safe Harbors agreements for private landowners; *Mike Yamamoto*, Aquatic Biologist at Division of Aquatic Resources (DLNR), for his extraordinary knowledge and field experience of fishes and shellfishes of Hawai'i; *Dan Polhemus*, Director of the Division of Aquatic Resources (DLNR) for bringing expert knowledge to the section on wetland insects, and *Ron Englund*, Research Specialist at Bishop Museum, for his collaboration and extensive field work on Hawaii's insects.

To contributors of the botany section: *Clyde Imada,* Research Specialist at Bishop Museum, for first approaching me about the need to update the wetland indicator list in 2001, his superb field knowledge of wetland plants in Hawai'i, and his skill in editing; *Derral Herbst*, exceptional botanist and Research Associate at Bishop Museum, for his unique ability to remember almost every plant he's seen in Hawai'i, and his exceptional contribution to the wetland grasses and sedges in this field guide; *Laura Crago*, Research Specialist at Bishop Museum, for her photography and curation of wetland plant materials assembled for this field guide. As photographer for the project *Laura* was ably assisted in the "lands that are wet" by *Clyde Imada, Carole Chun, Barbara Kennedy, Susan MacMillan* and *Christina McGuire*.

As part of the project design, voucher specimens were collected from virtually every plant photographed for this guide. This grant paid for the collecting, processing and databasing of these specimens so that they could be used to verify the scientific names used in this field guide, and to be kept for future reference should nomenclatural changes occur. We thank the staff and volunteers at the *Herbarium Pacificum*, Bishop Museum, the State of Hawaii's repository for botanical specimens, for housing these specimens, for maintaining the databases, and making these specimens available as a public reference collection.

A few plant and other images alluded our wetland photography team; many thanks go to the other contributors of photographs: *Army Corp of Engineers, Australian National Botanic Garden, Michelle Clark, Kerry Dressler, Ron Englund, Gary Fewless, Jack Jeffrey, David Lorence, NRCS Guam Field Office, Kim Peyton, Dan Polhemus, Forest* and *Kim Starr, Jan Surface, University of Hawai'i– Botany, Kim Uyehara, Ron Walker, Rick Warshauer, Mike Yamamoto* and *Brenda Zaun.*

This publication could not have happened without the landowners and land managers of Hawai'i who know their wetlands and graciously provided access to them for photographs and plant specimens: *Hugo DeVries, Fern Duvall, Scott Fisher, Betsy Gagné, Ranae Ganske-Cerizo, Michael Gomes, Eric Guinther, Erik and Hillery Gunther, Mike Hawkes, Josephine Hoh, David Ivy, Richard Kuitunen, David Matsuura, Jayson* and *Alberta Mock Chew, David Orr, Mike Silbernagle, Morgan Toledo, Ron Walker, Matt Wong* and *Brenda Zaun.*

I would like to acknowledge nine years at the Natural Resources Conservation Service (NRCS) in Hawai'i for providing me a job that initiated wetland restoration projects and programs for private landowners. I thank my dedicated colleagues, particularly: *Chris Smith,* Soils Scientist, for the 11 years we worked and trained field staff together in Hawaii's wetlands; *Pat Shade* for her expert GIS analyses, collaboration on the Kīhei wetlands project, creating the hydric soils maps, and for providing Mana Plains maps and photos; and to *Adonia Henry* of Ducks Unlimited for providing the information about the Mana wetlands for this manuscript.

Many people were involved in providing assistance and review of the manuscript at its various stages of development. These include: *David Burney, Mary Butterwick, Paul Conry, Laura Crago, Ronald Englund, Ron Erickson, Katherine Ewel, Scott Fisher, Betsy Gagné, Wendell Gilgert, Sam Gon III, Eric Guinther, Derral Herbst, Clyde Imada, Jim Jacobi, David Leonard, Leslie Loo, Megan Laut, Christina McGuire, Susan MacMillan, Dan Polhemus, Michelle Reynolds, Chris Smith, Jan Surface, Kim Uyehara, Rick Warshauer, Wendy Wiltse* and *Mike Yamamoto.*

Finally, thanks to *Chris Puttock,* my husband, for making it all happen.

Terrell A. Erickson
March 13, 2006

CONTRIBUTORS

Ms. Laura M. Crago, Bishop Museum
1525 Bernice St, Honolulu, HI 96817
lcrago@bishopmuseum.org

Dr. Ronald A. Englund, Bishop Museum
1525 Bernice St, Honolulu, HI 96817
englund@bishopmuuseum.org

Ms. Terrell A. Erickson
4806 Cherokee St, College Park, MD 20740
terrellerickson@aol.com

Mr. Clyde T. Imada, Bishop Museum
1525 Bernice St, Honolulu, HI 96817
cimada@bishopmuseum.org

Dr. Derral R. Herbst, c/- Bishop Museum
1525 Bernice St, Honolulu, HI 96817
dherbst@bishopmuseum.org

Dr. Daniel A. Polhemus
Division of Aquatic Resources, DLNR
1151 Punchbowl St, Honolulu, HI 96813
dan.a.polhemus@hawaii.gov

Dr. Christopher F. Puttock
Hawaii Conservation Alliance
1151 Punchbowl St, Honolulu, HI 96813
puttock@hawaii.edu

Ms. Kimberly J. Uyehara, c/- PCSU-RCUH
73-1270 Awakea Street,
Kailua-Kona, HI 96740
kjukem@lava.net

Mr. Mike N. Yamamoto
Division of Aquatic Resources, DLNR
1151 Punchbowl St, Honolulu, HI 96813
mike.yamamoto@hawaii.gov

Photographs and Illustrations (used with permission)

Army Corp of Engineers (COE) — p.46
Australian National Botanical Garden
   (ANBG) — p.205
David Burney (DB) — p.51
Michelle Clark (MC) — p.18, 74
Kerry Dressler (KD) — p.217
Ron Englund (RE) — p.35–39
Terrell Erickson (TE) — p.4, 10–15, 21–26,
   31, 45, 46, 51
Gary Fewless (GF) — p.80, 225
GretagMacBeth — p.273
Clyde Imada (CI) — p.81
Jack Jeffrey (JJ) — p.38
Robert Mohlenbrock (RM) — p.72, 188
David Lorence (DL) — p.201
Dan Polhemus (DP) p.35, 36, 37

Kim Peyton (KP) — p.78
Christopher Puttock (CP) p.24, 26, 42, 126
Forest and Kim Starr (F&KS) — p.116, 193,
   247
Jan Surface (JS) — p.10, 28
University of Hawai'i (UH) — p.66
USDA NRCS Guam Field Office (NRCS
   Guam) — p.13
USDA NRCS Hawai'i (NRCS) — p.11, 22,
   40, 274
USGS (USGS) — p.41
Kimberly Uyehara (KU) — p.52, 81
Ron Walker (RW) — p.29
Rick Warshauer (FRW) — p.93, 117, 238,
   266
Mike Yamamoto (MY) — p.32, 33, 34, 43
Brenda Zaun (BZ) — p.29

All other photography by Laura M. Crago (LC)
All other illustrations by Christopher F. Puttock (CP)

PART I

Wetland Identification and Ecology

Terrell A. Erickson (editor)

CONTRIBUTORS
Terrell A. Erickson — ecology
Kimberly J. Uyehara — birds
Mike N. Yamamoto — fishes
Dan A. Polhemus and Ronald A. Englund — insects

PART I
Wetland Identification and Ecology

A. Introduction — What are Wetlands?

Wet .... lands. Wetlands are extraordinary places. Hawaii's wetlands are no exception. Climatic variation, a wide range of topographic settings and soil conditions, and a year-round growing season sustain a remarkable range of wetland ecotypes in this state.

Among the many definitions of wetlands[1] all contain one or more of the three basic elements: hydrology, soils and vegetation. These definitions differ because they are intended for particular purposes. Some are meant for field-determined regulatory boundary determinations, while others are meant for non-regulatory inventory and planning purposes.

Since the 1980s in the United States there has been much discussion and debate about wetlands definitions and the use of field manuals. Recently the debate on how to define a wetland has subsided and is now focusing on the kinds of activities or types of wetlands regulated by federal and state government. This has led to some stability in the definition of wetlands. The following are the three most commonly used definitions in Hawai'i:

Kanahā Pond, Maui (LC)

Definition 1 (regulatory): "Those areas that are inundated or saturated by surface or groundwater at a frequency and duration sufficient to support, and that under normal circumstances do support, a prevalence of vegetation typically adapted for life in saturated soil conditions. Wetlands generally include swamps, marshes, bogs and similar areas."

---

[1] For example, South Africa uses the USFWS definition. The Australia New South Wales government defines wetlands as "lands that are inundated, on a temporary or permanent basis, with water that is usually slow moving or stationary, is shallow and may be fresh, brackish or saline." Many countries use the 1971 Ramsar World Convention definition of "areas of marsh, fen, peatland or water, whether natural or artificial, permanent or temporary, with water that is static or flowing, fresh, brackish or salt including areas of marine water, the depth of which at low tides does not exceed six metres" and "may incorporate riparian and coastal zones adjacent to the wetlands and islands." (Ramsar is the Iranian town in which participating countries first agreed on the Convention.)

Primary users: U.S. Army Corps of Engineers (COE), U.S. Environmental Protection Agency (EPA) and Hawai'i State Department of Health (HDOH).

Purpose: Wetland delineations for the Clean Water Act (CWA) regulation, and specifically by the COE and EPA to determine jurisdictional wetlands, using the 1987 COE wetland delineation manual in the field to determine boundaries.

Note: This definition is used for Hawaii's pollution control program, which includes water quality certifications to ensure federal CWA permits meet the state water quality regulations. There is a distinction between what is found to be a wetland versus what is regulated under the CWA. For instance, the Supreme Court's decision for Solid Waste Agency of Northern Cook County (SWANCC) [2] effectively precludes CWA jurisdiction over certain isolated, non-tributary and non-adjacent wetlands. Contact the local COE regulatory branch (808-438-9258) for current interpretation of "tributary" and "adjacent" in the SWANCC rule.

Definition 2 (regulatory): "Areas that have a predominance of hydric soils and that are inundated or saturated by surface or ground water at a frequency and duration sufficient to support and under normal circumstances do support, a prevalence of hydrophytic vegetation typically adapted for life in saturated soil conditions, except lands in Alaska identified as having a high potential for agricultural development and a predominance of permafrost soils."

Farmed taro patches, Hanalei National Wildlife Refuge, Kaua'i (TE)

Primary user: U.S. Department of Agriculture Natural Resources Conservation Service (USDA NRCS).

Purpose: To ensure that cooperators of USDA comply with wetlands regulations under the National Food Security Act "Swampbuster" provisions, which exclude federal funding from landowners that manipulate wetlands for agricultural production.

Note: The COE *Wetland Delineation Manual* is used by USDA NRCS to determine wetland boundaries in the field.

---

[2] January 9, 2001 Supreme Court decision in <u>Solid Waste Agency of Northern Cook County vs. U.S. Army Corps of Engineers</u> (SWANCC).

Definition 3 (non-regulatory): "Lands transitional between terrestrial and aquatic systems where the water table is usually at or near the surface or the land is covered by shallow water." This definition includes unvegetated wet areas (e.g., beaches, mudflats, gravel streambeds, shallow ponds) that are not considered wetlands under other definitions.

Primary user: U.S. Fish and Wildlife Service (USFWS).

Purpose: Used when conducting wetland inventories and mapping trends in the National Wetlands Inventory (NWI), which includes a classification scheme for wetlands and other aquatic ecosystems. From the NWI, the USFWS aims to determine wetland hectarage (acreage) throughout the United States.

Note: In the State of Hawai'i, the last comprehensive wetland inventory for all of the islands was completed in 1975 and can be found at http://www.USFWS.gov/data/stadata/hidata.html.

Wetlands at the James Campbell National Wildlife Refuge, O'ahu (LC)

B. Key Components/Characteristics of Wetlands

1. Hydrology

Water creates and maintains all wetlands. Standing water or saturated soils for the entire year is not required for a site to be classified as a wetland. Wetlands can be inundated or saturated in the upper part of the soil for only a few consecutive weeks of the year. Determining whether a site has been wet long enough to be defined as a wetland is often the most difficult decision to make in the field. Because a determination is based on restricted observations, it depends on the day the field determination is made. Conclusions about the site will differ considerably depending on the time of year the assessment is done. Common sense, existing hydrology clues (**indicators**), and as much local knowledge as possible should be used when determining if water has been at a site long enough to meet the requirements of a legally defined wetland. Many factors influence hydrology at a site, including:

> **Landscape position**: where the wetland lies on the land, including its topography, elevation, position and aspect.

> **Limiting layers** (aquatards): the layers near the surface that limit water movement downward. Hawaii's bog systems often have a layer of hard iron precipitate within the top 60cm of the soil surface that increases ponding and saturation above that layer. Other limiting layers include organic layers created under ponds, that keep water at the surface.

> **Precipitation**: rainfall, snow and fog drip. The intensity of rainfall affects how much of that water becomes surface flow compared with how much is absorbed in the soil. Orographic rainfall, generated when air is forced to rise by mountains, is most common on the mid-elevation/windward slopes (northeast) of all islands.

> **Groundwater**: subsurface water. Wetlands can be influenced by shallow groundwater, particularly where groundwater meets with the surface (i.e., at the bases of mountains, along the coastline or where lateral lava flows daylight at the toe of an ʻaʻa flow that lies over a pahoehoe flow).

> **Surface flow**: water that floods the landscape from streams and rivers. Tides may also induce surface flow. The duration and frequency of flows, from permanent to intermittent or temporary, affect wetland hydrology.

> **Evapotranspiration**: the loss of water to the atmosphere. Water is removed from the soil or water bodies by evaporation and from plants by transpiration. Evapotranspiration rates vary seasonally and daily, and are different for each organism.

> **Vegetation**: the standing terrestrial and aquatic flora; it affects hydrology in wetlands by its ability to absorb and transpire water and to slow down flood flows and tidal surges.

Wetland hydrology conditions are evident in two ways:

(1) **Inundation** - water flooded (of short duration, typically flowing) or ponded (of longer duration, typically standing) at the surface, and

(2) **Saturation** - all easily drained pores between soil particles temporarily or permanently filled with water. In wetlands, soils become saturated by surface water or by a shallow water table (the height of groundwater determined by the water level in an unlined hole or soil pit). By most wetland definitions, saturation is confirmed when the water table is within 40cm (16") of the soil surface. This is considered as the upper part of the vegetation root zone.

In the field, saturation is determined by observing very moist conditions or glistening in the upper part of the soil. To understand wetland hydrology, one must understand a concept called the capillary fringe. Saturation can extend above the water table, depending on the soils at a site. The **capillary fringe** is the zone above the water table that draws water up to the root zone. The capillary fringe defines the level of saturation. If the capillary fringe is found within 30cm (12") from the top of the soil surface, the site can legally be defined as a wetland. The capillary fringe also influences the types of plants that can grow at the site. Many plants cannot grow under wetland conditions. The capillary fringe rises higher in soils with smaller pores (fine clays vs. sands); thus the water table in clayey soils does not have to be as close to the surface as in sandy soils (see below).

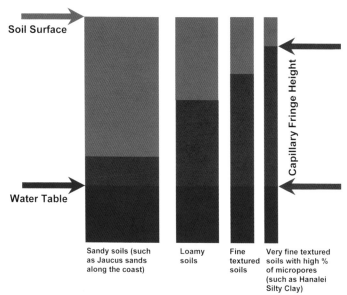

Capillary Action in Mineral Soils in Hawaiʻi

Soil Surface

Capillary Fringe Height

Water Table

Sandy soils (such as Jaucus sands along the coast)

Loamy soils

Fine textured soils

Very fine textured soils with high % of micropores (such as Hanalei Silty Clay)

In Hawaiʻi, verifying saturation can be difficult in the field because of the capillary fringe, particularly in soils with texture classes of "silty clay" and "silty clay loam," such as the Hanalei and Keālia series. In these cases, because glistening may be difficult to see, consult with a soil scientist to assist in the determination of saturation.

Water largely replaces air in the soil pores, leading to **anaerobic** (literally: without air) conditions. Soil microbes that require oxygen to survive deplete all free oxygen and then begin to obtain oxygen from mineral oxides in a process called **reduction**. Different oxide compounds liberate oxygen for microbe use more or less readily and a sequence of reduction occurs that is dependent on the duration of saturation and the condition of the soil environment (e.g., amount of organic food sources). The sequence of reduction is as follows:

Oxidation-Reduction sequence
1. Oxygen within the pores is consumed
2. Nitrogen is reduced by microbes — nitrate (NO_3^-) to nitrite (NO_2^-) to nitrous oxides (N_2O) and (NO) to nitrogen (N_2)
3. Manganese is reduced — (Mn^{+4}) to (Mn^{+2})
4. Iron is reduced causing a change in chroma (bright to pale) colors — ferric (Fe^{+3}) to ferrous (Fe^{+2})
5. Sulfur is reduced, causing a "rotten egg" smell — sulfate (SO_4^{-2}) to sulfide (H_2S)
6. Finally, carbon is reduced — organic matter to methane (CH_4), creating methane gas

A wetland must have water at or near the soil surface long enough and frequently enough to cause reductions in the soil and constrain the types of plants that can grow there. At a minimum a wetland must be saturated or inundated for at least two weeks to cause the microbes to reduce iron in mineral soils. The 1987 COE wetland delineation manual, most frequently used nationally in field determinations of wetlands, states that saturation or inundation must last at least 5% of the growing season, which for most of the

A white-faced ibis enjoys long-term duration of open water on the National Wildlife Refuge at Pearl Harbor, Oʻahu (LC)

Hawaiian Islands is year-round. This equates to at least 18.5 consecutive days of inundation or saturation per year. This condition should also occur in a minimum of 51 in 100 years (or more than 1 in 2 years). The NRCS further describes duration for farmed wetlands as 15 consecutive days of inundation, and for pasturelands at least seven days of saturation or 14 days of inundation.

In Hawai'i, since most delineations are based on restricted observations and data to determine longevity of hydrology at a particular site may be lacking, **indicators** of hydrology are used to identify wetlands. Indicators are clues for determining whether or not the site is "wet" enough to meet the requirements of a wetland. If data from shallow monitoring well sites or other flow data are available, use them to determine longevity of hydrology at the site. When these data are not available, use the indicators provided below.

The following table summarizes the national indicators used in the 1987 COE *Wetland Delineation Manual*. Only one primary indicator or two or more secondary indicators are needed to make a "wetland hydrology" determination of a regulatory (or jurisdictional) wetland. Secondary indicators, including regional conditions specific to Hawai'i, are explained below.

HYDROLOGY INDICATORS (1987 COE *Wetland Delineation Manual*)

Primary (only one is required):

Visual inundation (flooding or ponding) or saturation within the upper 20cm (8") of the soil pit

Water marks (e.g., dark or rust stains along rocks, fence posts, trees)

Drift lines (e.g., litter lines from surface flow — check flood frequency)

Sediment deposits (e.g., sand or small rock accumulations or lines from surface flow — check flood frequency)

Drainage patterns (e.g., lack of vegetation or flow patches in wetlands)

Secondary (two are required):

Oxidized root channels (rhizospheres) surrounding live roots in the upper 30cm (12")

Water-stained leaves (e.g., blackened mangrove or *hau* leaves)

Local survey data (i.e., site-specific hydrology information from previous studies)

FAC-Neutral Test (vegetation) (i.e., from the list of dominant species, remove the FAC designated plants and see if over 50% of those species remaining are hydrophytic). See page 18 for a detailed explanation of this indicator test.

Regional conditions distinctive in Hawai'i can also be used as indicators of hydrology. Many of them indicate ponding, such as black manganese staining or fluffy cracked surface of the soil in tidally influenced areas or remnant nests or wallows left by tilapia fish. Clues to long-term saturation include micro-hummocks in grazed pastures made by cattle or other ungulates. The following photos demonstrate indicators of hydrology in Hawai'i.

Black manganese staining on a fluffy cracked surface at Keālia National Wildlife Refuge, Maui, indicates ponding in brackish to saline mudflats, a regional hydrology indicator (TE)

Oxidized root channels in a gley matrix in rice fields on Kaua'i, a secondary hydrology indicator (TE)

Tilapia wallows at the Kawaiele State Wildlife Sanctuary, Mana Plain, Kaua'i, a regional hydrology indicator (JS)

Cattle-induced micro-hummocks in a farmed wetland pasture, Waimea, Hawai'i, a regional hydrology indicator (TE)

2. Soils

Soils are influenced by climate, parent material, topography, organisms, time and human manipulation. Wetland soils are most often poorly drained and/or have slow permeability rates, meaning that movement of water through the soils takes time and stays on site long enough to create wetland conditions. The standard references for drainage classifications and permeability rates of soils in Hawai'i are contained in the 1972/1973 Soil Conservation Service's (SCS, now named NRCS) soils surveys, found at: http://www.hi.nrcs.usda.gov/soils.html. Two major categories of soils exist based upon their origins: organic and mineral.

Organic soils form from decomposing plants and other organisms. These soils are often found in wetlands because plant debris decomposes less rapidly in anaerobic conditions. Highly decomposed organic materials result in soils that are very black, porous and light-weight and are "peats" or "mucks." Organic soils are typically grouped on the amount of organic carbon they contain, typically 12 to 18 percent (see NRCS Soil Taxonomy 1999).

Parts of a buried *hau* tree (*Hibiscus tiliaceus*) demonstrate how plant materials decompose less rapidly in hydric conditions at Hanalei, Kaua'i (TE)

Mineral soils, on the other hand, form from rocks or material transported by wind, water or landslides. These soils consist of amounts of sand, silt and clay and constitute the majority of the soils in the world.

The Histosol soil order includes most of the world's **organic soils**, with 'Hist' (from Greek *histos*, meaning tissue) indicating the presence of organically derived soil material. Most of these organic soils are hydric, with one exception. The suborder Folist (from Latin *folia*, meaning leaf) describes a group of organic soils that have formed under non-flooded conditions, composed of leaf litter and decaying wood fragments that have structure and are found in younger landscapes, particularly on the islands of Hawai'i and Maui.

Wetland ecologists and soil scientists have developed methods to determine if a hydric soil exists at a site. Since water changes soil characteristics, indicators of these characteristics are sought. Typically, the upper part of the soil or the top 45cm (18") is observed, which is also the typical root zone of herbaceous vegetation.

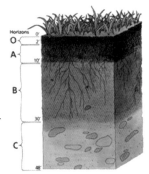

Basic soil profile: O - organic horizon; A - surface horizon; B - subsoil; C - substratum (NRCS)

The key factors to observe are **texture, smell and color**. All three of these features change with the frequency and duration of water in the upper part of the soil profile.

Texture is the relative percentage of sand, silt and clay. One can usually differentiate organic from mineral soils in the field by feel: organic soils typically are greasy or

slippery, lack stickiness and deform easily when wet, while mineral soils feel gritty or can be textured into a ribbon. Mineral soil textures are categorized into clay, silt and sand. Clay feels sticky and is plastic (pliable), silt is slick and non-sticky and sand is gritty (see Appendix 1 for texture triangle and description of texturing).

One part of the chemical sequence of reduction described in the previous section can be detected with your nose. When sulfur reduces, it **smells** like a burned match or rotten eggs and is a

Dark organic soil in Pearl Harbor, Oʻahu, is greasy, lacks stickiness and deforms easily when wet (TE)

clear indicator of wetland conditions. Other anaerobic odors differ from aerated soil odors, but these have no terms to help describe them.

Color is the most obvious soil feature used to determine hydric soils. Soil scientists use the Munsell Soil Color Charts (see Appendix 2 for a sample page), which consist of individual paint chips that show differences in color (hue), contrast (value) and color richness or brightness (chroma, pale to bright). Chroma is a key component for wetland determinations in mineral soils. High chroma soils are typically found in non-wetlands, while soils with low chroma colors (/1 or /2) are often hydric. Soils

should be "moist," not glistening, wet or dry, when the Munsell chart is used to read color. The predominant color, also called the "matrix," should be defined first, followed by those parts of the soil that differ from the matrix. These other colors, once called "mottles," are now called "redoximorphic features." For wetlands, the features to note are those that are formed under reduction/ oxidation processes and not those due to parent material or charcoal.

Note the dark redoximorphic features (manganese nodules, a soil indicator), a color different from the matrix. Hydrogen peroxide (3%) will make a strong effervescence upon contact with manganese, unlike charcoal (TE)

One word of caution about low chroma or "gleyed" colors: some parent materials contain virtually no iron minerals. These parent materials have a gray color and will remain gray regardless of whether the soils that develop in them become reduced or not. This situation can be encountered while conducting wetland soil determinations on volcanic soils in the tropics (e.g., Palau, Guam). The best way to determine if the low chroma or gley colors are indeed due to hydric

The Dechel series from Palau; a hydric soil that changes color (from dark grey to rust) upon drying (NRCS Guam)

conditions is to leave them exposed to the air for a while. Soil colors should turn rusty or bright if the gley color is due to reduction and wetland conditions. Hydric soils can change color in as little as 15 minutes when exposed. Other gray soils may have had all of the iron leached away or may have never had iron present (such as carbonate sands). These soils will not change color when exposed to air.

In Hawai'i at least two other situations make it difficult to read soils because natural conditions obscure hydric soil indicators. Mollisols or Vertisols, which include the

Hanalei series, typically are very dark in color and have a large amount of organic material. The organics tend to mask any reduction-oxidation features (mottles) that would indicate the soil is hydric. Caution should be used when assessing these types of soils; a soil scientist or someone knowledgeable about using an Eh/pH meter to check for "reducing conditions" may be needed.

The Eh/pH meter tests for reducing conditions in wetland soils where indicators of hydric soil may be masked or obscured (TE)

Also, Spodisols, which are found at the tops of Hawaii's volcanic mountains, often have a shallow organic layer on top, a horizon of bleached soil immediately below, then a red mineral layer below that.

Some soils high in iron concretions (e.g., Hāli'i series) may or may not be hydric. Fine-textured soils with high iron content may not show gray colors, even if iron reduction is occurring, because the iron content is so high that the reddish colors mask the effects of any reduction. Again, a soil scientist should be called to assist in wetland soil verification in these situations.

Determining hydric soils in the field:

1.	Dig a hole to a minimum of 45cm (18") depth
2.	Pick representative samples of soil throughout the soil profile and for each different soil horizon perform the following process
3.	Pick out a moist, not smeared sample of the soil (called a ped)
4.	Determine the matrix (>50%) first, then mottles (redoximorphic features) if they exist
5.	Describe mottle contrast (faint, distinct or prominent), abundance (few, common or many) and size (fine, medium, coarse, very coarse or extremely coarse)
6.	Describe texture, concretions (secondary concentric precipitates of Fe & Mn), structure and roots, if applicable
7.	Document profile data on a wetland data form or in a notebook

After completing the soil profile description of the soil pit at the site, next determine if indicators for hydric soils exist, using the following table:

Hydric Soil Indicators from the 1987 COE wetland delineation manual (one is sufficient)
• Histosol, an organic soil >40cm (16" deep), otherwise named a saprist, hemist, fibrist, but not a folist
• Histic epipedon, an organic surface 20 to 30cm (8 to12") thick
• Sulfidic odor, either SO_2 (a burnt match smell) or H_2S (a rotten egg smell)
• Aquic moisture regime, a soil taxonomy term specifying long duration of flooding, ponding or saturation at or near the surface, found in the description of the soil in the soil survey
• Currently present reducing conditions. This indicator can only be used if alpha-alpha dipyridyl is dropped onto the soil ped and it turns pink, or if an Eh/pH meter is used and the chart at Appendix 3 shows reduction
• Gleyed or low-chroma colors, that is, the soil is found on a gley page on the Munsell Soil Color Charts (black, gray, blue, green) or low chroma (gray, dark), including: ◊ Chroma 1 or less with or without redoximorphic concentrations (mottles)   ◊ Chroma 2 or less with redoximorphic concentrations (mottles)
• Concretions: Fe/Mn nodules (caution: in Hawai'i, Palau and the Federated States of Micronesia, these can be relic, meaning they indicate previous wetland conditions that are now dry and upland)

Hydric Soil Indicators, continued
• High organic matter in sandy soils
• Organic streaking in sandy soils
• Listed on local hydric soils list. Verify that it is the listed and mapped soil and not an inclusion or other soil type by checking your profile with the profile in the USDA SCS Soil Survey. See pg. 16 for a map of NRCS-listed hydric soils and soils with a predominance of hydric inclusions in Hawai'i
• Listed on national hydric soils list (the list of obligate hydric soils). Again, verify that it is the soil on the list

Hydric soils can also be identified using field indicators tested and distinct to regions across the nation in a document entitled *Field Indicators of Hydric Soils in the United States,* developed by NRCS soil scientists, in cooperation with the USFWS, the COE, the EPA and various regional, state, local agencies, universities and the private sector. It was tested in Hawai'i by an interagency team in 1994 to confirm its applicability in the islands. This publication contains the hydric soil indicators approved for use by the NRCS and the National Technical Committee for Hydric Soils.

Copies of the publication can be obtained from: Director, National Soil Survey Center, USDA NRCS, Rm 152, 100 Centennial Mall North, Lincoln, NE 68508-3866 or on the web at http://soils.usda.gov/soil_use/hydric/main.htm.

Gleyed mineral (sandy) soil in the upper part of the profile from Hanapepe salt flats, Kaua'i (TE)

Redox features in the upper part and low chroma colors below in hydric soil from Lawa'i, Kaua'i (TE)

Hydric soils of Hawai'i

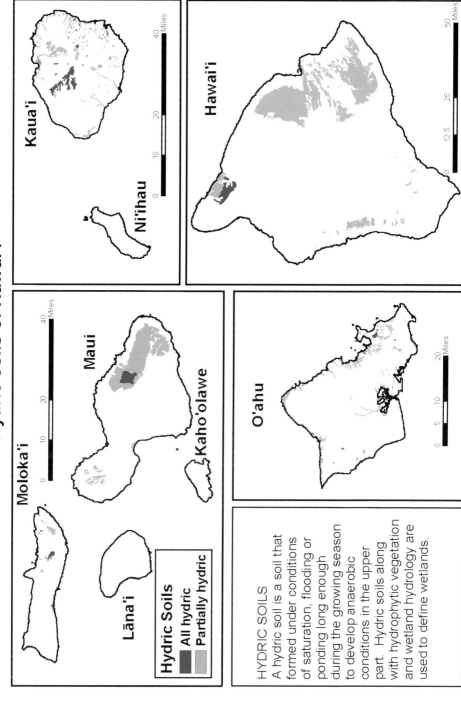

HYDRIC SOILS

A hydric soil is a soil that formed under conditions of saturation, flooding or ponding long enough during the growing season to develop anaerobic conditions in the upper part. Hydric soils along with hydrophytic vegetation and wetland hydrology are used to define wetlands.

Hydric Soils
All hydric
Partially hydric

Kaua'i

Ni'ihau

Hawai'i

Moloka'i

Maui

Kaho'olawe

Lāna'i

O'ahu

3. Vegetation

Plants are often the first clues to determining whether a wetland exists at a site. Hydrophytes (wetland plants) have developed unique evolutionary strategies for survival in wetlands, and have adapted to grow, effectively compete, reproduce and/or persist in areas subject to prolonged inundation or saturation. Hydrophytes are either able to withstand conditions of no oxygen (anoxia) or can oxygenate their roots and persist by morphological, physiological and reproductive adaptations.

(a) Morphological or physical characteristics of hydrophytic plants visible in the field include the following:

- Buttressed or multiple tree trunks: swollen or additional tree trunks to reinforce and support the plant.

- Hypertrophied lenticels: oversized pores on the surface of stems of woody plants through which gases are exchanged between the plant and the atmosphere. The enlarged lenticels serve as a mechanism for increasing oxygen to plant roots during periods of inundation and/or saturation.

Buttressed tree trunk (LC)

- Adventitious roots: roots found on plant stems in positions where they normally do not occur, to stabilize the plant or increase transpiration. Some plants normally have adventitious roots not due to water stress (e.g., *Pandanus tectorius*).

- Shallow root systems: roots sprawling and close to the surface to increase respiration and to support the plant.

Adventitious roots of *Rhizophora* sp. (LC)

- Pneumatophores and knees: modified roots that function as respiratory organs.

- Aerenchyma: "spongy tissue" or stem plant tissue in which cells are unusually large and arranged in a manner that results in air spaces in the plant.

- Polymorphic leaves: leaves of several different forms on a plant as an adaptation to aquatic habitats.

- Floating leaves: leaves with enlarged cells capable of floating on water (e.g., water lilies, water lettuce).

(b) Physiological adaptations allow hydrophytic plants to cope with living in water or saturated soil by processing energy through modified metabolic pathways, a complex of internal chemical reactions associated with life-sustaining functions.

Mangrove pneumatophores (LC)

(c) Reproductive adaptations allow plants to take advantage of their ability to reproduce in water or saturated conditions. For instance, seeds of some hydrophytes are able to germinate or survive under water or to float and disperse via water.

Morphological, reproductive and physiological adaptations can be noted and used as *indicators* of hydrophytic vegetation. Also, you can check a regional list that groups plants into categories (indicator ratings) by the frequency with which each plant species has been found in a wetland, otherwise known as its wetland indicator status.

Cape blue water lily in Kawaihau wetlands, Kaua'i (*Nyphaea capensis* var. *zanzibariensis*) have leaves adapted to floating on water (MC)

The Wetland Indicator Status of Plants

The USFWS is in charge of designating a wetland indicator status for each plant species found in Hawai'i. While these indicator ratings, which are set nationally, describe the frequency at which a species is found in wetlands, they do not necessarily describe the amount of "wetness" a species can tolerate. In Hawai'i, the presence of an obligate species generally reflects a year-round saturated or ponded wetland condition. Many weedy species by their nature are pioneering, adaptive and able to live in many different kinds of hydrological conditions. Typically, these are designated as facultative (FAC) species.

Obligate Wetland Species (OBL)	>99% found in wetlands
Facultative Wetland Species (FACW)	67-99% found in wetlands
Facultative Species (FAC)	33-66% found in wetlands
Facultative Upland Species (FACU)	1-33% found in wetlands
Obligate Upland Species (UPL)	<1% found in wetlands
No Indicator Status (NI)	Ignored in count
(-) means found in drier conditions; (+) means found in wetter conditions, within the rating	Important for wetlands, particularly if it is a FAC-
(*) means more data needed	Use indicator listed

Plants designated as OBL, FACW and FAC (except for FAC-) are considered hydrophytes. The sequence is from the most likely to be found in wetlands to the most likely to be found in uplands: **(OBL)—(FACW+)—(FACW)—(FACW-)—(FAC+)—(FAC)**—(FAC-)—(FACU+)—(FACU)—(FACU-)—(UPL). Those ratings in blue are hydrophytic.

In Hawai'i, the USFWS, in cooperation with other agencies and wetland botanists, developed a list and categorization process for plants typically found in local wetlands, resulting in the *National List of Plant Species That Occur in Wetlands, Region H* (Reed 1988), called the "Green Book." This book divides plants into the above five indicator status categories, based on their frequency of occurrence in wetlands. It includes two columns, one which shows the indicators of each species in other states (NAT-IND) and one which shows regional (Hawaiian) indicators (RHIND). The column of regional indicators is used in wetland delineations in Hawai'i. In this column, plants that are categorized as "UPL" (upland) are left off the list, so that if a plant is not found on the list, it is assumed to be an UPL species.

Hawai'i has had many new plant introductions and naturalizations since the publication of the Green Book in 1988, some of which are restricted to wetlands (e.g., *Salvinia molesta*). Because these plants were not included in the regional column of the Green Book, they were, for legal purposes, considered UPL plants. Puttock and Imada (2004) reviewed all plant species recorded for Hawai'i and provided each with a revised wetland indicator status. This field guide uses the new indicator statuses developed under that contract.

Usually, vegetation in the field is determined by strata (layer). In this way, one can surmise the longevity of the current conditions at the site. For instance, if the tree layer is dominated by UPL species, but the herb layer is dominated by OBL species, there has probably been a recent change in the hydrologic regime (i.e., becoming wetter).

The 1987 COE manual defines tree/shrub/herbaceous layers differently than standard botanical definitions. Both strata categories are as follows:

1987 COE *Wetland Delineation Manual*	Standard botanical terminology
Trees: woody plants with diameter-at-breast-height (DBH) greater than 8cm (3")	**Trees**: plants with a single woody stem or trunk
Shrubs: plants with DBH less than 8cm (3") and greater than 1m (3.2') tall	**Shrubs**: plants with several woody stems arising at ground level
Herbaceous layer: woody and non-woody plants less than 1m (3.2') tall	**Herbs**: plants not producing above-ground woody stems (includes plants with underground woody stems)

A wetland may consist of more than one plant community, indicating diversity. Representative sites should be chosen to determine whether each community is or is not dominated by wetland species. The focus of these analyses is on dominant communities –the most prevalent group of plants – rather than on single indicator species. To characterize the dominant species in the plant community two processes are most commonly used: the dominance ratio method and the prevalence index method.

Most wetland delineations performed at lower elevations in Hawai'i use the dominance ratio method for vegetation sampling, which entails estimating total percent cover of vegetation and substrates. All cover must be assessed. For instance, in many coastal wetlands only 80 percent of the site may be covered by plants (often just one species, e.g., *Batis maritima*) with 10 percent mudflat and 10 percent open water. Also, because of the layering effect of vegetation, the total plant cover may be more than 100 percent. Usually a simple statistical method is used to find the relative percentage of each species (i.e., how each relates to one another in terms of dominance). Divide the actual percentage of each species by actual total percentage to derive the relative percentage of the dominant plant species and their indicator statuses.

The other method that can be used is the **prevalence index**, a weighted average of the wetland indicator status of all plants present. This method is often used during an NRCS delineation appeal or COE violation case. In this method, each plant along a transect or within a plot must be identified, then given a score relating to its indicator status (OBL= 1.0, FACW=2.0, FAC=3.0, FACU=4.0 and UPL=5.0). Scores are then summed and averaged to determine the overall indicator rating of the area.

Once the dominant species are determined using either method, Hawaii's 2004 updated plant indicator status list is checked to determine the number of listed hydrophytes. **If hydrophytes make up more than 50 percent of vegetation at the site, it meets the wetland vegetation parameter, one of the three required to legally classify it as a wetland.**

Diversity of plants in water at Pouhala Marsh, O'ahu (TE). Either the prevalence index or dominance ratio method could be used at this site to determine if hydrophytes make up more than 50 percent of the dominant vegetation. Dominant species in this photo (*Batis maritima, Bolboschoenus maritimus* and *Typha latifolia*) are all OBLs and therefore indicate a hydrophytic plant community (LC)

C. Methods for Wetland Determination

Determination methods for all three of the components of wetlands (hydrology, soils and vegetation) depend upon the intent of the study or use of the information. These methods include:

(1) Off-site examination of a variety of maps and imagery, including soil surveys, aerial photos, topographic surveys, the NWI maps, and any other graphical information about the site. Previous reports or environmental assessments conducted within the watershed should also be obtained and reviewed, if available. Typically, one develops a general transect and sampling plan to coincide with representative plots of similar plant signatures, soils, or hydrology signs.

(2) On-site field investigation (by representative plot) is then done for each plant community, change in topography or change in soils from the soil survey. At each plot, first the vegetation community is analyzed, then the soil pit is dug to examine soils and then hydrology indicators are documented. If all three parameters are not obscured and can be evaluated, the site meets "**normal circumstances**," as defined in the 1987 COE wetland delineation manual, and wetland conditions are determined. If one or more of the parameters are obscured, one will need to find historical data previous to the disturbance, conduct the analysis in a similar adjacent site, or sometimes, dig beneath the fill (see "atypical situations," pg. 40).

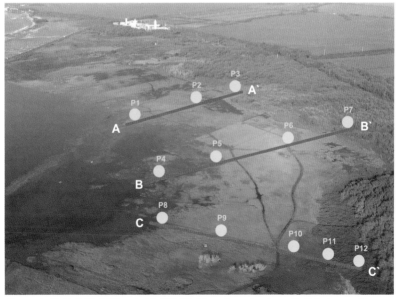

Transects (A-A`, B-B`, C-C`) and plots (P1, P2, P3, ...) may be planned initially from aerial photographs to conduct soil, vegetation community and hydrology indicator work. Once on the ground one must refine transects and plots locations (TE)

D. Wetland Analysis Protocol

A new wetland analysis protocol is proposed herein. This protocol describes wetlands in Hawai'i by providing basic functional assessment guidance to differentiate wetland types. The protocol can be used to guide monitoring, mitigation, restoration, or preservation projects (see pgs. 44–53). It can also be used to ensure functional habitat features exist (or are developed) for native fish (pgs. 32–34) or for rare insects (pgs. 35–39).

The wetland analysis protocol integrates the key elements of three classification schemes described below:

- The USFWS *Classification of Wetlands and Deepwater Habitats of the United States* (Cowardin *et al.* 1979) classifies wetlands in the nation based on vegetation and other habitat zones (i.e., unvegetated mudflats) rather than on abiotic functions. It defines frequently used terms such as palustrine (freshwater-influenced) and estuarine (saltwater-influenced, greater than 5 parts per thousand), used in the Hawai'i wetland analysis protocol.

Unvegetated mudflats, such as these at Pouhala Marsh, O'ahu, are included in the Cowardin Classification Sysyem (TE)

- The COE *Hydrogeomorphic Classification System* (Brinson 1993) focuses on hydrogeomorphology and other abiotic features of wetlands. Relevant concepts such as landscape position and flow regime were incorporated into the Hawai'i wetland analysis protocol.

- *An Ecosystem Classification of Inland Waters for the Tropical Pacific Islands* (Polhemus *et al.* 1992) classifies streams, lakes, wetlands and anchialine pools in the tropics. It includes all inland waters and focuses on streams. Unique island wetland types, such as anchialine pools, were incorporated into the Hawai'i wetland analysis protocol.

Polhemus *et al.* classifies in detail unique lotic (stream) systems in Hawai'i, including these intermittent streams near Hāna, Maui (TE)

The new Hawai'i wetland analysis protocol requires an answer for each of five wetland condition questions, starting from the top of the flow diagram (opposite page) and noting each answer. The five key questions are:

1. **What is the predominant flow regime**? In Hawai'i water moves in three primary ways: from below (groundwater, including tidal influence), from above (precipitation and cloud forest drip), and horizontally across the surface (surface flow).

2. **What is the water chemistry of the wetland**? Does it have a salinity reading of more than five parts per thousand and is thus saline or brackish, or is it fresh? If testing soils, do they have a pH range of 8.6 to 10?

3. **What is the geomorphology of the site**? This takes into account the geology and landscape position. Is it a depression with no outlet or inlet? Is it on a level floodplain or mudflat? Is it a wetland along a steep slope (greater than 25% or 4:1)? Is it the riparian area around the perimeter of a pond, reservoir or lake, called a "fringe" along a lentic system? Is it a riparian area along a stream, canal or flowing water body, called a riverine system? Is it a wetland along a stream or flowing water body with tidal influence, called a coastal riverine system? Or is it a wetland directly adjacent to the coast that is influenced by the tides?

Slope wetlands, Ko'olau Mountains, O'ahu (CP)

4. **What is the predominant substrate of the site**? Is it lava (*'a'a* or *pahoehoe*)? Is it a mineral soil (clay, silt, sand)? Is it organic (derived from plants, either a peat or a muck)?

5. **What is the type of wetland**? Is it a bog? A marsh, swamp or other freshwater, palustrine wetland? Is it an estuarine wetland, anchialine pool or coastal flat, meaning it is tidally influenced?

Fringe wetlands, Kohala Mountains, Hawai'i (TE)

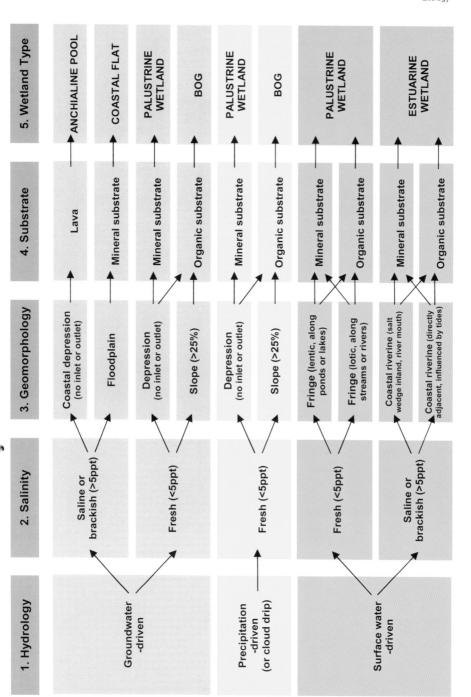

The following are a few examples of wetland types in Hawai'i, described using the wetland analysis protocol.

Taro patches (*lo'i kalo*) at the base of the mountains in Hanalei, Kaua'i (TE)
Groundwater-driven/ freshwater/ depression/ mineral substrate/ palustrine wetland

Hanging slope wetlands in the Ko'olau Mountains, O'ahu (CP)
Precipitation-driven/ freshwater/ slope/ organic substrate/ bog

Open water and riparian wetlands adjacent to the coast in Hāna, Maui (LC)
Groundwater-driven/ brackish /coastal depression/ lava substrate/ anchialine pool

Seasonal wetlands and mudflats at the Keālia National Wildlife Refuge, Maui (TE)
This large wetland system includes several wetland types, including near outlets: *Surface water-driven/ brackish/ coastal riverine/ mineral substrate/ estuarine wetland*; and within the depressional mudflat: *Precipitation-driven/ freshwater/ depression/ mineral substrate/ coastal flat*

E. Wetlands Functions and Values

Using the wetland analysis protocol can lead to a better understanding of the intricate functions and values provided by wetlands in Hawai'i. Not all wetlands are alike and therefore not all wetlands function alike. Flow, salinity, geomorphology and substrate influence wetland services provided and have resulted in a remarkable variety of wetlands found throughout the state.

For instance, riparian wetlands along Hule'ia River on Kaua'i, a *surface water-driven/ freshwater/ riverine/ mineral substrate/ palustrine wetland*, primarily provides sediment, nutrient and flood attenuation functions. In contrast, Pēpē'ōpae Bog on Moloka'i, a *precipitation-driven/ freshwater/ depression/ organic substrate/ bog*, mainly functions as a groundwater recharge area, providing plant community abundance and diversity and wildlife habitat.

Wetland functions are abiotic and biotic processes provided by wetlands. Wetland values define the usefulness of wetlands to humans, usually derived from wetland functions. In the example above, the riparian wetlands along Hule'ia River are valued for erosion control, property protection, water quality benefits and flood control. The bog provides groundwater for human consumption as well as recreational and Hawaiian cultural values. Functions and values are to be considered separately when assessing wetlands in Hawai'i. The following table defines and describes the differences between functions and values:

Wetland Function	Wetland Value
Sediment attenuation and reduction	Erosion control, better water quality in streams and ocean for recreation, fisheries and drinking water
Nutrient and chemical attenuation and reduction	Better water quality in streams and ocean for recreation, fisheries and drinking water, cleansing of waste materials, including nutrients, pesticides and herbicides
Flood attenuation and storage	Flood control, public safety within flood zones, groundwater recharge
Plant community abundance and diversity	Education and research, agriculture, urban quality of life, open space and aesthetics, timber production, historical and cultural importance, protection of native, threatened or endangered resources
Fish and wildlife habitat	Education and research, bird watching, urban quality of life, aesthetics, hunting and fishing, historical and cultural importance, protection of native, threatened or endangered resources
Groundwater recharge and discharge	Groundwater use potential, increased water supply
Shoreline or stream bank anchoring	Protection of property

Water flow, salinity, geomorphology and substrate largely determine the kinds of plants and animals on the landscape. Sediment, nutrients and organic matter inputs in wetlands provide raw materials and the basis for the food web. The resulting plant community greatly influences the distribution, abundance and species composition of animals, including birds, fish and insects.

Hawaii's wetlands provide unique biotic ecosystem functions and values, including endangered, threatened and rare species habitat. Some of the species found in wetlands in the state are found nowhere else in the world. The following sections describe some of the exceptional birds, fish and shellfish, and insects that depend on wetlands in Hawai'i.

1. Waterbirds in Hawaii's Wetlands — *K.J. Uyehara*

Wetlands of the Hawaiian Islands provide important habitat for seven native resident waterbird species, six of which are endemic and listed as endangered species. They also provide critical stopover or wintering habitat for migratory waterfowl and shorebirds. Over 80 species of migratory waterfowl and shorebirds have been recorded in the Hawaiian Islands. According to the fossil record the Hawaiian Islands have supported at least 13 species of endemic Hawaiian waterfowl. Four of these species, descendents of ancient dabbling ducks, were flightless terrestrial herbivores the size of large swans, known as the *Moa-nalo*, that evolved from aquatic filter-feeder to occupying the role of large herbivore in upland habitats, foraging primarily on leaves of low-growing plants and ferns. Today only three waterfowl species remain, one goose and two ducks.

Hanalei National Wildlife Refuge, Kaua'i *Nēnē* can be seen grazing on the fringes of taro patches (JS)

The endangered *Nēnē* or Hawaiian Goose (*Branta sandvicensis*), a close relative of the Canada Goose, is an upland browsing grazer that feeds on a variety of shrubs, grasses, legumes and other forbs. *Nēnē* use fresh to brackish wetlands and can be observed in reservoirs, fishponds, taro patches and golf course ponds. Wetland plants foraged by *Nēnē* include sedges (e.g., *Cyperus polystachyos*) and grasses (e.g., *Cynodon dactylon*, *Paspalum* spp.).

The critically endangered **Laysan Duck** (*Anas laysanensis*) was once widely distributed in the Hawaiian Islands. Laysan Duck is now isolated on Laysan and Midway Atoll, the latter a result of recent experimental reintroductions. Wetland habitats include tide pools, a hypersaline lake, brackish and saline ponds, freshwater seeps and ephemeral precipitation-driven pools. Laysan Duck often loafs in upland vegetation during the day and forages for brine flies, brine shrimp and other invertebrates in wetlands and uplands at night. Wetland plants are an important component of the adult's diet during the nonbreeding season (e.g., seeds of *Cyperus laevigatus*, *Sporobolus virginicus*) and provide habitat for invertebrate foods (e.g., *Sesuvium portulacastrum*, *Ipomoea pes-caprae*).

Koloa at Hanalei National Wildlife Refuge, Kaua'i (BZ)

Of the three Hawaiian waterfowl species, the endangered **Koloa** or Hawaiian Duck (*Anas wyvilliana*) is the most dependent on wetlands for survival. *Koloa* use a diversity of palustrine wetland types, including those on agricultural lands, from low to high elevations. *Koloa* is rarely observed in brackish and saline wetlands. Like most dabbling ducks, this species is an opportunistic forager and breeder and plant use is likely to be related to availability. Wetland plants provide escape cover from predators and microhabitats for invertebrate foods. *Koloa* feeds on algae, submerged plants and many grasses, sedges, legumes and other forbs, such as *Paspalum* spp., *Bolboschoenus maritimus*, *Schoenoplectus* spp. and *Persicaria* spp. *Koloa* nests on the edge of wetlands or in uplands. Nests have been found in *Urochloa mutica*, *Diplazium esculentum*, *Commelina diffusa* and other herbaceous plants near wetlands.

At least 14 endemic rail species are known from Hawaii's fossil record; 12 species were flightless. Four survived until the arrival of the Europeans, and two are extant today. The *'Alae 'ula* or Hawaiian Moorhen (*Gallinula chloropus sandvicensis*) is an endangered subspecies of the Common Moorhen. It inhabits fresh and occasionally brackish wetlands, including man-made reservoirs, ditches and farmed wetlands, typically below 130m elevation. This species eats seeds of grasses and sedges, legumes and other forbs, algae, aquatic insects and snails. The *'Alae 'ula* is secretive, foraging at the edges of vegetation and nesting within 2m of open water. Nesting takes place in emergent vegetation over shallow water, on the ground or on floating vegetation mats. In taro patches, it nests where taro plants are more than four months old and on sizeable patches of other emergent plants.

'Alae 'ula or Hawaiian Moorhen (RW)

The endangered *'Alae ke'oke'o* or Hawaiian Coot (*Fulica alai*) is similar to the *'Alae 'ula* but has a rounder profile, a white frontal shield and an assertive personality. The *'Alae ke'oke'o* uses wetlands with more open water than the *'Alae 'ula*, but generally the same wetland types, up to 400m elevation. Plant foods for the *'Alae ke'oke'o* include the seeds and leaves of a wide variety of aquatic plants such as *Ludwigia octovalvis*, *Persicaria* spp., *Echinochloa* spp. and sedges. *'Alae ke'oke'o* typically constructs semi-floating nests anchored to emergent plants near open water, or floating nests on dense mats of vegetation (e.g., algae, *Bacopa monnieri*) and are capable of building multiple and substantial nest platforms using *Bolboschoenus maritimus*, *Schoenoplectus* spp., *Typha* spp., grasses or *Batis maritima*, depending on local availability of suitable materials.

Endangered Hawaiian Coot (LC)

The *Ae'o* or Hawaiian Stilt (*Himantopus mexicanus knudseni*) is an endangered subspecies of the Black-necked Stilt of the Americas. *Ae'o* has a higher salt tolerance and is more prevalent than coots in seasonal open water areas of all salinity levels. They are found in anchialine pools and palustrine and estuarine wetlands. This species prefers wetlands with sparse vegetation, open mudflats and wetlands with water less than 10cm deep. Plants generally associated with *Ae'o* habitats include *Sesuvium portulacastrum*, *Heliotropium curassavicum* and *Cyperus laevigatus*. *Ae'o* eats aquatic invertebrates, including water boatmen, aquatic beetles, midges, brine flies, polycheate worms, crustaceans and occasionally small fish. The species usually nests on open mudflats in depressions sometimes lined with pebbles and twigs from nearby plants.

The only Hawaiian native waterbird not on the endangered species list is the *'Auku'u* or Black-crowned Night-Heron (*Nycticorax nycticorax*). This native heron uses a wide variety of wetlands and can be found wading or stalking prey from sea level to approximately 620m elevation. *'Auku'u* is a solitary forager and predator of marine and freshwater organisms including fish, frogs, crustaceans, mollusks, dragonflies and small vertebrates such as waterbird and seabird eggs and chicks. *'Auku'u* roosts and nests in trees such as *Prosopis pallida*, *Casuarina* spp., *Thespesia populnea*, *Rhizophora mangle* and *Hibiscus tiliaceus*, usually within 2km of the coastline. Its nests are complex platforms built from sticks and leaves placed on large tree limbs.

Black-crowned Night-Heron (LC)

Late summer to spring is the time to see migratory waterfowl and shorebirds in Hawai'i, in all wetland types. **Migratory shorebirds** feed primarily on aquatic and terrestrial invertebrates. Though commonly referred to as "visitors," some species, such as the **Kōlea** or Pacific Golden-Plover (*Pluvialis fulva*), spend eight months away

from Hawai'i each year and then return to the same grassland or wetland. Both Alaska-breeding *Kōlea* and **'Akekeke** or Ruddy Turnstone (*Arenaria interpres*) can cross the Pacific Ocean to Hawai'i in less than three to four days. The **Hunakai** or Sanderling (*Calidris alba*) breeds as far north as the high arctic (e.g., northern Siberia and Canada) and winters as far south as southern Chile and Peru. However, the specific breeding grounds for Hawaii's *Hunakai* are unknown. Significant numbers of *Kōlea*, **'Ulili** or Wandering Tattler (*Heteroscelus incanus*) and **Kioea** or Bristle-thighed Curlew

Wandering Tattler (TE)

(*Numenius tahitiensis*) winter in the Hawaiian Islands. An estimated 800 *Kioea* winter in the Northwestern Hawaiian Islands. *Kioea* is unusual in that it breeds in two small areas in Alaska and winters exclusively on the Pacific Islands.

The three most common species of migratory waterfowl in the Hawaiian Islands are the **Northern Shoveler** or *Koloa mohā* (*Anas clypeata*), **Northern Pintail** or *Koloa māpu* (*A. acuta*) and **Lesser Scaup** (*Aythya affinis*). The shoveler and pintail are both dabbling ducks found in fresh and brackish wetlands, such as seasonal coastal flats, cultivated wetlands, reservoirs and montane stock ponds. The shoveler is primarily a surface feeder, using its specialized bill to strain for small invertebrates and plant matter. Specific plants important to wintering shoveler and pintail include *Ruppia maritima*, *Potamogeton* spp., and *Schoenoplectus* spp. The Lesser Scaup is a diving duck found in deep water habitats. For a complete list of Hawaii's migrants and vagrants see Pyle (2002) and Engilis *et al.* (2004).

Bristle-thighed Curlew (LC)

2. Fish and Shellfish in Hawaii's Wetlands — *M.N. Yamamoto*

There are few native Hawaiian fish and shellfish and many introduced species that use wetlands as part of their life cycle. Five endemic Hawaiian stream fishes evolved from marine forms and live in differing salinity levels throughout their lives. In a life cycle referred to as **amphidromy**, the adults live and breed in freshwater streams, while the newly hatched larvae drift out to sea and remain there several months before returning to freshwater.

'O'opu naniha (MY)

The **'o'opu naniha** (*Stenogobius hawaiiensis*) and *'o'opu 'akupa* (*Eleotris sandwicensis*) are two endemic freshwater fishes often found in wetlands. The *'o'opu naniha* is a goby and can be differentiated from the *'o'opu 'akupa* by its fused pelvic fins, which form a disc. It has a brown to yellowish-brown body and a black bar extending downward through the eye. During courtship behavior the 9 to 11 bars on the side of its body become very distinct and the dorsal fins develop a red edging. *'O'opu naniha* are omnivorous, feeding on both plant and animal matter.

The **'o'opu 'akupa** has separate pelvic fins and is an eleotrid. Like the *'o'opu naniha*, it is a poor climber and is usually found in the lower reaches of *surface water-driven/*

'O'opu 'akupa (MY)

fresh to saline/ riverine and fringe/ mineral and organic substrate/ palustrine and estuarine wetlands. The *'o'opu 'akupa* is an ambush predator, usually half-burying itself in the substrate or under a rock, waiting for its prey to pass. It is also a highly opportunistic predator, feeding on abundant and slow-moving animals like thiarid snails and freshwater clams.

Another native species restricted to lowland wetlands is the **'ōpae 'oeha'a** (*Macrobrachium grandimanus*). This native shrimp grows to about 8cm and can be

'Ōpae 'oeha'a (MY)

easily recognized by its large and uneven-sized pincers or chelae. Its Hawaiian name, *'oeha'a*, means to "walk crookedly." A second native shrimp, the **'ōpae huna**, is found in estuarine wetlands. It has a transparent body marked with rows of white spots and black lines and blotches. Unlike the *'ōpae 'oeha'a*, it does not have large pincers. It grows to about 3cm in length and is favorite

bait for shoreline fishermen. Finally, the *'ōpae 'ula* is a very small red, pink or clear native shrimp about 1cm long that is restricted to anchialine pools on O'ahu, Maui and Hawai'i.

The most common aquatic fishes found in all lowland wetlands in Hawai'i are intentionally or accidentally introduced species. Two groups that are particularly well represented are the topminnows and tilapias. Six species, collectively referred to as **topminnows,** have become established in Hawaiian freshwaters. Topminnows were introduced early in the 1900s mostly as a biological control for mosquitoes. These species include the mosquitofish (*Gambusia affinis*), rainbow fish (*Poecilia reticulata*), sailfin molly (*P. latipinna*), liberty molly (*P. salvatoris/mexicana*), Cuban molly (*Limia vittata*) and green swordtail (*Xiphophorus helleri*). Some of these species hybridize making identification difficult. Of these six species, the mosquitofish and the three species of mollies (illustrated top to bottom right) are the topminnows most likely found in low-lying wetlands.

[From to top down] Mosquitofish, sailfin, liberty and Cuban mollies (MY)

At least 10 species of **tilapia** are found in Hawaiian waters. Several species were intentionally released for food, sport and vegetation control, and to serve as baitfish for the local *aku* (skipjack tuna, *Katsuwonus pelamis*) fishery. Others represent escapes from aquaculture. In wetlands three of the most common species include the Mozambique tilapia (*Oreochromis mossambicus*), black-chin tilapia (*Sarotherodon melanotheron*) and the redbelly tilapia (*Tilapia zillii*). The tilapia's hardiness, adaptability and reproductive potential, make them pests in wetlands, threatening native plants and animals, and other wetland-dependent species.

Redbelly tilapia (MY)

They out-compete more desirable native species, resulting in many more tilapia than the wetland ecosystem can sustain. During warm summer months, elevated water temperatures, combined with reduced water levels, can lower dissolved oxygen levels and result in large fish kills (see page 43).

More than 550 marine fish species are native to Hawai'i, some of which are found in estuarine wetlands. *Surface water-driven/ brackish to saline/ coastal riverine and fringe/ estuarine wetlands*, such as parts of Kawai Nui Marsh on O'ahu and Waiākea Pond on Hawai'i, also provide habitat for marine species, such as the gray mullet

(*Mugil cephalus*), *āholehole* (*Kuhlia xenura*), mangrove goby (*Mugilogobius cavifrons*), fang-tooth blenny (*Omobranchus ferox*), blue-pincer crab (*Thalamita crenata*) and Samoan crab (*Scylla serrata*).

Two eel-like introduced fishes can also be found in lowland wetlands. The **ricepaddy eel** (*Pisodinophis cancrivorous*) can grow up to 1m in length and is usually red or brown with a sprinkling of dark specks across its backs. It has a small mouth, small eyes, gill slits on its throat and lacks fins, and is nocturnal and very secretive. The rice paddy eel often goes unnoticed until forced out of its burrows during periods of high water or during stream-clearing operations. The other eel-like fish is the ***dojo*** or Oriental weatherfish (*Misgurnus anguillicaudatus*). Originally from eastern Asia, the *dojo* is yellow-brown to brown in color with greenish-gray to dark brown marbled markings. It can reach up to 20cm in length, but is most often smaller.

Thiarid snails, also called Malaysian live-bearing snails, are tall, thin, pointed and usually up to 2.5cm long. These snails can be found in brackish water and streams. They have been found to comprise a significant part of the *'o'opu 'akupa* diet.

Four introduced species of **apple snails** (three *Pomacea* spp. and *Pila conica*) have become invasive in Hawai'i. *Pomacea canaliculata* is the most prevalent of the four. It is a ravenous plant-eater that reproduces quickly and devastates taro plants. It is a large snail with a round, dark brown to pale yellow shell 2 to 5cm long. Apple snail egg cases are pink masses on emergent surfaces of all kinds.

Pomacea canaliculata eggs and adult (LC)

The **Asiatic freshwater clam** (*Corbicula fluminea*) is one of the most widespread and invasive clams in Hawai'i. Introduced from eastern Asia, it is usually 1 to 2cm in

diameter and ranges in color from dark blackish-brown to pale yellowish-brown. In wetland taro patches, juvenile or small *Corbicula* clog irrigation lines and broken shells can cut farmers' feet.

Asiatic freshwater clams in shallow water and in an irrigation line (MY)

3. Insects in Hawaii's Wetlands — *D.A. Polhemus and R.A. Englund*

Hawaiian wetlands support a wide diversity of aquatic insects, although they lack several major groups such as water striders and mayflies found in North America.

Lowland wetlands in Hawai'i are now primarily inhabited by introduced insect species, while upper elevation wetlands (above 480m) support mainly native taxa. There are 300 to 400 native aquatic insect species in Hawai'i, with the majority of these occurring in streams rather than wetlands. In addition approximately 200 species have been introduced, undoubtedly changing to some degree community dynamics of Hawaiian wetland ecosystems by displacing the native biota. Across the range of Hawaiian wetland types, several insect groups consistently dominate, most notably Odonata, Diptera, Heteroptera and Coleoptera.

Globe skimmer, *Pantala flavescens* (DP)

The Hawaiian **dragonfly** and **damselfly** (**Odonata**) fauna has 33 endemic species in the genera *Megalagrion*, *Anax* and *Nesogonia*, three introduced damselflies in *Ischnura* and *Enallagma*, one native dragonfly in *Pantala*, and four introduced dragonflies in *Tramea*, *Orthemis* and *Crocothemis*. The seven introduced species are common, particularly in lowland wetlands and ephemeral aquatic habitats, such as stock tanks and stream pools. Few of these introduced species have penetrated mountain habitats above 500m. The exceptions are *Orthemis ferruginea* and *Enallagma civile* which have been found breeding in stock ponds at elevations up to 1000m.

Orthemis ferruginea, an introduced dragonfly native to North America, is easily recognized by its lavender-pink coloration (RE)

Dragonflies are large and obvious in lowland wetlands. The most common species is the **globe skimmer** (*Pantala flavescens*), a native dragonfly that cruises widely and is widespread throughout the

Crocothemis servilia, a bright red introduced dragonfly native to China, is a common species in lowland wetlands on O'ahu (DP)

Anax junius nymph uses its extendable lower lip armed with sharp hooks to snare prey (RE)

tropics. The globe skimmer is a generalist familiar to many homeowners because it breeds in swimming pools and ornamental *koi* ponds. In wetlands such as Kawai Nui Marsh the globe skimmer is found with introduced species, including the bright red *Crocothemis servilia*, lavender-pink *Orthemis ferruginea*, large green and blue *Anax junius* and *Tramea lacerata* with its distinctive dark spots at the wing bases. The nymphs of all these species are fierce underwater predators that feed on small fish and aquatic invertebrates.

Damselflies, smaller relatives of dragonflies, are also abundant in Hawaii's lowland wetlands. Although these wetlands once provided habitat for endemic damselfly species such as *Megalagrion xanthomelas*, most are now dominated by three introduced species: *Ischnura ramburii, I. posita* and *Enallagma civile*. These American continental species have co-evolved with many of the introduced freshwater fishes, particularly mosquitofish, now prevalent in Hawaiian wetlands and as a result have superior predator avoidance behaviors in comparison to native species. In relatively intact lowland wetlands, such as those of the Ka'u coast, both the endemic *Megalagrion* species and the introduced *Ischnura* and *Enallagma* can be found flying together, indicating that predation from invasive aggressive species, not competition between damselfly species, affects the native species composition in disturbed wetland systems. In the relatively intact lowland wetlands at Kalaupapa and Pelekunu on the north shore of Moloka'i, where the introduced cane toad (*Bufo marinus*) is present but mosquitofish are absent, *Megalagrion xanthomelas* remains abundant. Prior to the arrival of mosquitofish, *M. xanthomelas* was probably the dominant damselfly in both natural lowland wetlands and in historically human-manipulated wetlands such as taro patches. In *groundwater-driven/ brackish/ coastal depression/ lava substrate/ anchialine pools*, such as those found along Puna and Kona, *M. xanthomelas* has a distinct advantage over introduced damselflies due to its ability to tolerate waters with salinities in the range of 2 to 8 parts per thousand.

In contrast the upper elevation wetlands have almost entirely native dragonfly and damselfly species. The giant Hawaiian damselfly, *Anax strenuus*, is commonly seen patrolling bogs throughout the islands, sometimes in company with the small black-and-red

Ischnura posita is commonly found perching in grasses in lowland fringe wetlands (DP)

36

endemic dragonfly *Nesogonia blackburni.*
Upper-elevation damselflies comprise an
even richer assemblage, including single-
island endemics. In the bog systems of the
Alakaʻi Plateau of Kauaʻi, one can find
Megalagrion paludicola, which breeds in
bog pools beneath the tangled roots of *Met-
rosideros* spp., in company with *Megalagrion oresitrophum*, which frequents fringe
wetlands. On Oʻahu, Mount Kaʻala in the
Waiʻanae Mountains provides wetland
habitat for *M. hawaiiense*, while in the
Koʻolau Mountains the Poamoho fringe
wetland supports *M. nigrohamatum ni-
grolineatum.* The bogs of Molokaʻi, Maui
and Hawaiʻi are predictably reliable habitats for *M. hawaiiense* and *M. calliphya*,
which can often be found flying together.
Although these species can sometimes also
be encountered at elevations as low as
100m, such as in *uluhe* (*Dicranopteris lin-
earis*) swamps in otherwise forested areas

Native dragonfly *Nesogonia blackburni* (DP)

Native damselfly *Megalagrion oresitrophum* (DP)

or along overflow channels in flat-bottomed valleys such as Waipiʻo on Hawaiʻi, they
are not typical inhabitants of the coastal wetlands, where *Megalagrion xanthomelas*
formerly dominated.

There are 19 species of aquatic **true bugs (Heteroptera)** in Hawaiʻi, 11 of which are
native. These are hardy insects that disperse readily and some are locally common in
Hawaii's lowland wetlands. All are generalists that prey on both introduced and native
insects, using their lance-like sucking beaks. These taxa include:

- one microveliine water skater in the family Veliidae,
- three water treaders in the family
  Mesoveliidae,
- one monophyletic radiation of ten
  shore bugs in the family Salididae,
  plus another introduced species,
- one species of Pleidae,
- one species of Corixidae,
- three backswimmers in the family
  Notonectidae. Notonectids are voracious predators that have primarily
  colonized artificial basins such as

Introduced water bug *Mesovelia mulsanti* (RE)

stock ponds or sewage treatment plants where they may be controlling larvae of introduced mosquitoes.

Low elevation *freshwater/ depression and fringe/ mineral and organic substrate/ palustrine wetlands* are inhabited by the introduced **Micracanthia humilis**, an ovate-shaped bug with a dark black body and small white flecks on the wings, and flies away quickly when approached. On adjacent open waters one will frequently find the introduced **water treader**, *Mesovelia mulsanti*, a small, narrow-bodied, pale green insect that runs swiftly on top of the water and may be abundant in large mats of floating aquatic weeds (e.g., *Salvinia molesta* or *Eichhornia crassipes*).

In upper elevations, exposed substrate (peat/muck) in bogs provide habitat for three native **saldids**, *Saldula exulans*, *S. procellaris* and *S. oahuensis*, all of which have ovate body shapes and complex patterns of pale markings on a brown or black body. The open water within bogs also frequently supports large numbers of the small black-and-silver native **water bug**, *Microvelia vagans*.

Members of the Order **Diptera** or flies, are the most common aquatic insects in the Hawaiian Islands, although most species are associated with rocky higher elevation streams. In wetlands, there is a diverse array of **midges** in the family Chironomidae and along fringes or on open water pools there is often an assemblage of taxa in the families Dolichopodidae and Ephydridae, which may compose a mixture of both native and introduced species, some of which are useful indicator species of habitat quality. In lowland wetlands, the majority of dipteran species present are introduced, and some, such as the **spotted wing midge** (*Polypedilum nubiferum*) at Kanahā Pond in the central isthmus of Maui, may occasionally breed to reach nuisance levels for nearby property owners.

Native midge *Chironomus hawaiiensis* (RE)

Introduced mosquito *Culex quinquefasciatus* (JJ)

All seven species of **mosquitoes** present in Hawai'i are introduced; five blood feeders in the genera *Aedes*, *Culex* and *Wyeomyia*, introduced accidentally, and a nectar feeder in the genus *Toxorhynchites*, intentionally introduced as a biological control because their larvae eat other larval mosquitoes. *Wyeomyia* is a bromeliad-breeding genus that is not associated with wetlands. *Aedes* and *Culex* are generally found breeding in habitats free of fishes, such as isolated stagnant pools that form in tire ruts, along wetland margins.

None of the human-biting mosquitoes breed in the intolerable numbers seen in comparable continental wetlands, such as the Everglades and in fact most are more of a nuisance in Hawaii's forested areas than in Hawaii's wetlands.

In addition, other more benign species belonging to other dipteran families have been introduced and may be found in wetlands. These include 39 members of nine families. Among them are the small native **chironomid**, *Cricotopus bicinctus*, with its distinctively white-banded abdomen, the introduced **ephydrid**, *Ochthera circularis*, with its diagnostically enlarged raptorial forelegs and the introduced **stratiomyid**, *Odontomyia ochropa*, which appears to breed primarily in taro patches. Similarly, the introduced large **midge**, *Chironomus esakii*, is widespread at higher elevations, such as in the summit bog on Mount Ka'ala, or at Violet Lake below Pu'u Kukui on West Maui, although it does not appear to be having an obvious impact on the native species that dominate these ecosystems.

Introduced water beetle *Rhantus gutticollis* (RE)

There are 19 species of **water beetles (Coleoptera)** known from the Hawaiian Islands: five native species in the families Dytiscidae and Hydrophilidae and 14 introduced species. Most are small and uncommon, found in lowland wetlands amid submerged floating weeds (e.g., *Salvinia molesta*) that provide escape cover from predaceous fishes. The spread of such weeds may be facilitating the establishment and persistence of these and other introduced aquatic insects in the lowland wetlands. In comparison, upper-elevation wetlands host large native water beetles in the hydrophilid genus *Limnoxenus* and the dytiscid genus *Rhantus*. *Limnoxenus* are elongate and shiny black in color and the Alaka'i bog on Kaua'i supports at least two undescribed species. The three native Hawaiian *Rhantus* species are also black, in contrast to the introduced *R. gutticollis* which is tan. *Rhantus gutticollis* and the native *R. pacificus*, both predators with similar body size and ecology, are sometimes found together in places such as the Mount Ka'ala bog on O'ahu.

In highly altered lowland systems, such as Kawai Nui Marsh on O'ahu, the introduced dragonflies add a dash of color and are interesting creatures to observe due to their complex behavior and amazing aerial maneuverability. In the few intact examples of Hawaiian lowland wetlands that remain (e.g., along the north shore of Moloka'i, the coast of Ka'u on Hawai'i and as anchialine pools of leeward Maui), native aquatic insects may still be present and in some cases even dominant. In upperelevation wetlands, by contrast, there is still the opportunity to observe many native species, which though generally unobtrusive, will reward the patient observer with a glimpse into yet another subtle facet of Hawaii's wetlands and their natural history.

F. Wetland Trends in Hawai'i

The most recent comprehensive wetland mapping effort (Dahl 1990) identified at least 9100 hectares (22,474 acres) of lowland wetlands and 14,700 hectares (36,328 acres) of upper/mid-elevation wetlands in the state of Hawai'i, using the National Wetlands Inventory. These inventory data are old (late 1970s) and do not adequately take into account small wetlands not seen from aerial images (e.g., forested wetlands) or inclusion of hydric soils not captured in the 1965 soil surveys. These inventories also did not differentiate between artificial and natural wetlands (e.g., they included reservoirs created from uplands).

1. Wetland Losses

Estimating wetland trends in Hawai'i is difficult, particularly because data for baseline hectarages are far from comprehensive. Twelve percent of lowland and upper-elevation wetlands from the 1780s to 1980s have been lost (Dahl 1990). Kosaka (1990) analyzed wetlands below 1000 ft (305m) elevation and estimated over 31 percent coastal wetland loss for the same time period. There has never been a complete or detailed on-site survey of wetland loss in the Hawaiian Islands.

Most wetland losses in the islands have been human induced, from discharging fill, building dams, channelizing, pumping, grubbing, grading, deep ripping and other agricultural or military landuse practices. The 1987 COE wetland delineation manual states that these types of disturbances can cause "**atypical situations**." Atypical situations include alterations to vegetation, soil and/or hydrology. Under these situations one or more indicator is obscured.

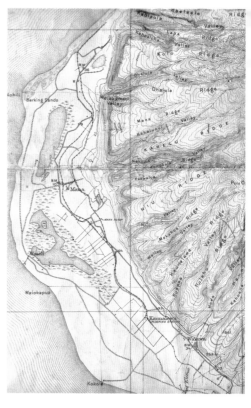

Along the Mana Plain on Kaua'i, over 650ha (c.1600 acres) of wetlands originally existed; note the open water areas and swamp symbols (1910 map, NRCS)

The regulatory response to an "atypical situation" depends on when the disturbance occurred.

- After 1972 (Clean Water Act) a person is subject to civil and criminal penalties unless they received a permit or are exempt from the regulations.

- After 1985 (NRCS Swampbuster provisions) a person could lose or become ineligible for USDA program benefits.

Calculations of wetlands obliterated in Hawai'i, such as those on the Mana Plain (illustrated below) do not include estimates of wetland functions lost. Most wetlands in the state have suffered from functional losses, although calculating the magnitude of degradation is difficult. Wetland functions decline as an indirect result of activities that alter the hydrological regime, such as ditching and diversions, groundwater withdrawals and nearby hardening of surfaces.

Recent USGS topographic map shows extent of ditching and draining; 80ha (c.200 acres) of wetland remain

2004 Digital Global QuickBird satellite imagery shows the extent of upland vegetation on the Mana plain (NRCS)

Also, because of the year-round growing season in most of Hawai'i, wetlands are continually threatened by invasive plant species. Especially damaging are **aggressive-invasive** species that completely out-compete other plant and animal species, often resulting in single-species (monotypic) stands.

A thorough understanding of wetland functions and the underlying causes of degradation will assist anyone interested in maintaining, restoring or mitigating for wetlands. Identifying and addressing some of the causes of declines in wetland fish and wildlife habitat functions in Hawai'i are especially important for these efforts.

2. Invasive Species and Their Habitat Modifications

The most destructive habitat modifiers now present in wetlands are species that have been introduced to Hawai'i. They first came as passengers with the world's ultimate predator, *Homo sapiens*. Some examples of invasive animals are given below. Invasive plants also adversely affect wetlands; many are described in Part II of this guide.

• Feral pigs (*Sus scrofa*) are present on all main islands with the exception of Lāna'i and Kaho'olawe. Pigs have impacted wetlands since the first settlement of the islands. They rototill wetlands to expose fleshy roots and worms, create wallows and disperse invasive species.

• House mice (*Mus musculus*) and rats (*Rattus* spp.) are present on all main islands.

A pig at work in a wetland at 650m above Hāna, Maui (CP)

lands. Rats are particularly active around bird nesting sites, robbing nests of eggs. The Polynesian or Pacific rat (*R. exulans*) and humans are responsible for the complete removal of wetland *loulu* forests (*Pritchardia* spp.). Rats devour the entire annual crop of *loulu* fruits, preventing their re-establishment. Mice are seasonally present in plagues competing for fruits and vegetation.

• Feral dogs (*Canis lupus familiaris*) are present on all main islands with the exception of Kaho'olawe. Dogs, even those under human control, disturb nesting sites for waterbirds and seabirds.

• Feral (and not so feral) cats (*Felis silvestris catus*) are present on all main islands. These mostly nocturnal hunters are particularly active around bird nesting sites.

• North American bullfrogs (*Rana catesbeiana*) and cane toads (*Bufo marinus*) are present on all main islands with the exception of Kaho'olawe. Bullfrogs and cane toads are

Cane toads (*Bufo marinus*) amplexing (MY)

carnivores and eat insects, shrimps, frogs and eggs of fish. They will also take young chicks and almost anything with a soft body. The cane toad has poison glands on the back of its head.

- Small Indian mongooses (*Herpestes auropunctatus*) are present on Kaua'i, O'ahu, Moloka'i, Maui and Hawai'i. They live in burrows, are diurnal, and are particularly active around bird nesting sites, robbing nests of eggs and taking small birds. They are voracious and opportunistic omnivorous predators and have been known to take sea turtle eggs, fruit and vegetation.

Mongoose (*Herpestes auropunctatus*) (LC)

Tilapia die-off (MY)

- Invasive fishes deplete native invertebrates and algae. High population densities of invasive fishes, combined with summer high temperatures and lower water levels, decrease dissolved oxygen levels needed for fish and other aquatic life.

- Cattle egrets (*Bulbulcus ibis*), introduced to Hawai'i in 1959 to control agricultural pest insects, feed on a variety of native and introduced invertebrates and small vertebrates such as fish, skinks, frogs and waterbird and seabird chicks.

- Mallards (*Anas platyrhynchos*) were introduced to the Hawaiian Islands in the 1800s for sport and food. They are closely related to the endangered *Koloa* and readily hybridize producing fertile offspring. Genetically pure *Koloa* may still remain on Kaua'i and on parts of Hawai'i, however, the O'ahu and Maui populations appear to have significant genetic introgression, with few, if any, pure *Koloa* remaining.

- Humans, apart from being responsible for hydrological modifications, have unintentionally or deliberately introduced many invasive plants (e.g., *Urochloa mutica*, *Rhizophora mangle*), insects, diseases, pesticides, herbicides and other contaminants, that are responsible for changes in wetland dynamics. Global warming will also bring changes in climate patterns, shifts in drought and floods, submergence of current coastal wetlands, and even new wetlands to places where there was once dry land.

G. Wetland Mitigation

Soon after passage of the CWA in 1972, the EPA issued wetland mitigation regulations in its Section 404(b)(1) guidelines. These are the foremost rules regarding wetlands mitigation. They provide a considerable wealth of legal information about wetland **avoidance** (precluding impacts), minimization and mitigation.

In all individual permit actions the applicant is required to prove that impacts to wetlands cannot be avoided and that the proposed activities are in the best interest of the public. This obligates finding the least environmentally damaging, practicable alternative.

Those wetland habitat impacts that cannot be avoided must be **minimized**. For wetland impacts that cannot be avoided or minimized, agencies must next consider whether to require mitigation. **Mitigation** is compensation through wetland restoration, enhancement, creation and/or preservation in direct response to wetland functions and values lost. Mitigation is generally interpreted as alleviating or reducing severity or harm. In environmental contexts, mitigation generally refers to the efforts employed in reducing or offsetting the negative environmental consequences of activities that are permitted despite their negative impact (Environmental Defense Fund 1999).

Mitigation or compensation of wetland impacts can be accomplished in a variety of ways:

Restoration: re-establishing wetland conditions, including hydrology, hydric soils or hydrophytic vegetation to an area where a wetland had previously existed.

Enhancement: altering an existing wetland to increase specific functions and values. Enhancement includes new capabilities, management options, structures or other actions that benefit one or more functions and values.

Creation: developing the hydrologic, geochemical and biological components necessary to support and maintain a wetland where a wetland did not previously exist, including wetlands established in non-hydric soil.

Preservation: protecting an existing and functioning wetland from prospective future threats for a set time (e.g., in perpetuity) through the implementation of appropriate legal and physical mechanisms, including easements, land trusts, conservation funds for management or state conservation overlays (e.g., the Natural Area Partnership Program or Natural Area Reserves System through Hawaii's Department of Land and Natural Resources).

"In lieu" fees: providing direct payment to a mitigation bank, usually offsite from the wetland to be impacted.

1. Wetland Mitigation Successes

In its report *Compensating for Wetland Losses Under the Clean Water Act* (June 2001) the National Research Council (NRC) of the National Academy of Sciences attempted to evaluate the success of wetland mitigation efforts in the U.S., but encountered a problem of poor or no data for such efforts. Without such data the NRC could not determine that the goal of "no net loss of wetlands" was being achieved. Similarly, mitigation projects in Hawaiʻi have been constrained by lack of data and knowledge of the ecology, functions and values of specific wetland types. To date, mitigation successes have been few. Learning from mitigation and restoration projects enhances our ability to move forward with successful projects.

2. Wetland Mitigation Case Study: Kīhei, Maui

Numerous wetland mitigation projects in Kīhei, Maui, provide lessons for future compensatory mitigation plans. From an analysis of aerial imagery and case files, Kīhei had approximately 85 hectares (210 acres) of seasonal wetlands/mudflats in 1965, prior to major urban development. From 1965 to 1976, approximately 15.3 hectares (38 acres) of wetlands were converted to uplands and another 9 hectares (22 acres) of wetlands were lost from 1976 until 1991. In 1990, the first mitigated wetlands in Hawaiʻi were created and enhanced in Kīhei (Longs' and Azeka's ponds) to compensate for wetland loss. Between 1991 and 2003, another 19 hectares (46 acres) of wetlands were converted to upland and compensated by approximately 4 hectares (9 acres) of enhanced wetlands. Thus, between 1965 until 2003, Kīhei lost over 50% of its wetlands (Erickson & Shade 2004).

Wetland challenges in Kīhei are cumulative. Most of the more than 15 wetland-fill permit requests from 1989 to 2003 were for small lots of less than one hectare. The wetlands were fragmented, with diverse ownership (some business, some residential). Urban development the past decade has been considerable. Kīhei has been one of the fastest growing areas in the state. Functional benefits of these seasonal wetlands were considered to be few; many of the first wetland mitigation projects were devised to compensate simply for bird habitat or for flood storage functions. Also most mitigation projects were "out-of-kind," meaning a different wetland type, such as replacing seasonal *groundwater-driven/ brackish/ level flood-*

Failed mitigation project within the fence, Kīhei, Maui 2005 (TE)

plain/ mineral substrate/ coastal flats with permanent *groundwater-driven/ brackish/ depression/ mineral substrate/ palustrine wetlands.* Most of these wetland mitigation projects would be categorized today as enhancement, rather than restoration or creation projects.

3. Mitigation Planning

When planning mitigation, the first decision is to determine location. A legal agreement between the COE and EPA establishes a preference for on-site mitigation of wetlands impacts. Some argue that for small, patchwork losses (e.g., in an urban environment), off-site mitigation or mitigation banking better compensates for the loss. Currently in Hawai'i there are no mitigation banks established for use. Location of the compensatory wetland should take into consideration all factors, including functionality within the *ahupua'a* (Hawaiian land division system that extends from the

An initial COE wetland violation case, mitigation of the Nukoli'i wetland, on Kaua'i, included grading and microtopography work in 1995 (COE)

The Nukoli'i mitigation eight years later. Dominant plant species are native, while *Casuarina equisetifolia* is aggressively invading the buffer area (TE)

mountains to the sea), functions and values, practicality of mitigation and cost.

The next decision will quantify "how much is enough." Ratios are often used to diffuse the impact of wetland loss from development by creating or restoring more wetlands prior to the proposed impacts in order to compensate for the functional time loss. Mitigation ratios are usually based on area and sometimes on functions and values and time. Because mitigation projects may not be fully functioning before impacts to the wetland occur, agencies often require a larger mitigation area, for instance, three hectares of mitigation for one hectare of wetland loss.

The temporal lag is especially keen for certain types of wetlands. For instance, a one hectare loss of a grazed wetland pasture in Hanalei, Kaua'i (described as *groundwater-driven/ freshwater/ depression/ mineral substrate/*

palustrine wetland) would be mitigated differently from one hectare of a hanging wetland in the Koʻolau Mountains, Oʻahu (described as *groundwater-driven/ freshwater/ slope/ organic substrate/ bog*). One might argue that the potential for success of mitigating for the bog would be nil because of the time it would take to develop like conditions elsewhere. Wetland classification and functional attributes of the wetlands to be impacted are therefore crucial in analyzing and understanding any wetland mitigation planning scheme.

At least five factors should be addressed when deciding upon mitigation ratios:
- existing levels of wetland functions at the mitigation site prior to mitigation;
- resultant levels of wetland functions expected at the mitigation site after the project is fully successful;
- length of time before the mitigation is expected to be fully successful;
- risk that the mitigation may not succeed; and
- differences in the location of the wetland lost and the mitigation wetland that would affect wetland functions.

Mitigation plans should include everything needed in a restoration plan (see the following section) as well as an analysis and description of the wetland to be impacted to ensure appropriate and successful compensation occurs.

• Locate wetland mitigation sites in similar wetland classifications
• Consider both current and future watershed hydrology
• Choose wetland restoration over creation (more feasible and sustainable)
• Avoid over-engineered structures (high maintenance)
• Choose sites with connectivity or closeness to other wetlands over isolated sites
• Consider control of invasive plants and animals
• Consider the need for buffers (upland and riparian)
• Know your plants and plant life requirements
• Know your target animal species requirements
• Pay attention to the subsurface (soil and geomorphology and water quality)
• Consider costs
• Consider long-term protection of the site, and
• Consider long-term monitoring and maintenance

4. Wetland Mitigation/Restoration Planning Guidelines

The following outline includes the most pertinent elements of a mitigation or restoration plan. It can be used as a guide during project planning and implementation.

Wetlands Mitigation/Restoration Plan Outline
Responsible Party_____
Date_____
1. Goals and objectives of mitigation/restoration
2. Clear rationale of purpose and need
3. (If a mitigation plan) Description of wetland to be lost or impacted, including area and extent of proposed impacts; existing soils, hydrology and plants; wetland classification (all function and value attributes); surrounding current and future land uses; and cultural resource locations
4. Performance standards for determining success (or compliance, if mitigation)
5. Financial or real estate assurances to provide for maintenance and monitoring and long-term protection of the site
6. Ecological descriptions of habitat types and functions to be mitigated/restored, including any unique habitat types and target species for which the project is designed
7. Explanation of watershed function and how the restoration will fit into the *ahupua'a*
8. Description of practices required for wetland compensation/restoration and management of the site, such as planting plans, water control structure locations and capacities, cut-and-fill re-contouring designs, levee locations, management tools and schedules
9. Schedule of dates for implementing practices and measures
10. Erosion control and other temporary measures to reduce short-term effects of restoration or mitigation
Wetlands Mitigation/Restoration Plan Outline — continued next page

Wetlands Mitigation/Restoration Plan Outline (continued)
Responsible Party_____
Date_____
11. Site plan map, including:
A.   adjacent land uses and previous land uses at site
B.   certified wetland delineation map with labels
C.   access routes
D.   utility location
E.   Hawaiian cultural resource locations, and
F.   planned wetland system(s) and proposed design layout
12. Photographs documenting site conditions before, during and after restoration. Photo points should be documented on restoration plan map
13. Identification and assessment of potential effects that any public drainage rights or water rights may have on the wetland and buffer area
14. Management and maintenance plan which can including mowing, grazing, invasive species and pest control strategies
15. Monitoring plan
16. Contingency plan to correct unanticipated site conditions or changes
17. List of required permits to be obtained to comply with Federal and State laws, including the National Environmental Policy Act, Endangered Species Act, Section 106 of the National Historic Preservation Act, NAGPRA, Clean Water Act Section 404, Coastal Zone Consistency Review, 401 Water Quality Certification and other applicable laws

H. Wetland Restoration

Since the 1990s, there has been an emerging interest in wetland restoration in Hawai'i. Ongoing projects include those on National Wildlife Refuges, such as Keālia Pond on Maui, James Campbell Refuge on O'ahu and the Hanalei Refuge on Kaua'i; State Wildlife Sanctuaries, such as Pouhala, Hāmākua and Kawai Nui Marshes on O'ahu; and private lands, such as Umikoa Ranch on Hawai'i, Ka'elepulu Pond on O'ahu, Hāna Ranch on Maui and Kawaihau wetlands on Kaua'i. Partnerships between private landowners, state and federal agencies, nongovernmental organizations, community groups and volunteers make wetland restoration possible in the state.

Because wetland restoration in Hawai'i is relatively new and each project is complex, lessons are continually being learned about how to better plan and implement wetland restoration projects. Nationally, wetland societies, interagency groups and private entities have written extensively about restoration ecology and planning. This section provides a summary of the information available and the important issues in Hawai'i.

1. Wetland Restoration Goals and Objectives

The most important part of restoration planning is to clearly define goals and objectives of the project. What do you want to restore to and how far back in time do you go? Will you practically be able to restore the site to your defined previous condition? Why are you restoring the wetland? Are there specific wetland types (see wetland analysis protocol pg. 25) functions and values on which to focus? In Hawai'i there are many ways to determine historic baseline wetland conditions to answer the question, "how far back do you go?"

The science of **paleoecology** can provide the most extensive chronology. A paleoecological survey draws on the fossil record to reconstruct ecosystems of the past. Paleoecology has dispelled some widely held beliefs in Hawai'i (e.g., little to no herbivory or fires prior to human arrival) and has helped to "rediscover" species previously not known to exist on certain islands. Analyses of fossils, casts and pollen cores can provide information not apparent on the current landscape about past wetland ecosystems, particularly those that existed prior to human settlement in the islands. Paleoecology entails sediment coring and analysis. It can reveal indicators of hydrology, soils and types of vegetation (usually to genus) as well as faunal changes, particularly the changes from pre-human to present times.

The pollen and spore diagram on the next pages is an example of information that can be provided through paleoecology studies (Burney 2004). It shows the percentages of major plant groups identified in a sediment core taken from the Kawaihau wetlands on Kaua'i. *Pritchardia* palms and diverse woody vegetation dominate the mid-Holocene (pre-human) period. Calendar years from the core are from 6600BP to present, depth of coring and soil texture type are noted on the left vertical axis, and the distinction between pre-human and human time frames is noted on the right vertical axis. This information can be vital to restoration, if the goals and objectives of the project are to restore native plant communities that once existed at the site.

BMT-4: Major Pollen and Spore Types

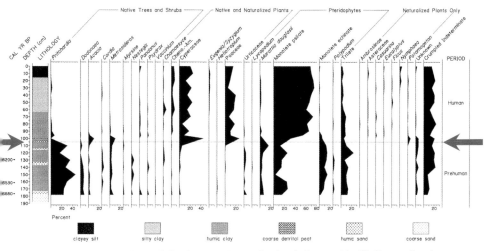

A typical pollen and spore diagram indicating percentages of major plant groups identified in a sediment core taken from the Kawaihau wetlands, Kaua'i (DB). Note drastic changes with human arrival indicated by arrows

Other methods use more recent information, including local knowledge, old maps, photographs, hydrology, soils and plant data, and personal communications with experts. For instance, there has been an increased interest in restoring historic taro patches in Hawai'i, and there are numerous publications that explain the restoration process, such as *"Taro, mauka to makai: a taro production and business guide for Hawaii growers"* (CTAHR 1997), that can be used to restore wetlands to historic taro-farming conditions.

Goals and objectives of wetland restoration projects in the state often focus on specific wetland functions and values. Most Hawaiian lowland wetlands represent highly altered systems, that for the most part retain little semblance of their original hydrology or vegetation and are in many cases heavily managed for human values, such as flood control, native riparian plant restoration or endangered waterbird habitat.

There is an increased interest in restoration of Hawaiian taro patches, such as on this farm in Waipi'o Valley, Hawai'i (TE)

51

One should be clear about restoration goals and objectives, and recognize the potential gaps or fallacies in defining wetland restoration to specific values, compared with striving for the comprehensive restoration of all wetland functions and values.

2. Wetland Restoration Challenges

Wetlands in Hawai'i are difficult to restore. To begin with it is essential to restore the basic elements that define the wetland, that is, its structural integrity: hydrology, soils and plants, as discussed in previous sections. A wetland restoration plan should be developed (see pages 48–49, Mitigation/Restoration Plan Outline).

The driving force in wetlands – hydrology – is the most confusing and yet is probably the single most important determinant of the establishment and maintenance of specific types of wetlands and wetland processes. Especially in Hawai'i, very little long-term hydrological data are documented and we still do not know detailed information about the influence of fluctuations in hydrology on soils, plants and animals. Because water plays such a vital role, it is crucial to re-establish the kind of hydrologic regime desired, based on goals and objectives.

Soils provide a rooting medium for germination, a seed bank, water and nutrient-holding capacity and habitat for soil micro-organisms (e.g., bacteria, fungal mycorrhizae and algae). Soils at a proposed wetland restoration site may be devoid of organic matter and nitrogen and may lack biological microbes important to plants, in which case they should be supplemented. A soil analysis can be completed prior to restoration to ensure the soils contain enough organic materials for the desired plant and invertebrate communities.

After restoration of this *surface water-driven/ freshwater/ fringe/ mineral substrate/ palustrine* wetland in Kohala, Hawai'i, plant diversity was low and out-planting was required. Wetlands complexes were constructed primarily to provide functions and values for *Koloa* through the NRCS Wetlands Reserve Program (WRP). *Koloa* responded almost immediately and were seen foraging within weeks of inundation (KU)

If possible, the original hydric soil can be stockpiled and later redistributed on the surface or along fringe areas during the final grading stages. This can provide organic materials necessary for microbial and wetland plant and invertebrate communities. Sometimes when restoring a wetland that has become an upland after a long period of time, hydric soils may be at a great depth, but can still be stockpiled and spread to provide a rooting medium for plants.

Sometimes the seed bank can be relied upon for volunteer vegetation to reestablish after restoring hydrology and hydric soils (called **passive restoration**). However, in Hawai'i it is often the case that the seed bank contains aggressive-invasive plants. Therefore, weeding and planting of desired species are often required.

Depending on the restoration goals of the project, a plant list can be developed from a paleoecology report or can be developed based on function and value objectives. This plant list should correlate to a plan map that details plant density and community design. Site drainage, water chemistry (i.e., salinity), proximity of invasive plant species and maintenance needs should be clearly described in a planting plan. In Hawai'i, meticulous inspection should also take place to insure all plants delivered to the site do not include "hitchhikers" of the worst variety, such as invasive ants (e.g., little fire ants) or coqui frogs.

If passive restoration is not possible, extensive planting will need to occur. A **wetland restoration planting plan** should be developed, to include:

- The type of propagule used for each species of plants (e.g., seed, bare root, rhizome, bagged, plug, potted)
- Timing of planting to achieve maximum survival (e.g., avoid dry season)
- Source of plant materials
- Expected volunteer vegetation (including weed species)
- Methods of planting
- Potential use of mulch
- Potential soil amendments needed
- Proposed benefit of each plant species (e.g., for endangered waterbirds)
- Potential supplemental water needs for establishment
- Maintenance and weeding specifics (species, methods and timing)
- Herbivore protection/fencing plan

Lessons are continually being learned about wetland restoration and mitigation in Hawai'i. As this guide has discussed, the main concepts to keep in mind are to use a watershed and ecosystem approach, and to use functional assessment procedures to ensure the appropriate wetland type is restored or mitigated. Completing the wetland restoration/mitigation plan outline on pages 48 and 49 and the above planting plan outline, provide comprehensive guidance to commence a wetland restoration or mitigation project.

PART II

Wetland Plant Identification

Christopher F. Puttock (editor)

CONTRIBUTORS
Christopher F. Puttock — ferns, monocots, dicots
Clyde T. Imada — monocots, dicots
Derral R. Herbst — sedges, grasses

Wetland plants

PART II
Wetland Plant Identification

Arrangement

The wetland plants in this field guide are arranged into seven sections. The sections are essentially life-forms and subdivisions of them. These sections are fairly intuitive: submerged and floating herbs, ferns and fern allies, woody plants, dicot herbs, monocot herbs, sedges and grasses. As life-forms rarely fit neatly into human definitions some species may be on the border-line between two sections. These plants are keyed out in more than one place, with redirection to the section in which their descriptions and photographs can be found. Within each section the plants are arranged alphabetically by the scientific name of genus and species.

Identification keys

Identification keys are provided for all species included in this field guide. For the use of any identification keys a good representation of vegetative, flowering and fruiting material is required. Attempting to identify plants from what some describe as "eco-scraps" is at best unreliable, if not impossible. Plants are not always cooperative, although the virtually continuous growing season for many plants in Hawai'i make the chances of finding adequate material better than in many other places in the world.

The keys are dichotomous, providing an either/or choice at each lead. Each lead will either give you a genus or species name, or direct you to the next lead. Follow the number to the next lead question, and continue the process until the lead runs to a species name. Where possible the keys have used vegetative morphology first. In some groups, particularly the grasses and sedges, this has not been possible as vegetative morphology is highly variable, so minute floral and fruit details are needed almost immediately. Take notes about your plants. Observations should be made from several plants to find the range of variation within the population and to assure that, for example, the flower you are using has not lost a petal before (or after) you got to it. Parts will fall off in your collecting bags. For making herbarium specimens the use of a field plant press is essential. Collecting permits are required for taking plant material from most places in Hawai'i. Check with the Department of Land and Natural Resources (DLNR) for what permits may be needed. Once you have obtained the collecting permits to make specimens for a research professional or for an herbarium (e.g. Bishop Museum), take more notes and use a GPS to pinpoint the location of each of your specimens. This will make the specimens more useful for further taxonomic research. Use pruning shears to minimize injury to the plant.

Everything that you will need to see to identify the plants in this field guide can be discovered using a 10X hand-lens (jeweler's loupe). Attach one to your field guide.

You WILL need it. Practice using the keys and descriptions, as these are much more reliable for determining the species than matching photographs and illustrations. Images will only bring you close to the real identity of a plant. If you have any doubt about the identity of a plant, professional identification services are available from botanists at the *Herbarium Pacificum*, Bishop Museum, in Honolulu. The *Herbarium Pacificum* is the State of Hawaii's repository for botanical collections.

Scientific name: The scientific names used for species in this field guide are those currently accepted by botanists in Hawai'i. The vast majority of these names are the current names used by the Integrated Taxonomic Information System (ITIS). Discrepancies between the names used in this field guide and ITIS may occur when local botanists believe that the nomenclatural changes have been taken up before the scientific evidence has undergone sufficient scrutiny. When more than one scientific name has been used for a species in Hawai'i during the past few decades that name is listed as a **Note** and the reason for its dismissal indicated. The scientific name for a species consist of two parts: a genus name and a specific epithet. In this field guide these are always in *italics*. This is followed by the name of the author of the species (the person who originally described the species in a publication) and, if the placement of the species has changed, by the name of the person who made that change. Author abbreviations follow Brummitt and Powell (1992) and updated on the International Plant Name Index (IPNI) website http://www.us.ipni.org/index.html.

Vernacular name: Most species have at least one common name in use in the local vernacular languages. For widespread species many other names and variations may exist. For all introduced (non-Hawaiian) and native species in this field guide the most widely used common name is provided. For species endemic to the Hawaiian Islands the most commonly used Hawaiian name is provided. For native species both Hawaiian and English name (or in some instances Chinese or Japanese names where they have cultural significance) are also provided. Recently coined names in the Hawaiian language for introduced species are considered secondary to the most widely used vernacular name and are generally not included.

Description: The plant descriptions are provided in telegraphic style, using minimal punctuation. Complex botanical terms have been simplified or generalized wherever possible (see Glossary). This sacrifices some precision in terminology. The same information for all descriptions across each section is provided. As this has not been done in other publications this field guide assembles some information not found elsewhere. For a small number of species that differ from another in very few details, short diagnoses highlighting the differences are provided.

Distribution: Where known, the center of origin for each species is given to a subcontinent or continent. The current Hawaiian Island distribution is based on Wagner *et al.* (1999), supplemented by updates published in the Hawai'i Biological Survey Records. Wetland plants may exist outside the island ranges described. Such new

58

information should be reported to the Hawai'i Biological Survey at Bishop Museum, preferably accompanied by a voucher specimen.

The extent of species distributions are classified as:

- **Endemic**: used for plants only occurring in the Hawaiian Islands and nowhere else before human arrival. Narrower endemism is indicated by island distribution (endemic is a subset of native).

- **Native**: used strictly for plants occurring naturally in the Hawaiian Islands AND somewhere outside the Hawaiian Islands before human arrival (= indigenous).

- **?Native**: used for plants that are possibly native, but may have arrived unnoticed with humans, and therefore considered to be cryptogenic (having hidden origins).

- **Introduced**: used for any species that was brought to the Hawaiian Islands by humans or through human intervention, as deliberate or unintentional cargo on canoes, ships and planes, and on livestock, etc (= alien, and when well established, naturalized).

Invasiveness is defined by how a species reacts in the environment:

- **Aggressive-invasive**: species that are actively moving towards single-species stands and will eliminate habitat occupied by other plants.

- **Passive-invasive**: species that replace themselves, but are not actively moving toward forming single-species stands.

- **Non-invasive**: species that are overtaken by aggressive-invasive species and may be considered under threat of habitat loss and eventual extirpation.

Wetland indicator ratings (OBL, FACW, FAC and FACU) are defined on page 19. The wetland indicator status of each plant is that from the revised *Wetland Status List for Hawaiian Plants* (Puttock & Imada 2004).

Terminology used in Keys and Descriptions

Many people are daunted by what appears to be a difficult language used by botanists. This field guide uses very few specific botanical terms. Some terms are similar to common medical terms, such as reniform (kidney-shaped) and cordate (heart-shaped). The majority of terms that may be difficult are actually geometric terms used widely in many scientific disciplines. Terms used in this field guide are indicated in **bold** and can be found in the glossary; those avoided are in normal type.

Stems: Terms used for above-ground axes of flowering plants include **trunks**, **branches**, **cladodes**, stalks, fronds [*sic*], **peduncles**, **pedicels**, inflorescence axes, floral axes, **culms**, rachises, rachillas, and so on. Surface stems are called **stolons**, runners and **corms**. Underground stems include such terms as suffruticose stems, **rhizomes** and **tubers**. To confuse matters the stems of ferns, whether above ground or below, are called rhizomes.

Although stems of ferns and flowering plants have different vascular types, their function to support leaves is the same. The points at which leaf-bases arise on the stem are called **nodes**. The intervals between leaves are called **internodes**. In flowering plants each node produces a leaf and an **axillary bud**—the bud for a new stem. This stem may become a vegetative branch, inflorescence or pedicel of a flower. Fern leaves do not produce axillary buds and their branches arise differently. The only leaves in flowering plants that never have axillary buds are the cotyledons (seed-leaves).

Leaves: The leaf begins at the **leaf-base** or point of departure of the vascular traces of the leaf. The leaf-base includes the **stipules**—lateral extensions at the leaf-base. The central axis of a leaf is called the **petiole, midvein**, phyllode, **rachis**, etc. The leaf-blade may be **simple** or subdivided to the axis to form compound leaves, consisting of **pinnae** or **leaflets**. Axillary buds are never present between leaflets and the central axis in a compound leaf. As an absolute rule every branch on a flowering plant has or had at one time a subtending leaf.

Leaves arising on stems above ground level are called **cauline**. Those arising at or near ground level are called **basal**. Leaves on inflorescence axes are usually much smaller in size. These reduced leaves are generally called bracts; hence **floral bracts, involucral bracts**, floral scales, **spathes, glumes, lemmas** and **paleas** are all forms of leaves.

Flowers: The reproductive parts of flowering plants are highly modified fertile leaves that terminate a specialized stem called a **pedicel**. At the apex of the pedicel, the **receptacle**, is the female part of the flower, consisting of one to many **carpels**, and collectively known as the **gynoecium** or pistil. The parts of the carpel are the **stigma, style** and **ovary**. The ovary encloses one to many **ovules**. Subtending the carpels is the male part of the flower, consisting of one to many stamens, and collectively known as the **androecium**. The parts of the stamen are the **filament** and **anther**. The anthers enclose two sacs of **pollen**. Subtending the androecium are several whorls of specialized sterile leaves, collectively known as the **perianth**. The perianth generally consists of two whorls, the inner **petals** and the outer **sepals**. When each whorl is partially or entirely joined together (fused) they are called the **corolla** and **calyx**. When the ovary is visible above the attachment of the outer floral parts, the ovary is called **superior**. In flowers where ovary is not visible, that is, the outer floral parts arise above the ovary, the ovary is called **inferior**. Flowers differ in shapes and numbers of parts present. When both gynoecium and androecium are present, the flower is **bisexual**, perfect or hermaphrodite. When only one sex is present the flower is **unisexual**: male (**staminate**) or female (**pistillate**).

The different numbers of floral parts give clues to relationships between plants. These numbers can be written out as floral formulas. Many families of plants have fairly stable floral formulas and can easily be recognized by the number and arrangement of the floral parts.

Flowers, when not solitary in the axil of a leaf or terminating a stem, are borne on branches in various types of inflorescences. For the purposes of this field guide the terms **head**, **umbel**, **spike**, **raceme**, **cluster** and **panicle** have been used. More complicated terms such as cymes and thyrses, have been largely avoided.

Fruit: The fruit is the structure that develops from the one or more ovaries and associated parts of a flower, and sometimes the parts of many flowers together. These parts can include the peduncles, pedicel, receptacle, bracts, perianth and stamens. The fruit is the unit that protects the developing seed/s and may assist in seed dispersal. In general fruits may be fleshy or dry, dehiscent or indehiscent.

Fruit terminology is complex and very confusing. There are many terms in use (and often misuse) for different and even the same types of fruits. In this treatment we have condensed the 95 currently recognized fruit types (Spjut 1994, 2003) into six broad categories. Common names for fruits are not usually helpful in understanding fruit terminology. The six general terms used in this field guide are:

- **Berry**: includes all fruit that are the product of one or more carpels and are fleshy throughout, such as: berries, pomes and pepos (e.g., blueberries, apples, oranges, bananas, tomatoes, and grapes).

- **Drupe**: includes all fruit that are the product of one or more carpels and have a fleshy or leathery outer layer and a hard stone-like inner layer, sometimes called a pit (e.g., peaches, almonds, cherries, coffee cherries, macadamia nuts, pecans, mangos and olives).

- **Nut**: includes all dry fruit that are the product of one carpel that does not break open along a natural line of weakness at maturity, such as: achenes, caryopses, cypselas, utricles and samaras (e.g., coconuts, acorns, hazelnuts, strawberries, sunflower seeds and grass grains).

- **Schizocarp**: includes all dry fruit that are the product of more than one carpel and split into the separate carpels (mericarps) at maturity (e.g., coriander seeds).

- **Pod**: includes all dry fruit that are the product of one carpel that breaks open along natural lines of weakness at maturity, such as: follicles, coccums and legumes (e.g. string beans and peanuts).

- **Capsule**: includes all dry fruit that are the product of more than one carpel and break open to release the seeds at maturity along natural lines of weakness, such as: true capsules, siliques and loments (e.g., gumnuts).

In rare instances the seedlings germinate on the parent plant, thus giving it a headstart by having their hypocotyls already well advanced before being released by the parent plant. This is called vivipary (**viviparous**) in plants and is analogous to the production of live young rather than eggs in animals.

KEY TO SECTIONS
Common Ferns and Flowering Plants of Hawaii's Wetlands

Included in this field guide are the common lowland obligate (OBL) to facultative (FAC) plants encountered in Hawaii's wetlands. We have also included several facultative upland (FACU) species that may stray into wetlands but are essentially dried out for most of their life. Mosses, liverworts, hornworts and algae, although present in wetlands, are not included in this field guide.

Key to the sections

1   Plants growing in water with leaves and stems completely submerged, or plants floating on the water surface ... ***Submerged and floating herbs*** (Section 1, p.63) Plants growing in water with leaves and stems held above the water surface, or terrestrial plants growing in moist or saturated soils prone to inundation 2

2(1)   Plants not producing flowers and seeds; leaves without branches or buds between leaf-base and stem .... ***Ferns and fern allies*** (Section 2, p.84) Plants producing flowers and seeds; leaves with branches arising only from axillary buds 3

3(2)   Trees (including palms and screwpines), shrubs and woody vines; plants with above-ground stems producing wood and bark .... ***Woody plants*** (Section 3, p.101) Annual or perennial herbs; plants with above-ground stems lacking wood and bark 4

4(3)   Flower parts usually in twos, fours or fives; leaves with net-like (reticulate) veins (dicots, mostly broad-leaved plants) .... ***Dicot herbs*** (Section 4, p.138) Flower parts usually in threes; leaves usually with parallel veins (monocots, mostly narrow-leaved plants) 5

5(4)   Flowers arranged in heads, dense spikes or clusters but never spikelets .... ***Monocot herbs*** (Section 5, p.180) Flowers arranged in laterally flattened or terete spikelets 6

6(5)   Stems 3-sided and solid, rarely terete or hollow; leaves 3-ranked; leaf-sheath usually closed; each flower subtended by a single floral bract; carpels usually 3 .... ***Sedges*** (Section 6, p.202) Stems usually terete and hollow; leaves 2-ranked; leaf-sheath usually open; each flower subtended by two floral bracts (lemma and palea) and other inflorescence bracts (glumes); carpels usually 2 .... ***Grasses*** (Section 7, p.244)

SECTION 1 — SUBMERGED and FLOATING HERBS
Plants fully submerged or free-floating

This section treats plants that are fully or partially submerged, their stems being supported by the water column, and plants that are free-floating on the water surface. This is a diverse group arising independently in a small number of families. There are two floating ferns in Hawai'i, *Azolla* and *Salvinia*. They are keyed out here and also in Section 2 (Ferns and fern allies) and are described in that section. Recent molecular studies place the duckweed family Lemnaceae (i.e., *Landoltia*, *Lemna*, *Spirodela*, *Wolffiella* and *Wolffia*) as a distant relative of the water lettuce (*Pistia*) in the family Araceae.

Key to the submerged and floating plants of Hawaii's wetlands

1 Plants free-floating on the surface, not attached to the bottom 2
  Plants attached to the bottom, or sometimes detached 11

2(1) Leaves absent; plant consisting of small floating stems less than 10mm long ... 3
  Leaves present; stems more than 10mm long 7

3(2) Plants without roots; stems less than 0.8mm long .... *Wolffia globosa*
  Plants with 1 or more roots; stems more than 1mm long 4

4(3) Plants with 1 root only 5
  Plants with 2 or more roots 6

5(4) Stems green, never red .... *Lemna aequinoctialis*
  Stems purplish-red below, often with red spots on upper surface ....
  .... *Lemna obscura*

6(4) Stems with 3–5 veins and 3–5 roots .... *Landoltia punctata*
  Stems with 7–12 veins and 7–16 roots .... *Spirodela polyrhiza*

7(2) Plants producing sporangia on leaves or sporocarps on submerged leaves 8
  Plants producing flowers 9

8(7) Leaves 1–2mm long .... *Azolla filiculoides* (Section 2)
  Leaves more than 7mm long .... *Salvinia molesta* (Section 2)

9(7) Leaves in whorls of 3–12 at each node .... *Ceratophyllum demersum*
  Leaves alternate 10

10(9) Leaves sessile .... *Pistia stratiotes*
  Leaves with long petioles .... *Eichhornia crassipes*

11(1) Plants without leaves .... *Utricularia gibba*
       Plants with leaves 12

12(11) Leaves floating on water surface or at least some leaves emergent 13
       Leaves entirely submerged 14

13(12) Leaves sessile, divided into feathery pinnae above and below the water surface .
       .... *Myriophyllum aquaticum*
       Leaves petiolate, entire or dentate, with some leaves floating on the water sur-
       face .... *Nymphaea* spp.

14(12) Leaves alternate 15
       Leaves opposite or whorled 17

15(14) Flowers 2 per peduncle; tepals absent; stamens 2; fruit stalked ....
       .... *Ruppia maritima*
       Flowers many per peduncle; tepals 4; stamens 4; fruit sessile 16

16(15) Stipules attached at the leaf-base; leaves predominantly 1-veined ....
       .... *Stuckenia pectinata*
       Stipules not attached at the leaf-base; leaves predominantly 3–5-veined ....
       .... *Potamogeton foliosus*

17(14) Plants growing in sea water 18
       Plants growing in fresh water 19

18(17) Petioles 15–25mm long; leaf-blades elliptical to spathulate with entire margins .
       .... *Halophila hawaiiana*
       Petioles 3–15mm long; leaf-blades obovate with minutely serrate margins ....
       .... *Halophila decipiens*

19(17) Leaves less than 4cm long 20
       Leaves more than 20cm long 21

20(19) Leaves in whorls of 3–5, 2–5mm wide; flowers on the water surface ....
       .... *Egeria densa*
       Leaves in opposite pairs or subopposite, less than 2mm wide; flowers in axils
       below the surface .... *Najas guadalupensis*

21(19) Leaves less than 1–3cm wide; male flowers stamens upright with filaments par-
       tially or wholly united; female flowers with stigmas not fringed ....
       .... *Vallisneria americana*
       Leaves less than 2cm wide; male flowers stamens obliquely extended with fila-
       ments free; female flowers with stigmas fringed .... *Vallisneria spiralis*

Ceratophyllum demersum L.
Coontail, hornwort

CERATOPHYLLACEAE

Description: Submerged aquatic perennial herb 0.5–3m long; stems terete, slender, many-branched and forming large submerged masses. **Leaves** cauline in whorls of 3–12 per node; stipules absent; petioles inconspicuous; leaf-blade 1–3-pinnate; leaflets 1–2cm long, linear with toothed margins. **Flowers** males in pairs, females solitary, axillary on the same plant; bracts connate; pedicels 0–1mm long; sepals 8–15, 1–2mm long, linear; petals absent; stamens 10–20; ovary superior, 1-celled. **Fruit** a dark green to reddish-brown nut 4–6mm long, 1–2.5mm wide, laterally compressed-ellipsoid.

Distribution: Coontail is probably native to Eurasia, now cosmopolitan in still or slow-moving freshwater habitats; in the Hawaiian Islands it is found on Oʻahu, Maui and Hawaiʻi. First collected on Oʻahu in 1934, it is now common in ponds, reservoirs, canals and taro patches from near sea level to 10m elevation. Introduced passive-invasive; OBL.

Note: Coontail has no major economic uses, but does provide food and shelter for aquatic birds and fish. It is used as a cultivated ornamental in aquaria and outdoor ponds and is easily propagated by pieces of the brittle stems. It prefers to grow in slightly acidic water.

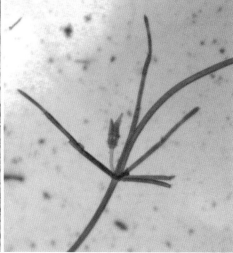

Egeria densa Planch.
Common waterweed, elodea

HYDROCHARITACEAE

Description: Submerged freshwater perennial herb 0.5–3m long, glabrous, with surface-floating flowers; stems slender, 1–3mm diam., terete with few branches, rooting in mud or drifting when broken loose. **Leaves** in whorls of 3–5, curled; leaf-sheath 2–3mm long; petioles absent; lower leaf-blades 3–7mm long, 1–2mm wide, ovate; upper leaf-blades 1–4cm long, 2–5mm wide, ovate to linear with serrate margins. **Flowers** 2–4 males and females on separate plants (females not known from Hawai'i), subtended by a bract (spathe) 11–12mm long, borne on 3–6mm long

peduncles; sepals 3, green, 3–4mm long; petals 3, white, 9–11mm long; stamens 9–10. **Fruit** a capsule 7–15mm long, 3–6mm wide, ellipsoid.

Distribution: Common waterweed is native to tropical South America, now a worldwide escape from cultivation; in the Hawaiian Islands it is found on Kaua'i, O'ahu, Moloka'i, Maui and Hawai'i. First recorded on Hawai'i in 1937, it occurs in coastal wetlands, freshwater ponds and ditches, from near sea level to 50m elevation. Introduced aggressive-invasive; OBL.

Note: This species was previously widely known as *Elodea densa* (Planch.) Casp. and *Anacharis densa* (Planch.) Victorin, and is also commonly known as elodea and Brazilian waterweed. This nuisance species of waterways is widely sold in the aquarium trade.

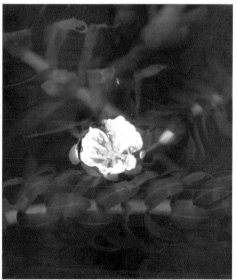

66

Eichhornia crassipes (Mart.) Solms
Water hyacinth   PONTEDERIACEAE

Description: Free-floating freshwater perennial herb 10–25cm high, glabrous; stems (stolons) 1–2cm diam., tufted, long-creeping, occasionally branching and rooting on mud. **Leaves** mostly basal, whorled; leaf-bases with sheathing stipules 2.5–14cm long; petioles 7–30cm long, inflated at the base; leaf-blades simple, 3–16cm long, 4–14cm wide, ovate to orbicular with entire margins. **Flowers** 4–15, bisexual on 10–40cm long spikes; peduncles 5–12cm long; perianth violet, 3.5–4cm long; stamens 6; ovary superior, 3-celled. **Fruit** a green capsule 1–2mm long, ellipsoid, surrounded by persistent perianth.

Distribution: Water hyacinth is native to Central America, now a worldwide aggressive nuisance weed; in the Hawaiian Islands it is found on Kaua'i, O'ahu, Moloka'i, Maui and Hawai'i. First recorded in Hawai'i in the late 1800s, and now locally abundant in coastal wetlands, freshwater ponds and ditches, from near sea level to 50m elevation. Introduced aggressive-invasive; OBL.

Note: *Eichhornia crassipes* is a declared noxious weed in the United States and many other countries. It is considered one of the world's most serious aquatic weeds.

Halophila spp.
Salt-leaf seagrasses
HYDROCHARITACEAE

Halophila hawaiiana Doty & B.C.Stone
Hawaiian seagrass

Description: Fully submerged saltwater perennial herb 10–30cm long, glabrous; erect stems absent; rhizomes prostrate, 1–2mm diam., terete, rooting at nodes in mud and sand. **Leaves** opposite, erect; leaf-base scales sheathing; petioles 15–25mm long; leaf-blades light green, 1–4cm long, 2–6mm wide, elliptical to spathulate with entire margins. **Flowers** 1 male and 1 female, axillary on the same plant, enclosed by a bract (spathe), borne on pedicels 1–2cm long; tepals 3, white, 3–4mm long; stamens 3; ovary inferior, 1-celled. **Fruit** a green capsule 3–6mm diam., ellipsoid, transparent.

Distribution: Hawaiian seagrass occupies sandy reef-flats and in marine fish ponds, and is found in shallow waters around Midway, Pearl and Hermes, Kaua‘i, O‘ahu, Moloka‘i and Maui. The habitat of this species is under threat from siltation, increased nutrient loads and mangrove invasion. Endemic non-invasive; OBL.

Note: This species is very closely related to the widespread South Pacific species, *Halophila ovalis* (R.Br.) Hook.f.

Halophila decipiens Ostenf.
Paddle grass

Diagnosis: This species differs from *Halophila hawaiiana* by shorter petioles 3–15mm long; leaf-blades 2–3cm long, 3–8mm wide, obovate with minutely serrate margins.

Distribution: Paddle grass is native to tropical oceans worldwide; in the Hawaiian Islands it is known from Midway, Kaua‘i and O‘ahu, generally from deeper water. Native non-invasive; OBL.

Note: Some researchers believe that *Halophila decipiens* is a recently arrived invasive species in Hawai‘i, others that it is a deeper water species only recently noticed.

Photo: UH — *H. hawaiiana*

Photo: UH — *H. hawaiiana*

68

Landoltia punctata (G.Mey.) Les & D.J.Crawford
Spotted duckweed   LEMNACEAE

Description: Free-floating perennial herb, glabrous; stems (cladodes) in clusters of 2–6 together, green above, purplish-red below, 1.5–8mm long, 1–4mm wide, obovate with 3–5(–7) veins and distally pointed, 2 branching (budding) pouches near the proximal end, leafless, bearing 2–5 roots. **Flowers** (rarely seen) usually 2 males and a female within a cup-like bract (spathe); perianth absent; male flowers a single stamen; female flowers a 1-celled superior ovary. **Fruit** a pale brown capsule 0.8–1mm long, 0.3–0.5mm wide, ellipsoid, winged.

Distribution: Spotted duckweed is na-tive to tropical and temperate Africa, now cosmopolitan; in the Hawaiian Islands it is found on Oʻahu and Hawaiʻi. First collected on Oʻahu in 1976, it is currently sporadically naturalized in coastal wetlands, freshwater ponds and ditches, from near sea level to 50m elevation. Introduced passive-invasive; OBL.

Note: Previously known as *Spirodela punctata* (G.Mey.) C.H.Thomps. under a broader generic concept. This species provides high-protein food for water birds.

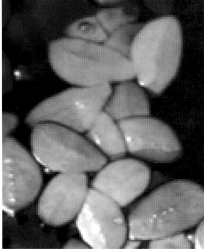

Lemna spp.
Duckweed   LEMNACEAE

Lemna aequinoctialis Welw.
Tropical duckweed

Description: Free-floating perennial herb, glabrous; stems (cladodes) single or in clusters of 2–5 together, green above and below, 2–3.5mm long, 1–2mm wide, elliptic-obovate with 3 veins, 2 budding pouches near the proximal end, leafless, bearing 1 rootlet only. **Flowers** (rarely seen) usually 2 males and a female, within a cup-like bract (spathe); perianth absent; male flowers a single stamen; female flowers a 1-celled superior ovary. **Fruit** a pale brown capsule 0.5–0.8mm long, 0.3–0.5mm wide, ellipsoid, winged.

Distribution: Tropical duckweed is native to tropical and warm temperate Africa, now cosmopolitan; in the Hawaiian Islands it is found on Kaua'i, O'ahu, Moloka'i, Maui and Hawai'i. First recorded in Hawai'i in 1895, it occurs in coastal wetlands, freshwater ponds and ditches, from near sea level to 150m elevation. Introduced or possibly native, non-invasive; OBL.

Note: *Lemna perpusilla* Torr. has been misapplied to this species in Hawai'i. This species provides high-protein food for water birds.

Lemna obscura (Austin) Daubs
Little duckweed

Diagnosis: This species differs from *Lemna aequinoctialis* by stems reddish-purple below, often with red spots on upper surface.

Distribution: The little duckweed is native to the tropical Americas; in the Hawaiian Islands it is found on O'ahu and Hawai'i. First recorded on Hawai'i in 1987, it occurs in coastal wetlands, from near sea level to 50m elevation. Introduced passive-invasive; OBL.

Note: High protein duck food.

L. aequinoctilis

L. aequinoctilis

Myriophyllum aquaticum (Vell.) Verdc.
Parrot feather
HALORAGACEAE

Description: Aquatic perennial herb 0.5–1.8m long, glabrous; stems unbranched, reddish-green with erect growing tips, rooting in the substrate, becoming free-floating. **Leaves** in whorls of 3–6 at each node; stipules and petioles absent; submerged leaf-blades 1-pinnate, 2–3.5cm long; leaflets 25–36, 3–8mm long, linear. **Flowers** a solitary male and female on the same plant, sessile in leaf axils above water surface; calyx 4-lobed; petals 4; stamens 8; ovary inferior, 4-celled. **Fruit** not yet known in Hawai'i.

Distribution: Parrot feather is native to temperate South America; in the Hawaiian Islands it is found on Kaua'i, O'ahu and Hawai'i. First collected on O'ahu in 1919, it is common in still, fresh water habitats, such as ponds, taro patches and upland marshes, from near sea level to 1280m elevation. Introduced aggressive-invasive; OBL.

Note: Grown as an aquatic ornamental in outdoor freshwater ponds. Previously known in the islands by the two younger names *Myriophyllum brasiliense* Cambess. and *M. proserpinacoides* Gillies ex Hook. & Arn.

71

Najas guadalupensis (Spreng.) Magnus
Southern naiad   NAJADACEAE

Description: Completely submerged freshwater annual herb 0.3–1m long, glabrous; stems slender, 0.2–1mm diam., terete, not scabrous, rooting on mud. **Leaves** opposite or subopposite, light green; leaf-base sheathing; petioles absent; leaf-blades 1–3.3cm long, 0.2–2mm wide, linear with minutely serrate margins. **Flowers** 1–3 unisexual, axillary on the same plant; pedicels of male flowers 1–2mm long, females sessile; tepals 2–4, c.1mm long; stamen 1; ovary superior, 1-celled. **Fruit** a purplish-brown nut 1–2mm long, conical.

Distribution: Southern naiad is native to North America, now a worldwide escape from cultivation; in the Hawaiian Islands it is found on O'ahu and Hawai'i. First recorded on Hawai'i in 1987, it is currently sporadically naturalized in coastal wetlands, freshwater ponds and ditches, from near sea level to 50m elevation. Introduced passive-invasive; OBL.

Photo: RM

Nymphaea spp.
Water lilies
NYMPHAEACEAE

Water lilies are very popular cultivated aquatic plants worldwide. Apart from their charismatic appeal as water features, the seeds and rhizomes of several species are eaten in some countries. There are approximately 35 species in the genus and many cultivars and hybrids. The taxonomy at present is intractably confused. Six species appear to be present in Hawai'i; five of which are currently considered as garden escapes. Four of these are day-flowering plants and there are two night-flowering species, one of which (*Nymphaea rubra* Roxb.) has yet to stray from parks and gardens. It is included in this treatment, as it will only be a matter of time before it appears in some wetland.

Key to the species of *Nymphaea* in Hawai'i's wetlands

1   Petals white .... *N. lotus*
     Petals colored (blue, lavender, purple, pink or red) 2

2(1)   Stamens more than 100 3
     Stamens less than 80 4

3(2)   Leaf-blades with dentate margins; petals pink .. *N. capensis var. zanzibariensis*
     Leaf-blades with entire to sinuate margins; petals violet ....
     .... *N. capensis var. capensis*

4(2)   Leaf-blades with sinuate, acutely dentate margins; flowers purplish-red ....
     .... *N. rubra*
     Leaf-blades with entire margins; flowers pale blue to bluish purple 5

5(4)   Leaves more than 30cm diam. .... *N. caerulea*
     Leaves less than 15cm diam. .... *N. ×daubenyana*

Nymphaea spp.
Water lilies

NYMPHAEACEAE

Nymphaea caerulea Savigny
Egyptian blue water lily

Description: Aquatic perennial herb, glabrous; rhizomes unbranched, erect. **Leaves** basal, whorled; stipules absent; petioles reaching the water surface; leaf-blades dark green above, pale green with purple dots below, 30–40cm diam., circular with entire or undulate margins. **Flowers** scented, solitary, 8–15cm diam., on axillary pedicels rising above the water surface; sepals 4, dark green with purple lines, lanceolate; petals 14–20, pale blue, 5–8.5cm long, lanceolate; stamens 50–75, the outer ones above blue and yellow below middle, and inner stamens bright yellow throughout; ovary superior, 14–20-celled. **Fruit** a berry 2.5–3.8cm long, compressed-ovoid.

Distribution: Egyptian blue water lily is native to northern and tropical Africa, now cultivated worldwide; in the Hawaiian Islands it is found on Hawai'i. First collected in 1992 in a stock pond near Kehena Reservoir on Parker Ranch, now in wetlands from 700 to 800m elevation. Introduced aggressive-invasive; OBL.

Nymphaea capensis Thunb.
Cape blue water lily

Diagnosis: This species differs from *N. caerulea* by leaf-blades with entire to dentate margins; flowers 7–8cm diam., petals 12–27; stamens 100–250, yellow throughout; ovary 14–50-celled; fruit 2–3cm long, compressed-ovoid.

var. *capensis* with leaf-blades with entire to undulate margins; flowers 7–8cm diam.; petals violet; stamens 100–200.

N. capensis
var. capensis

var. *zanzibariensis* (Caspary) Conard with leaf-blades dentate; flowers 15–25cm diam.; petals vivid pink; stamens 120–250.

Photo: MC

N. capensis
var. zanzibariensis

Distribution: Cape blue water lily is native to eastern Africa and Madagascar, now cultivated worldwide; in the Hawaiian Islands both varieties are only found on Kaua'i, from Hanalei National Wildlife Refuge in 2000 and Kawaihau District in 1989, in slow-moving streams, from near sea level to 50m elevation.

Introduced passive-invasive; OBL.

Nymphaea ×*daubenyana* W.T.Baxter ex Daubeny　**Dwarf blue water lily**

Diagnosis: This hybrid differs from *N. caerulea* by petioles bearing plantlets at the top; leaf-blades brownish-green blotched dark brown, 9–13cm long, 9–10cm wide, elliptical with entire margins; flowers 5–13cm diam., petals 12–15, pale blue; stamens 40–55 with bright yellow anthers; fruit not formed.

Distribution: Dwarf blue water lily is cultivated worldwide; in the Hawaiian Islands it is found on Maui, first collected in 1999 at Ukumehame, in a flood control canal near sea level. Introduced passive-invasive; OBL.

Note: A sterile hybrid created in the Oxford Botanical Garden in 1856.

Nymphaea lotus L.
White water lily, Egyptian lotus
Diagnosis: This species differs from *N. caerulea* by leaf-blades reddish-green above, purplish-green or bronze below, 10–32cm long, 11–28cm wide, subcircular with sinuate, dentate margins; flowers foetid, 10–25cm diam.; sepals green; petals 16–20, white, cream or pink; stamens 40–80, yellow; ovary superior, 20–30-celled.

Distribution: White water lily is native to tropical Africa and Australia, now cultivated worldwide; in the Hawaiian Islands it is found on Oʻahu, where it was first collected in 2000, in freshwater ponds and slow-moving streams, from near sea level to 100m elevation. Introduced passive-invasive; OBL.

Nymphaea rubra Roxb.
Red water lily
Diagnosis: This species differs from *N. caerulea* by leaf-blades reddish to greenish-brown, 20–50cm diam., circular with sinuate and acutely dentate margins; flowers odorless, 15–25cm diam.; sepals broadly ovate; petals 15–20, purplish-red; stamens c.55 with cinnabar red becoming brownish-red anthers; ovary 30-celled; fruit not formed.

Distribution: The red water lily is cultivated worldwide; in the Hawaiian Islands it is currently only found in cultivation; OBL.

N. lotus

N. rubra

Pistia stratiotes L.
Water lettuce   ARACEAE

Description: Free-floating aquatic herb 3–20cm high, 5–30cm long, soft-hairy; stems (stolons) 2–4mm diam., tufted and bearing roots at nodes. **Leaves** basal, spongy; petioles absent; leaf-blade simple, 3–15cm long, 1.5–8cm wide, oblong to obovate, with 5–7-ribbed parallel veins, entire margins and rounded or indented apex; upper side pale green, underside paler. **Flowers** 2–8 male and a solitary female on the same plant, in sessile clusters (spadix) 1–2cm long on 2–7 axillary peduncles 15–50cm long; spathe white, 1–2cm long; stamens 2; ovary superior, 1-celled. **Fruit** a berry 6–9mm long, 3–5mm diam., obovoid to ellipsoid.

Distribution: Water lettuce is widely cultivated, and now widespread in waterways in the tropics; in the Hawaiian Islands it is currently found on Kaua'i, O'ahu, Moloka'i, Maui and Hawai'i. First collected on O'ahu in 1938, it is now common in open ditches, ponds and other watercourses, from sea level to 50m elevation. Introduced aggressive-invasive; OBL.

Note: Water lettuce is grown as a very popular aquatic ornamental. It is poisonous to humans. The leaves spread horizontally by day and stand erect at night. Water lettuce readily proliferates by offsets, and can become a serious pest in still or slow-moving freshwater habitats.

Potamogeton foliosus Raf.
Leafy pondweed
POTAMOGETONACEAE

Description: Submerged freshwater perennial herb 0.1–1m long, glabrous; stems slender, 2–3mm diam., slightly laterally compressed, many-branched, arising from slender rhizomes, rooting in mud. **Leaves** alternate, cauline; leaf-base with sheathing stipules 5–15mm long; leaf-blades simple, 1–10cm long, 0.5–2mm wide, linear with 3–5 veins and entire margins. **Flowers** few, bisexual, clustered on 1–5mm long spikes, terminating peduncles 0.3–2cm long; tepals 4, green, 0.5–1mm long, oblong; stamens 4; ovary superior with 4 separate carpels. **Fruit** a green sessile drupe 1.5–2.5mm long, obovoid.

Distribution: Leafy pondweed is native to North and Central America, now a worldwide weed; in the Hawaiian Islands it is found on Kaua'i, O'ahu, Maui and Hawai'i. First recorded on O'ahu in 1888, it is locally abundant in man-made ponds, ditches and taro patches, from near sea level to 700m elevation. Introduced or ?native passive-invasive; OBL.

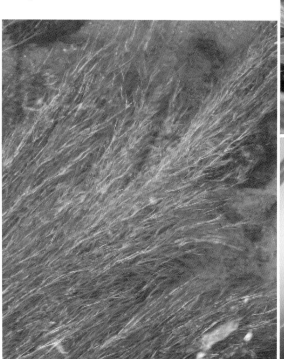

Ruppia maritima L.
Widgeon grass
RUPPIACEAE

Description: Submerged brackish water perennial herb 0.2–1m long, glabrous; stems slender, 1–3mm diam., terete, many-branched, arising from creeping rhizomes, rooting in mud. **Leaves** alternate; leaf-base with a sheath 0.2–7cm long; leaf-blades simple, 1–10cm long, 0.2–1mm wide, linear with 1 vein and entire margins. **Flowers** 2, bisexual, on 1–17mm long spiraling axillary peduncles; perianth absent; stamens 2; ovary superior with 4 separate carpels. **Fruit** a green pedicellate drupe 1.5–4mm long, 1.5–2mm wide, ovoid to pyriform.

Distribution: Widgeon grass is native to the Americas, Africa and Eurasia, now a worldwide weed; in the Hawaiian Islands it is found on seven main islands (not Kahoʻolawe). It is currently locally abundant in man-made ponds, ditches and anchialine pools, from sea level to 15m elevation. Native passive-invasive; OBL.

Photo: KP

Photo: KP

Spirodela polyrhiza (L.) Schleid.
Greater duckweed

LEMNACEAE

Description: Free-floating perennial herb, glabrous; stems (cladodes) solitary or 2–5 together, green above, purplish-red below, 3–10mm long, 2–6mm wide, orbicular-ovate with (5–)7–16 veins and entire margins, 2 budding pouches near the proximal end, leafless, bearing 6–21 roots. **Flowers** (rarely seen) usually 2 males and a female within a sac-like bract (spathe); perianth absent; male flowers a single stamen; female flowers a 1-celled superior ovary. **Fruit** a pale brown capsule 1–1.5mm long, 0.6–0.8mm wide, winged.

Distribution: Greater duckweed is native to tropical and warm temperate regions of the Americas, Africa, Eurasia and Australia; in the Hawaiian Islands it is found on Kaua'i, O'ahu, Maui and

Hawai'i. First recorded on O'ahu in 1918, it occurs in coastal wetlands, freshwater ponds and ditches, and taro paddies, from near sea level to 50m elevation. Introduced or ?native non-invasive; OBL.

Note: Provides high protein food for water birds.

Stuckenia pectinata (L.) Börner
Sago pondweed

POTAMOGETONACEAE

Description: Submerged freshwater perennial herb 0.3–1m long, glabrous; stems slender, 1–2mm diam., terete to slightly compressed, many-branched, arising from slender creeping rhizomes and white tubers, rooting in mud. **Leaves** alternate, cauline; leaf-base with a sheathing stipule 1–3cm long; leaf-blades simple, 2–15cm long, 0.2–1mm wide, linear with 1–3 veins and entire margins. **Flowers** many, bisexual, on 1–3cm long spikes, borne on peduncles 1–25cm long; tepals 4, brownish-green, 1–1.5mm long, oblong; stamens 4; ovary superior with 4 separate carpels. **Fruit** a green, sessile drupe 2.5–4mm long, 1–2mm wide, obliquely obovoid.

Distribution: Sago pondweed is native to the Americas, Africa and Eurasia, now a worldwide weed; in the Hawaiian Islands it is found on Ni'ihau, Kaua'i and Hawai'i. First recorded on Kaua'i in

1947, it is currently locally abundant in man-made ponds, ditches and taro patches, from near sea level to 6m elevation. Introduced passive-invasive; OBL.

Note: This species was previously known as *Potamogeton pectinatus* L.

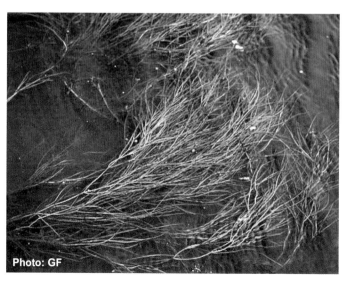

Photo: GF

80

Utricularia gibba L.
Humped bladderwort

LENTIBULARIACEAE

Description: Aquatic herb 5–10cm high, glabrous; stems slender, 0.5–1mm diam., branching into 2–3 slender segment 1–5mm long with scattered bladders. **Leaves** absent. **Flowers** 1– 4, bisexual, clustered on slender peduncles 5–15cm long; pedicels 10–25mm long; sepals 5, lobes 2–4mm long; petals 5, yellow, 6–12mm long, united to form an upper and lower lip that project forward and are usually unequal in size; stamens 2; ovary superior, 1-celled. **Fruit** a green capsule 2–5mm long, 2–4mm diam., ovoid.

Distribution: Humped bladderwort is native to the tropics worldwide, and now also in temperate Europe and Australasia; in the Hawaiian Islands known only from Hawai'i, where it was first collected in 1983 along the Stainback Highway and in Puna, in mucky soil in wet forest, from 100 to 1000m elevation. Introduced passive-invasive; OBL.

Note: This is a carnivorous plant and household "pet". The bladder fills with water when an aquatic invertebrate sets off trigger hairs, sucking the creature inside, where it is digested.

Photo: KU

Photo: CI

Vallisneria spp.
Tape grass   HYDROCHARITACEAE

Vallisneria americana Michx.
Water celery

Description: Submerged brackish to fresh water perennial herb 1–5m long, glabrous; rhizomes slender, 2–4mm diam., terete, rooting at nodes in mud and sand. **Leaves** opposite; leaf-base sheathing; petioles absent; leaf-blades 0.2–2m long, 0.6–3cm wide, linear with serrate margins. **Flowers** many males in clusters, and female solitary, on different plants, terminating long peduncles reaching the surface; sepals 3, 0.1–0.25mm long; petals 3, 1–1.5mm long, ovate; stamens 2, upright with filaments partially or wholly united; ovary inferior, 1-celled; stigmas not fringed. **Fruit** a capsule 8–18cm long, 1–2mm diam., terete.

Distribution: Water celery is native to the tropical Americas, east Asia and Australia; in the Hawaiian Islands it is found on Kaua'i, where it was first recorded in 1933. It occurs in coastal wetlands, freshwater ponds and ditches, from near sea level to 40m elevation. Introduced passive-invasive; OBL.

Note: Widely used in the aquarium trade, and also eaten as a vegetable.

Vallisneria spiralis L.
Tape grass

Diagnosis: This species differs from *V. americana* with leaves less than 2cm wide; male flowers stamens obliquely extended with filaments free; female flowers with sepals 0.08–0.13mm long and stigmas fringed.

Distribution: Tape grass is native to eastern North America, central America, east Asia and Australia; in the Hawaiian Islands it is found on O'ahu, where it was first recorded in 2000 from coastal wetlands, from near sea level. Introduced passive-invasive; OBL.

V. spiralis

V. spiralis

Wolffia globosa (Roxb.) Hartog & Plas
Tropical watermeal
LEMNACEAE

Description: Free-floating perennial herb, glabrous; stems (cladodes) single or 2 together, green above and below, 0.4–0.9mm long, 0.3–0.5mm wide; elliptical to obovate without veins; 1 budding pouch near the proximal end, leafless and rootless. **Flowers** (rarely seen) usually 2 males and a female, bract (spathe) and perianth absent; male flowers a single stamen; female flowers a 1-celled superior ovary. **Fruit** not yet known in Hawai'i.

Distribution: Tropical watermeal is native to tropical east Asia, now widespread in the tropics and subtropics; in the Hawaiian Islands it is found on O'ahu and Moloka'i. First recorded on Moloka'i in 1916, it is now naturalized in coastal wetlands, freshwater ponds and ditches, from near sea level to 50m elevation. Introduced passive-invasive; OBL.

Note: Provides high protein food for water birds.

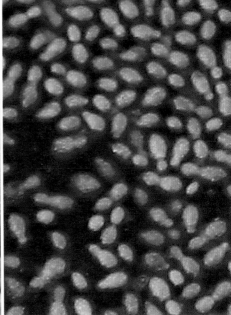

SECTION 2 — FERNS and FERN ALLIES
Plants reproducing by spores

Ferns and fern allies differ from other macroscopic plants by their method of reproduction. They do not produce flowers and fruits. The plants that we normally encoun-
ter are the spore-producing phase of the lifecycle. The sexual phase takes place on a
small green or colorless plant called the gametophyte. Gametophytes look somewhat
like heart-shaped liverworts, or small pieces of root. The leaves of ferns are generally
called fronds; the central axis of a divided leaf is called the rachis (rhachis); the leaflets of a divided leaf are called pinnae; and the scale-like hairs are called trichomes.
For identification purposes the most diagnostic feature of the fern is the position of
the sporangia: how they are arranged on the leaf, and whether they have a protective
covering (indusium). Two floating fern species are included here: *Azolla* and *Salvinia*.

Key to ferns and fern allies of Hawaii's wetlands

1   Plants floating on the water surface 2
    Plants rooted in soil 3

2(1) Leaves less than 2mm long .... *Azolla filiculoides*
      Leaves more than 7mm long .... *Salvinia molesta*

3(1) Leaves simple, not divided to the rachis 4
      Leaves variously pinnate 7

4(3) Leaves linear, more than 10cm long .... *Isoëtes hawaiiensis*
      Leaves triangular, less than 1cm long 5

5(4) Leaves on vegetative parts all the same .... *Lycopodiella cernua*
      Leaves on vegetative parts not all the same 6

6(5) Rhizome with ascending or erect branches; lateral leaf margins entire ....
      .... *Selaginella arbuscula*
      Rhizome with procumbent branches; lateral leaf margins dentate ....
      .... *Selaginella kraussiana*

7(3) Leaves divided into 4 radiating pinnae, resembling clover 8
      Leaves pinnately divided into pinnae 9

8(7) Pinnae margins crenate; rachis and pinnae glabrous or sparsely hairy ....
      .... *Marsilea crenata*
      Pinnae margins entire; rachis and pinnae densely hairy .... *Marsilea villosa*

9(7) Leaves 1-pinnate 10
      Leaves more than 1-pinnate 14

10(9) Pinnae with crenate or serrate margins, not deeply lobed 11

Pinnae lobed at least halfway to the midvein 12

11(10) Trichomes (scales) uniformly brown, not 2-toned; rhizomes with tubers; pinnae with crenate margins and obtuse apices; midveins glabrous .... *Nephrolepis cordifolia*

Trichomes 2-toned with dark centers and pale margins; rhizomes without tubers; pinnae with serrate margins and acute apices; midveins hairy .... *Nephrolepis brownii*

12(10) Pinnae lobed almost to the midvein .... *Christella parasitica*

Pinnae lobed halfway to two-thirds to the midvein 13

13(12) Overall leaf shape elliptic in outline; rachis purplish-brown; pinnae lobes somewhat rectangular .... *Christella dentata*

Overall leaf shape ovate in outline; rachis creamy-brown; pinnae lobes somewhat triangular .... *Cyclosorus interruptus*

14(9) Leaves with prominent basal flanges at the base; rachis more than 1m long .... *Angiopteris evecta*

Leaves without flanges; rachis less than 1m long 15

15(14) Fertile pinnae 2–4mm wide, linear; sporangia circular, protected by the curled leaflet margin .... *Ceratopteris thalictroides*

Fertile pinnae 5–20mm wide, linear-lanceolate; sporangia linear, protected by a linear indusium .... *Diplazium esculentum*

Angiopteris evecta (G.Forst.) Hoffm.
King fern   MARATTIACEAE

Description: Perennial herb 1.5–5m high, mostly glabrous; rhizomes erect, stout, short. **Leaves** clustered, ascending; leaf-base with 2 very prominent circular lateral flanges; rachis 1–7m long, yellowish to dark brown; leaf-blades deltoid in outline, 1-pinnate or 2-pinnate; pinnae 6–35 pairs, 10–30cm long, 1.5–2cm wide, linear to lanceolate with serrate margins. **Sporangia** in elliptic sori inside the lower margin along lateral veins, in double rows, lacking indusia.

Distribution: King fern is widespread in the tropics of Africa, southeast Asia, Australia and the western Pacific, typically in mesic and wet forests; in the Hawaiian Islands it is found on Oʻahu, Lanaʻi, Maui and Hawaiʻi. Imported from Australia to the Lyon Arboretum on Oʻahu in 1927, it is now locally common on mesic slopes and in wet forests, bogs, seeps and springs, from near sea level to 650m elevation. Introduced aggressive-invasive; FAC.

Note: The local vernacular name "mule's-foot fern" may have originated in Hawaiʻi for this species; elsewhere it is widely known as the king or giant fern. Mule's-foot fern is also the vernacular name for the Hong Kong endemic, *Angiopteris fokiensis* Hieron.

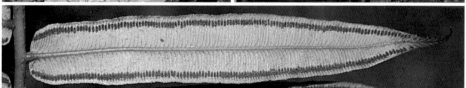

Azolla filiculoides Lam.
Large mosquito fern   AZOLLACEAE

Description: Aquatic annual herb 2–4mm high, 10–50mm long, glabrous; rhizomes prostrate, free-floating, many-branched, bearing many simple rootlets. **Leaves** sessile, overlapping, 2-lobed, the upper lobe emergent, green, 1–2mm long, 0.7–1mm wide, ovate with entire margins, the lower lobe submerged, transparent. **Sporangia** in circular sori in leaf axils, protected by a transparent indusium.

Distribution: Large mosquito fern is a native of the tropical and temperate Americas, where it reproduces rapidly by fragmentation and becomes a problem by clogging waterways; in the Hawaiian Islands it is found on six main islands (not Niʻihau and Kahoʻolawe). Deliberately introduced to Hawaiʻi in the 1920s for a mosquito control program, it is now very common in rice fields, taro patches, irrigation ditches, ponds and lakes, from near sea level to 500m elevation. Introduced aggressive-invasive; OBL.

Note: Other English common names for this species are duckweed fern and red waterfern, which are also applied to other mosquito fern species. The emergent leaf-lobes of all *Azolla* spp. contain *Anabaena azollae*, a nitrogen-fixing cyanobacterium, which are a natural fertilizer when dried. In Florida (USA), Europe, South Africa and Australia, *Azolla filiculoides* has been effectively controlled by the waterfern weevil, *Stenopelmus rufinasus* Gyll.

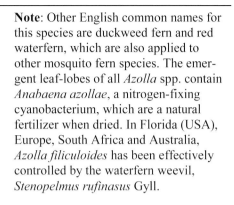

Ceratopteris thalictroides (L.) Brongn.
Water sprite   PTERIDACEAE

Description: Aquatic annual herb 5–40cm high, glabrous; rhizome erect, short. **Leaves** clustered, erect, glabrous, dimorphic; sterile leaves 10–40cm long; rachis succulent, light green; leaf-blades triangular in outline, simple to 4-pinnate; pinnae 3–12cm long, 4–10mm wide; fertile leaves 10–50cm long with narrower pinnae 2–4mm wide. **Sporangia** in circular sori on the underside of pinnae, parallel to the margin and protected by an indusium formed by the curled leaflet margin.

Distribution: Water sprite is widespread in the tropics of south and southeast Asia and America, growing in mud in lakes and slow-flowing streams; in the Hawaiian Islands it is found on Kaua'i and O'ahu in rice fields and taro patches. First recorded on Hawai'i in 1907 and probably brought to the islands by rice farmers in the early 1800s, it now occurs widely in streams and wetlands, from sea level to 300m elevation. Introduced passive-invasive; OBL.

Note: Also locally known as *hihia wai*, swamp fern and oriental water fern. The leaves are used as a vegetable in Asia and the western Pacific.

Christella dentata (Forssk.) Brownsey & Jermy
Downy maiden fern THELYPTERIDACEAE

Description: Perennial herb 0.3–1m high, short-hairy; rhizomes ascending to erect, slender, short-creeping. **Leaves** clustered, ascending or erect; rachis 0.5–1.2m long, purplish-brown; leaf-blades elliptic in outline, 1-pinnate; pinnae 20–35 pairs, greatly reduced below middle, 6–12cm long, 1–2cm wide, linear to lanceolate and deeply-lobed 2/3 to the midvein. **Sporangia** in circular sori in a row midway between the midvein and the margin, protected by reniform indusia.

Distribution: Downy maiden fern is a widespread species of the tropics and subtropics of Africa and Asia, now a weed in the Americas; in the Hawaiian Islands it is found on six main islands (not Ni'ihau and Kaho'olawe). First recorded on O'ahu in 1887, it is now a very common species in mesic to wet lowland habitats, from near sea level to 1250m elevation. Introduced aggressive-invasive; FAC.

Note: In recent times *Christella dentata* has been given the local name *pai'i'ihā*. This species is known to produce natural hybrids with the introduced species, *C. parasitica,* and the endemic species, *C. cyatheoides* (Kaulf.) Holttum. Some botanists include *C. dentata* in the genus *Thelypteris*, viz., *T. dentata* (Forssk.) E.P.St.John.

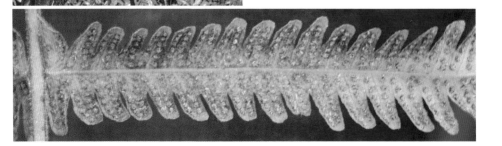

Christella parasitica (L.) H.Lév.
Maiden fern
THELYPTERIDACEAE

Description: Perennial herb 20–70cm high, long-hairy; rhizomes ascending, slender, short-creeping. **Leaves** well-spaced, erect; rachis 30–90cm long, creamy-brown; leaf-blades narrowly ovate in outline, 1-pinnate; pinnae 16–24 pairs, almost not reduced below, 12–16cm long, 1.2–2cm wide, oblong and deeply-lobed almost to the midvein. **Sporangia** in circular sori in a row midway between the midvein and the margin, protected by reniform indusia.

Distribution: This maiden fern is widespread in the tropics and subtropics of southeast Asia, Australia and the western Pacific; in the Hawaiian Islands it is found on six main islands (not Ni'ihau and Kaho'olawe). First recorded on O'ahu in 1926, it is now very common on sunny wet lowland stream banks, and in swamps and pasture, from sea level to 1200m elevation. Introduced aggressive-invasive; FAC.

Note: Some botanists include *Christella parasitica* in the genus *Thelypteris*, viz., *T. parasitica* (L.) Fosberg.

Cyclosorus interruptus (Willd.) H.Itô
Neke, **Willdenow's maiden fern**

THELYPTERIDACEAE

Description: Perennial herb 20–50cm high, stiff-hairy; rhizomes slender, prostrate, long-creeping. **Leaves** well-spaced, erect; rachis 30–90cm long, creamy-brown, scaly at the base; leaf-blades narrowly ovate in outline, 1-pinnate; pinnae 20–30 pairs, 45–150mm long, 10–18mm wide, lanceolate and lobed halfway to the midvein. **Sporangia** in circular sori in a row halfway between the midvein and the margin, protected by reniform indusia.

Distribution: *Neke* is widespread in the tropics and subtropics of southeast Asia, Australia and the western Pacific to Hawai'i; in the Hawaiian Islands it is found on six main islands (not Ni'ihau and Kaho'olawe). It is a common species in sunny wet lowland bogs, marshes, swamps and taro patches, from near sea level to 1000m elevation. Native aggressive-invasive; FACW.

Note: Some botanists include *neke* in the genus *Thelypteris*, viz., *T. interrupta* (Willd.) K.Iwats.

Diplazium esculentum (Retz.) Sw.
Vegetable fern, *paca*   ATHYRIACEAE

Description: Perennial herb 0.7–1.5m high, glabrous; rhizomes slender, erect, short, unbranched. **Leaves** clustered, ascending; rachis 0.2–1m long, dark brown; leaf-blades triangular in outline, 1-pinnate to 2-pinnate in the lower part; pinnae 10–20 pairs on lower fronds, 3–8cm long, 0.5–2cm wide, linear-lanceolate with serrate to deeply lobed margins. **Sporangia** in linear sori along veins of pinnae, protected by linear indusia.

Distribution: Vegetable fern is widespread in the tropics and subtropics of southeast Asia, Australia and the western Pacific; in the Hawaiian Islands it is found on Kaua'i, O'ahu, Lana'i, Maui and Hawai'i. First recorded on Kaua'i in 1910, this edible fern is now common along streams and in swamps from sea level to 200m elevation. Introduced aggressive-invasive; FACW.

Note: Mistakenly called *hō'i'o* locally, a Hawaiian name applied to the native *Diplazium sandwichianum* (C.Presl) Diels, whose young fiddleheads are also eaten in salads.

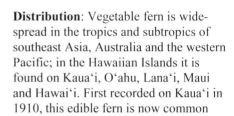

Isoëtes hawaiiensis W.C.Taylor & W.H.Wagner
Hawaiian quillwort   ISOËTACEAE

Description: Submerged or emergent aquatic grass-like perennial herb 10–25cm high, glabrous throughout; rhizome erect, very short. **Leaves** densely clustered, green above; leaf-bases spoon-shaped, translucent with a swollen sporangium on the upper surface; leaf-blade simple, 10–25cm long, 3–8mm wide, linear, gradually tapering to a point, with entire margins. **Sporangia** solitary, obovate, medial, covered by a translucent indusium.

Distribution: Hawaiian quillwort is currently known only from localities on West Maui and Hawai'i. It occurs in upper elevation bogs on Mt. 'Eke and in streams on the eastern slope of Mauna Kea, from 850 to 1375m elevation. Endemic non-invasive; OBL.

All photos: FRW

93

Lycopodiella cernua (L.) Pic.Serm.
Wāwae'iole, rat's-foot fern

LYCOPODIACEAE

Description: Perennial herb 0.3–1m high, 1–5m long, glabrous; rhizomes long-creeping with erect branches. **Leaves** clustered, sessile, dimorphic; vegetative leaves simple, 1–4.5mm long, 0.2–1mm wide, linear with entire margins and attenuate apex; sporangia-bearing leaves smaller than vegetative leaves, ovate, dentate, ciliate, forming strobili 5–15mm long. **Sporangia** solitary, basal on upper surface, without an indusium.

Distribution: *Wāwae'iole* is widespread in the tropics of Africa, Asia, Australia and the western Pacific, in mesic and wet forests; in the Hawaiian Islands it is found on six main islands (not Ni'ihau and Kaho'olawe). It is locally common in mesic and wet forests, swamp margins, bogs, seeps and springs from sea level to 2000m elevation. Native non-invasive; FAC.

Note: This species is widely known as the rat's-foot fern. Previously known as *Lycopodium cernuum* L. Some botanists maintain this broader generic concept.

Marsilea crenata C.Presl
Nadoo, dwarf four-leaf clover MARSILEACEAE

Description: Emergent aquatic herb 10–20cm high, glabrous or sparsely hairy; rhizomes long-creeping. **Leaves** clustered, dimorphic, erect; sterile leaves divided into 4-leaf clover-like pinnae; rachis wiry, green, 2.5–20cm long; leaf-blades 1-pinnate, radiate; pinnae 10–25mm long, 3–8mm wide, obovate to cuneate with crenate margins; fertile leaves stalked with one globular structure (sporocarp); rachis 1–3mm long. **Sporangia** clustered inside sporocarps.

Distribution: *Nadoo* is native to northern Australia and southeast Asia in monsoon seasonal wetlands and floodplains; in the Hawaiian Islands it appears to have become recently established in a demonstration taro patch in Makiki, Oʻahu, perhaps arriving in Hawaiʻi with some Asian *kalo* cultivars, from 50 to 80m elevation. Introduced passive-invasive; OBL.

Note: The sporocarps of *nadoo* were used as a survival food by Australian Aborigines.

Marsilea villosa Kaulf.
'Ihi'ihi

MARSILEACEAE

Description: Emergent aquatic herb 2.5–15cm high, densely hairy; rhizomes long-creeping. **Leaves** clustered, dimorphic; sterile leaves divided into 4-leaf clover-like pinnae; rachis wiry, green, 2.5–15cm long; leaf-blades 1-pinnate, radiate, pinnae 1–2.5cm long, 1–2.2cm wide, obovate with entire margins; fertile leaves stalked with one globular structure (sporocarp); rachis wiry, brown, 2–6mm long. **Sporangia** clustered inside sporocarps.

Distribution: *'Ihi'ihi* is endemic to Ni'ihau, O'ahu and Moloka'i, where it is a rare species, known to occur in several seasonal wetlands, from near sea level to 200m elevation. Endemic non-invasive; OBL.

Note: Some historical locations for this species around Kaimuki, Honolulu have disappeared under urban development. In an effort to conserve this federally listed endangered species, *'ihi'ihi* has been transplanted into several other wetland areas on O'ahu.

Nephrolepis spp.
Fishbone ferns

NEPHROLEPIDACEAE

Nephrolepis brownii (Desv.) Hovenkamp & Miyam. **Asian sword fern**

Diagnosis: Differs from *N. cordifolia* (below) by bi-colored brown trichomes; rhizomes without tubers; leaves ellipticlanceolate; rachis light brown; pinnae 20–80mm long, 6–15mm wide, linear with serrate margins and hairy midvein.

Distribution: Asian sword fern is widespread in wet forests of southeast Asia; in the Hawaiian Islands it is known from Nihoa and six main islands (not Ni'ihau and Kaho'olawe). First recorded on Hawai'i in 1923, it is common along roadsides, moist areas, seeps and springs, from sea level to 1500m elevation. Introduced aggressive-invasive; FAC.

Note: Previously known in Hawai'i by the younger name *N. multiflora* (Roxb.) F.M.Jarrett ex C.V.Morton.

Nephrolepis cordifolia (L.) C.Presl
Fishbone fern, *'ōkupukupu*

Description: Perennial herb 0.3–1m high, with brown trichomes; rhizomes mostly erect with occasional tubers. **Leaves** 0.3–1m long; rachis brown; leafblades 1-pinnate; pinnae 12–35mm long, 6–11mm wide, linear to falcate with basal auricle overlapping the leaf-stalk, crenate margins and glabrous midvein. **Sporangia** clustered in round submarginal sori, protected by a reniform indusium, opening towards pinna apex.

Distribution: Fishbone fern is widespread in the tropics of Asia, Australia and the western Pacific; in the Hawaiian Islands it is found on six main islands (not Ni'ihau and Kaho'olawe) and is common in mesic and wet forests, seeps and springs from 400 to 1500m elevation. Native passive-invasive; FAC.

Note: Also widely known as the tuber sword fern; potentially displaced by *Nephrolepis brownii*.

N. brownii

N. brownii

Salvinia molesta D.S.Mitch.
Giant salvinia   SALVINIACEAE

Description: Free-floating aquatic herb 5–20cm long, with stiff hairs; rhizomes short, bearing trailing rootlets. **Leaves** overlapping, dimorphic; lower submerged leaves bladeless, bearing a string of capsule-like sporocarps, upper emergent leaves stalked; leaf-blades green, 7–30mm long, 7–20mm wide, elliptical to obovate with long stiff, 4-haired papillae; **Sporangia** (not seen in Hawai'i) clustered inside globular sporocarps.

Distribution: Giant salvinia is native to tropical South America, and is now worldwide; in the Hawaiian Islands it is known from O'ahu and Hawai'i. First reported on O'ahu in the 1980s, it now seasonally covers ponds, lakes and wet-lands, from near sea level to 200m elevation. Introduced aggressive-invasive; OBL.

Note: This federally-listed noxious weed is used as an ornamental in aquaria and garden ponds. It reproduces rapidly by fragmentation and is a nuisance weed clogging waterways. It is also called Kariba weed since overtaking the man-made Lake Kariba on the Zambezi River in Africa. In Australia and elsewhere giant salvinia has been effectively controlled by the salvinia weevil, *Cyrtobagous salviniae* Calder & Sands.

Selaginella arbuscula (Kaulf.) Spring
Lepelepe-a-moa, spike moss
SELAGINELLACEAE

Description: Perennial herb 10–60cm long; rhizomes long-creeping with ascending or erect zig-zag branches. **Leaves** overlapping, glabrous, sessile, trimorphic, simple; medial leaves narrowly ovate to lanceolate, 1–3mm long, 0.5–1.5mm wide; lateral leaves ovate-oblong, 2–6mm long, 1–3.5mm wide with entire margins and acute apex; sporangium-bearing leaves smaller than vegetative leaves, acuminate, forming cones (strobili) 5–50mm long. **Sporangia** solitary, basal on the upper surface, without an indusium.

Distribution: *Lepelepe-a-moa* is native to French Polynesia and Hawai‘i; in the Hawaiian Islands it is found on six main islands (not Ni‘ihau and Kaho‘olawe). It is a common species in lowland mesic to wet habitats, particularly on wet shaded cliffs, slopes and swamp margins, from near sealevel to 1200m elevation. Endemic non-invasive; FAC.

Selaginella kraussiana (Kunze) A.Braun
Trailing spike moss
SELAGINELLACEAE

Description: Perennial herb 1–2cm high, 10–50cm long, glabrous; rhizomes long-creeping with procumbent branches. **Leaves** overlapping, sessile, trimorphic, simple; medial leaves 2–2.5mm long, 0.5–0.8mm wide, narrowly ovate with entire margins; lateral leaves 3–4mm long, 0.8–1.4mm wide, linear to elliptic with dentate margins and acute apex; sporangia-bearing leaves smaller than vegetative leaves, ovate to lanceolate, forming cones (strobili) 5–8mm long. **Sporangia** solitary, basal on the upper surface, without an indusium.

Distribution: Trailing spike moss is native to tropical Africa but is now widely cultivated and naturalized worldwide; in the Hawaiian Islands it is known from Oʻahu, Maui and Hawaiʻi. First reported as a garden escape on Hawaiʻi in 1938, it is now a weed in mesic and wet habitats, from sea level to 1200m elevation. Introduced aggressive-invasive; FACW.

SECTION 3 — WOODY PLANTS
Flowering plants with above-ground woody stems

This section treats the flowering plants that are woody at ground level and above. It also includes subshrubs, woody at the base and herbaceous above. Plants that are woody below ground level are included in herbs. Woody plants are generally short-lived to long-lived perennials. They possess a cambium, a cell division layer that produces secondary xylem to the inside (wood) and secondary phloem to the outside (bark). Although several tree-like monocotyledons do not produce wood in this manner, for convenience these have been included in this section because of their tree-like stature.

Subshrubs and vines (woody at the base but predominantly herbaceous), are included in both woody plant and dicot herb keys. Their descriptions are included in this section unless otherwise noted (e.g. *Cuphea carthagenensis*, *Ludwigia octovalvis*).

Key to the woody plants of Hawaii's wetlands

1 Adult plants trees (woody perennials with a single main trunk) 2
Adult plants shrubs (woody perennials with several to many stems arising from near ground level), or a woody creeper or vine (at least near the base) 12

2(1) Tree a palm, fronds fan-shaped, pleated (plicate) .... *Pritchardia martii*
Tree not palm-like, leaves not plicate 3

3(2) Tree supported by prop roots 4
Tree without prop roots 5

4(3) Leaves linear, more than 80cm long, prickly along margins .*Pandanus tectorius*
Leaves elliptic to obovate, less than 20cm long, without prickly margins ....
.... *Rhizophora mangle*

5(3) Tree with buttressed trunk and knee roots .... *Bruguiera sexangula*
Tree not as above 6

6(5) Leaves cordate 7
Leaves ovate, lanceolate, elliptic or spatulate, not cordate 8

7(6) Branches usually horizontally spreading, forming impenetrable thickets; fruit an ovoid capsule splitting into 5 parts at maturity .... *Hibiscus tiliaceus*
Branches not spreading as above; fruit a globose, woody capsule, only tardily splitting with age .... *Thespesia populnea*

8(6) Leaves opposite 9
Leaves alternate 10

9(8)   Leaves with 25–40 pairs of lateral veins, spaced 2–5mm apart; berry dark purple
       to black, oblong, 1.2–2cm long .... *Syzygium cumini*
       Leaves with 10–20 pairs of lateral veins, spaced 5–15mm apart; berry whitish-
       yellow to pinkish-yellow, globose, 2–4cm long .... *Syzygium jambos*

10(8) Leaves spatulate .... *Terminalia catappa*
       Leaves lanceolate or ovate to elliptic 11

11(10) Leaves lanceolate, aromatic when crushed, glabrous ....
       .... *Melaleuca quinquenervia*
       Leaves ovate to elliptic, not aromatic when crushed, usually densely silky-hairy
       .... *Conocarpus erectus*

12(1) Adult plant a shrub 13
       Adult plant a creeper or woody vine 29

13(12) Leaves opposite 14
       Leaves alternate 21

14(13) Leaves terete, succulent .... *Batis maritima*
       Leaves flat, not succulent 15

15(14) Leaves linear to lanceolate, more than four times longer than wide 16
       Leaves ovate, obovate or elliptical, less than four times as long as wide 17

16(15) Plants more than 40cm high, glabrous or sparsely hairy; leaf-blades with serrate
       margins ....*Verbena litoralis*
       Plants less than 40cm high, stems clothed with stiff red hairs; leaf-blades with
       entire margins .... *Cuphea hyssopifolia*

17(15) Leaf-blades broadly ovate, almost as wide as long ...... *Clerodendrum chinense*
       Leaf-blades narrower, ovate, elliptical and oblong, at least two times longer than
       wide 18

18(17) Plants with glandular or stiff hairs on stems and leaves 19
       Plants glabrous throughout or with a few scattered hairs 20

19(18) Plants with glandular (sticky) hairs .... *Cuphea carthagenensis* (Section 4)
       Plants with stiff hairs .... *Pterolepis glomerata*

20(18) Flowers solitary, axillary .... *Lythrum maritimum*
       Flowers many in a long spike .... *Stachytarpheta jamaicensis*

21(13) Leaves linear, 0.5–4cm long, grayish-green silky-hairy; calyx with 5 reddish,
       hooked spines .... *Bassia hyssopifolia*
       Leaves not as above; calyx lacking hooked spines 22

22(21) All parts of the plant stellate-hairy .... *Hibiscus furcellatus*
Plants glabrous or hairy, but not stellate-hairy 23

23(22) Leaves cordate to orbicular, 8–30cm long and wide .... *Hibiscus tiliaceus*
Leaves elliptic, ovate, obovate, lanceolate or linear, longer than wide 24

24(23) Branches lax, long-spreading; leaves glossy green, 3-veined from the base ....
.... *Colubrina asiatica*
Branches not as above; leaves not as above 25

25(24) Leaves linear to lanceolate, 1–14cm long, 0.5–4cm wide; flowers yellow ....
.... *Ludwigia octovalvis* (Section 4)
Leaves ovate, obovate, elliptic or oblong; flowers pink, purple to pale blue ... 26

26(25) Inflorescence a stout spike; flowers blooming singly along the spike, usually
pale blue .... *Stachytarpheta jamaicensis*
Inflorescence branching; flowers minute, crowded into heads, pink to purplish ..
.... 27

27(26) Plants low-spreading .... *Pluchea* x*fosbergii*
Plants erect 28

28(27) Leaves lustrous pale green with scattered hairs; margins coarsely dentate ....
.... *Pluchea indica*
Leaves grayish-green, densely hairy; margins entire to dentate towards the apex.
.... *Pluchea carolinensis*

29(12) Leaves opposite 30
Leaves alternate 32

30(29) Leaves elliptic to spatulate, 1–3.5cm long, 0.2–0.9cm wide; upper leaves alternate, lower ones opposite .... *Atriplex semibaccata*
Leaves linear to narrowly ovate or ovate-deltate, 3–16cm long, 1–6.5cm wide;
all leaves opposite 31

31(30) Leaves ovate-deltate, usually 3-lobed; ray florets 6–15mm long ....
.... *Sphagneticola trilobata*
Leaves linear to narrowly ovate, not lobed; ray florets 4–7mm long ....
.... *Lipochaeta succulenta*

32(29) Leaves compound 33
Leaves simple 35

33(32) Leaves pinnately compound; flowers in spherical heads, pink to lavender ....
.... *Mimosa pudica*
Leaves trifoliate; flowers pea-like, yellow 34

34(33) Leaflets broadly to more narrowly ovate, the apex rounded; pods linear-oblong, more or less curved, glabrous .... *Vigna marina*
Leaflets ovate, ovate-elliptic or ovate-lanceolate, the apex acute to acuminate; pods linear, more or less pubescent .... *Vigna luteola*

35(32) Creepers; leaves elliptic to spatulate, 1–3.5cm long; flowers inconspicuous ....
.... *Atriplex semibaccata*
Vines; leaves heart-shaped, ovate, orbicular or triangular, 4–16cm long; flowers conspicuous, tubular 36

36(35) Flowers white 37
Flowers yellow or purple 38

37(36) Corolla white with light green lines, tube 9–15cm long; sepal apex acute to acuminate; stems sometimes with short fleshy prickles .... *Ipomoea alba*
Corolla pure white, without visible lines, tube 6–10cm long; sepal apex obtuse; stems without prickles .... *Ipomoea violacea*

38(36) Corolla purple; flowers solitary or sometimes a few together; leaves thick, succulent, usually folded upward at the midrib .... *Ipomoea pes-caprae*
Corolla yellow; flowers few to many clustered and originating from a common point; leaves not as above .... *Merremia umbellata*

Atriplex semibaccata R.Br.
Creeping saltbush, Australian saltbush   CHENOPODIACEAE

Description: Perennial woody herb 5–80cm high, 60–150cm long, glabrous (scurfy when young); stems ascending to prostrate, many-branched, thornless, forming spreading mats. **Leaves** alternate, the lower ones opposite, grey-green; stipules and petioles absent; leaf-blades simple, 10–35mm long, 2–9mm wide, narrow-ovate to obovate with margins entire to dentate above the middle. **Flowers** few, males lacking bracts, 1–4 females surrounded by 2 bracts, on the same plant in separate axillary clusters; calyx lobes 3–5; corolla absent; stamens 3–5; ovary superior, 1-celled. **Fruit** an almost sessile red berry 3–6mm long, 3–5mm wide, rhomboid, enclosed within fleshy bracts 4–6mm long.

Distribution: Creeping saltbush is native to Australia and introduced worldwide to increase the productivity of saltmarshes; in the Hawaiian Islands it is found on all eight main islands. First collected on Moloka'i in 1910, but introduced on Lāna'i around 1895 as experimental forage for cattle. It now occurs in seasonally wet areas, such as coastal mudflats, from sea level to 150m elevation. Introduced passive-invasive; FAC.

Note: Creeping saltbush was introduced to Hawai'i and California with the hope that it would provide forage on saline and desert soils.

Bassia hyssopifolia (Pall.) Kuntze
Fivehorn smotherweed, fivehook bassia CHENOPODIACEAE

Description: Annual woody herb 10–60cm high, 20–50cm long, grayish-green silky-hairy, denser on younger parts; stems stiff, many-branching from the base, prostrate and ascending. **Leaves** alternate; petioles absent; leaf-blades simple, 0.5–4cm long, 1–3.5mm wide, linear to lanceolate with entire margins. **Flowers** 2–3, in bractless axillary clusters; calyx 5-lobed, each with a conspicuous reddish-green, hooked spine 0.5–1mm long; petals absent; stamens 5; ovary superior, 1-celled. **Fruit** a nut 1.5–2mm long, 1–1.5mm diam., globose, enclosed within the leathery calyx.

Distribution: Fivehorn smotherweed is native to Eurasia, now worldwide; in the Hawaiian Islands it is found on O'ahu, Moloka'i and Maui. First collected on O'ahu in 1982, it occurs only in coastal alkaline soils, from sea level to 50m elevation. Introduced passive-invasive; FACW.

Batis maritima L.
Saltwort, pickleweed   BATACEAE

Description: Perennial woody herb 30–50cm high, 0.5–4m long, glabrous; stems prostrate with ascending branches, often 3–5-angled. **Leaves** opposite, fleshy and succulent, filled with salty juice smelling of pickles; stipules and petioles absent; leaf-blades simple, 2–3cm long, terete, yellowish-green with entire margins. **Flowers** 15–30, unisexual on different plants, on axillary conical spikes 5–10mm long, each flower subtended by a 0.5–1mm long bract in males (smaller in females); perianth 4 in male flowers only, stamens 4; female flowers a naked superior ovary, 4-celled. **Fruit** a green drupe, 1–2cm long, 3–6mm diam., conical.

Distribution: Saltwort is native to coasts of tropical and subtropical America and the Galápagos Islands; in the Hawaiian Islands it is found on all eight main islands. First collected on Oʻahu in 1859, it is now very common in dense, monotypic stands in mud flats, fishponds, salt or brackish marshes and raised coralline beachrock, from sea level to 5m elevation. Introduced aggressive-invasive; OBL.

Note: More widely known in Hawaiʻi as pickleweed, this species is also known as beachwort and turtleweed. Saltwort and pickleweed are also vernacular names of several other unrelated plants. In recent time it has become known by the Hawaiian name *ʻākulikuli kai.*

Bruguiera sexangula (Lour.) Poir.
Mangrove, *kukunaokalā*

RHIZOPHORACEAE

Description: Tree 4–25m high, glabrous throughout; trunk buttressed and with knee roots. **Leaves** opposite and decussate, green; stipules lanceolate, reddish-green, 1–2cm long; petioles 1–3cm long, pale reddish-green; leaf-blades simple, 8–15cm long, 3.5–5cm wide, elliptic-oblong with entire margins. **Flowers** solitary or several, in axillary clusters; pedicels 1–2.5mm long; sepals 9–11, yellowish-orange, 15–20mm long, obtuse; petals 9–11, yellowish-brown, 12– 15mm long, bristled; stamens 18–22; ovary inferior, 3–4-celled. **Fruit** a drupe 2–2.2cm long, 1.2–1.5cm diam., bullet-shaped with a viviparous seedling 8–10cm long.

Distribution: A mangrove native to tropical south and east Asia, Australia and the western Pacific, typically of coasts and saltwater riparian habitats; in the Hawaiian Islands it is currently only found on Oʻahu, where it was introduced by the Hawaiian Sugar Planters' Association in 1922. Without intervention this species will take over fringing reefs and tidal strand, saltwater marshes and other maritime riparian habitats. Introduced aggressive-invasive; OBL.

Note: Until recently this deliberately introduced species had been incorrectly determined as *Bruguiera gymnorrhiza* (L.) Lam., a species widely known as the large-leaf mangrove. *Bruguiera sexangula* is a landscape-altering species of reef-flats, fishponds, estuaries and streams. The calyces are strung into *lei* and the tree has been given the Hawaiian name *kukunaokalā*—rays of the sun.

Clerodendrum chinense (Osbeck) Mabb.
Stickbush, *pīkake hohono*   VERBENACEAE

Description: Shrub 1–2m high, densely hairy (except corolla); stems erect, spreading by root-suckers. **Leaves** opposite, green above, light green below; stipules absent; petioles 2–23cm long; leaf-blades 6–30cm long, 5–28cm wide, ovate with margins irregularly dentate to weakly lobed. **Flowers** many, in terminal clusters, fragrant; peduncles absent; pedicels 1–2mm long; calyx 5-lobed, purple or red, 10–18mm long, campanulate; corolla pale pink to white, salverform; stamens 4, petaloid; ovary superior, 4-celled. **Fruit** not developing in Hawai'i.

Distribution: Stickbush, known locally as *pīkake hohono*, is a native of tropical southeast Asia, now worldwide in the tropics as an ornamental shrub; in the Hawaiian Islands it is found on six main islands (not Ni'ihau and Kaho'olawe). First reported from Hawai'i in 1864, this infertile cultivar spreads by root-suckers. It is naturalized in partly shaded disturbed areas at the edges of paddy fields and taro patches and wet to mesic forest, from 50 to 670m elevation. Introduced aggressive-invasive; FAC.

Note: This species forms dense thickets. Previously known in Hawai'i by the younger name, *Clerodendrum philippinum* Schauer.

Colubrina asiatica (L.) Brongn.
'Ānapanapa, latherleaf   RHAMNACEAE

Description: Shrub 1–3m high, 2–10m long, glabrous, glossy throughout; stems many-branched, decumbent, long-spreading, producing adventitious roots. **Leaves** alternate, bright green; stipules triangular, 0.8–1mm long; petioles 0.5–2cm long; leaf-blades simple, 3–12cm long, 2–7cm wide, ovate, 3-veined with serrate-dentate margins. **Flowers** 1–3, in short axillary clusters; peduncles 1–4mm long; pedicels 1–8mm long; sepals 5, green, 0.5–1.5mm long; petals 5, greenish-white, 1.2–1.4mm long; stamens 5; ovary inferior, 3-celled. **Fruit** a schizocarp 5–8mm diam., spherical, breaking into 3 mericarps.

Distribution: *'Ānapanapa* is a native of Hawai'i, also of tropical Africa, Asia and the western Pacific, now common in coastal and lowland wetland habitats; in the Hawaiian Islands it is found on Ni'ihau, Kaua'i, O'ahu, Moloka'i and Maui. It is a common species in coastal wetland margins and riparian areas, from sea level to 100m elevation. Introduced or ?native passive-invasive; FAC.

Note: *'Ānapanapa* or latherleaf is also known in the American literature as Asiatic snakewood and Asiatic nakedwood. It has the gestalt of an introduced species, persisting in riparian areas overcome with weeds. It is an invasive species in Florida.

Conocarpus erectus L.
Button mangrove, sea mulberry   COMBRETACEAE

Description: Tree 3–8m high, densely silky-hairy; trunk rough-barked, dark brown, deeply fissured. **Leaves** alternate; stipules absent; petioles 5–10mm long with 2 glands at the base; leaf-blades simple, 2.5–9cm long, 1–3cm wide, ovate to elliptic with entire margins. **Flowers** many, mostly bisexual, in 8–10mm diam. heads, subtended by many overlapping involucral bracts, on peduncles 2–15mm long on terminal racemes; sepals greenish-white, 1.5–2mm long; petals absent; stamens 5–10; ovary inferior, 1-celled. **Fruit** a brown, 2-winged leathery drupe, 3–4mm long, 3.5–4.5mm wide, laterally compressed, densely packed into brownish-red heads 1–1.5cm diam.

Distribution: Button mangrove is native to mangrove swamps of the American tropics and western tropical Africa; in the Hawaiian Islands, where it is more commonly known as sea mulberry, it is found on Kaua'i, O'ahu, Lāna'i and Maui. Introduced to Maui in the early 1900s, it occurs in brackish or saline, coastal silty habitats exposed to salt spray, from sea level to 5m elevation. Introduced passive-invasive; FACW.

Note: *Conocarpus erectus* is a popular street tree in Hawai'i, especially the form with a dense covering of silky hairs on the leaves.

111

Cuphea hyssopifolia Kunth
Mexican false heather   LYTHRACEAE

Description: Shrub 10–30cm high, 3–5cm long, stiff red-hairy or glabrous; stems erect to almost prostrate, many-branched. **Leaves** opposite; stipules absent; petioles 0–1mm long; leaf-blades simple, 10–30mm long, 2–4mm wide, entire, linear with 1 prominent vein, upper side glossy green, glabrous. **Flowers** solitary, axillary; calyx tube pale green, sometimes purple toward apex, 5–8mm long, terete, 12-ribbed, enlarged on one side at base; corolla 6-lobed, pale purple, white or pink, 3–4mm long. **Fruit** a capsule 3–4mm long, 1–2mm diam., oblong-ovoid.

Distribution: Mexican false heather is native to tropical North America, now widely cultivated elsewhere; in the Hawaiian Islands it is a garden escape on Hawai'i. First collected in 1909 as a cultivated plant, it now occurs sporadically in open, disturbed sites and along streambeds, from 60 to 380m elevation. Introduced passive-invasive; FACW.

Note: A common landscape ornamental in Hawai'i with a number of cultivated forms, used as a bedding plant, container plant, groundcover and bonsai. The flowers are sometimes used in *lei*.

Hibiscus furcellatus Desr.
'Akiohala, rosemallow — MALVACEAE

Description: Perennial shrub 1–2.5m high, stellate-hairy; stems with few branches. **Leaves** alternate; stipules 4–8mm long, filiform; petioles 4–25mm long; leaf-blades simple, 5–15cm long, 5–15cm wide, ovate to cordate with entire or shallowly to deeply 3–5-lobed margins. **Flowers** 1–2, in upper leaf axils or borne on flowering branches; pedicels 10–13mm long; bracts 10–14 surrounding calyx, 10–15mm long, linear; calyx 5-lobed, 18–25mm long; corolla pale magenta-rose, darker at base, not opening widely, 5–9cm long; stamens many fused into a column, maroon; ovary superior, 5-celled. **Fruit** a capsule 25–32mm long, 15–23mm diam., ovoid, enclosed by calyx, 5-valved.

Distribution: This species of rosemallow is native to tropical North America, South America and Hawai'i, primarily in marshy places near sea level; in the Hawaiian Islands, where it is known as *'akiohala*, it is found on Kaua'i, O'ahu, Maui and Hawai'i in wet forests and swampy disturbed sites, from 90 to 240m elevation. Native passive-invasive; FACW.

Note: A younger name previously used for this species in Hawai'i is *Hibiscus youngianus* Gaudich. ex Hook. & Arnott.

Hibiscus tiliaceus L.
Hau, sea hibiscus

MALVACEAE

Description: Shrub or tree 2–20m high, mostly glabrous; stems many-branched, spreading. **Leaves** alternate, coriaceous; stipules 1–6cm long, lanceolate; petioles 3–15cm long; leaf-blades simple, 8–30cm long, cordate to orbicular with entire margins and acute apex; upper surface glabrous, lower surface with short white hairs. **Flowers** 1–4, in axillary cymes; pedicels 1–3cm long; bracts surrounding calyx forming a 7–12-toothed cup 1–1.5cm long, finely hairy; calyx 5-lobed, 1.5–3cm long; corolla yellow, usually brownish-red at the base, changing to orange and dark red by day's end, 4–8.5cm long; stamens many, fused into a yellow column. **Fruit** a capsule 13–28mm long, 12–25mm wide, ovoid, 5-valved, finely yellowish-hairy.

Distribution: *Hau* is widespread in the tropics and subtropics worldwide, especially along coasts; in the Hawaiian Islands it is found on Midway, French Frigate Shoals, and six main islands (not Ni'ihau and Kaho'olawe), forming impenetrable thickets primarily along coasts, stream mouths, brackish swamps and along moist gullies and streambeds, from near sea level to 300m elevation. Introduced aggressive-invasive; FAC.

Note: *Hau* was used by Polynesians for canoe outriggers, fishnet floats, kite frames, adz handles and to produce fire by friction by rubbing it with the harder wood of *olomea* (*Perrotettia sandwicensis* A.Gray). The sap has laxative properties and the inner fiber of the bark was used to make ropes and *kapa* cloth. The leaf buds were chewed for dry throat. *Hau* branches were set along shorelines to indicate *kapu* fishing zones. The flowers and leaves were used in *lei* for *hula* ceremonies. It has been known in the islands by the younger name, *Hibiscus pernambucensis* Arruda.

Ipomoea alba L.
Moon flower

CONVOLVULACEAE

Description: Perennial woody vine 6m or more long, glabrous; stems smooth or covered with short fleshy prickles, twining, exuding a milky sap when cut, rooting adventitiously near nodes. **Leaves** alternate; stipules absent; petioles 5–25cm long; leaf-blades simple, 5–15cm long, cordate or with 3–7-lobed margins. **Flowers** 1–4, in axillary clusters; pedicels 7–15mm long; sepals 5, 10–20mm long, ovate to elliptical with a long tail-like appendage; corolla salverform, white with light green nectar guides, the tube narrow, 9–15cm long, flaring out to 8–10cm diam.; stamens 5; ovary superior, 2-celled. **Fruit** a dark brown cap-sule 2–3cm long, 1–2cm diam., ovoid with long-pointed apex.

Distribution: Moon flower is native to central America, now widely cultivated in the tropics; in the Hawaiian Islands it is found on six main islands (not Niʻihau and Kahoʻolawe). First recorded from Hawaiʻi in 1819, it now occurs in moist areas, from near sea level to 610m elevation. Introduced passive-invasive; FAC.

Note: Called moon flower because the flowers open at night and usually close up by mid-morning. This species has been known in Hawaiʻi by the younger name *Ipomoea bona-nox* L.

Ipomoea pes-caprae (L.) R.Br. ssp. *brasiliensis* (L.) Ooststr.
Pōhuehue, Beach morning glory
CONVOLVULACEAE

Description: Perennial woody vine 5m or more long, glabrous; stems not twining, exuding a milky sap when cut, often rooting at the nodes. **Leaves** alternate; stipules absent; petioles 2–10cm long; leaf-blades simple, 5–11cm long, 3–10cm wide, ovate to orbicular with entire margins. **Flowers** solitary or a few together bisexual, in axillary clusters; peduncles 4–14cm long; bracts 3–4mm long, caducous; pedicels 1–3cm long; sepals 8–13mm long; corolla pink to lavender-purple (rarely white) with a darker purple throat, 5–7cm long, tubular; stamens 5; ovary superior, 2-celled. **Fruit** a brown capsule 12–17mm long, 6–16mm wide, laterally compressed-ovoid.

Distribution: *Pōhuehue* is native to Central and South America, widely cultivated as a coastal groundcover; in the Hawaiian Islands it is found on Kure, Midway, Lisianski, Laysan, French Frigate Shoals, Nihoa and all eight main islands, commonly as a coastal strand plant but sometimes found in lowland saltwater marshes, from sea level to 460m elevation. Native aggressive-invasive; FAC.

Note: In Hawai'i the vine was mashed and used to bind sprains and the pounded roots were used as a cathartic. While the roots and leaves were said to have been used as starvation food, its cathartic effects would have been problematic. Short lengths of cut stems were used to slap the breasts of women who had just given birth to symbolically induce the flow of milk (mimicking *pōhuehue*'s milky white sap). The tough, flexible stems were used for cordage and to weave fishnets and baskets.

Ipomoea violacea L.
White morning glory

CONVOLVULACEAE

Description: Perennial herbaceous vine 5m or more long, glabrous; stems striate, twining, woody at the base, exuding a milky sap when cut, rooting at the nodes. **Leaves** alternate; petioles 1–3cm long; leaf-blades simple, 8–16cm long, 8–14cm wide, broadly cordate, margins smooth. **Flowers** 1–4, in axillary cymes; peduncles 3–7cm long; bracts small, caducous; sepals 15–25mm long; corolla salverform, white, the tube 6–10cm long, abruptly spreading at top of tube to 8–10cm diam.; stamens 5; ovary superior, 2-celled. **Fruit** a tan to brown capsule 2–3cm long, 2–2.5cm diam., ovoid to globose.

Distribution: White morning glory is pantropical; in the Hawaiian Islands it is found on O'ahu, Moloka'i, Maui and Hawai'i. First collected on Moloka'i in 1910, it is now common in coastal sites trailing among rocks and sand or in wet sites along brackish lagoon margins, from sea level to 5m elevation. Introduced passive-invasive; FAC.

Note: Synonyms include *Ipomoea grandiflora* (Choisy) Hallier f., *I. macrantha* Roem. & Schult. and *I. tuba* (Schltdl.) G.Don.

Photo: FRW

Lipochaeta succulenta (Hook. & Arn.) DC.
Nehe
ASTERACEAE

Description: Perennial subshrub 5–40 cm high, scattered stiff-hairy; stems ascending from woody rhizomes, decumbent, spreading, rooting adventitiously. **Leaves** opposite, grayish-green; stipules absent; petioles 2–10mm long, winged; leaf-blades simple, 6–16cm long, 1–6.5cm wide, linear to narrowly ovate with entire to serrate margins. **Flowers** 9–15 ray florets and 25–50 disk florets in heads 15–20mm diam., subtended by 8–10 involucral bracts in 2 rings, terminating simple or compound cymes; ray florets yellow, 4–7mm long; disk florets 3–4mm long; stamens 4; ovary inferior, 1-celled. **Fruit** a nut 2–3mm long, 1–2mm diam., ellipsoid with a ring of white connate, awned scales.

Distribution: *Nehe* is endemic to seven main Hawaiian Islands (not Lāna'i). It is an uncommon species of less disturbed coastal wetland, riparian and mesic habitats, from sea level to 100m elevation. Endemic non-invasive; FAC.

Lythrum maritimum Kunth
Pūkāmole, loosestrife
LYTHRACEAE

Description: Perennial shrub 0.3–1m high, mostly glabrous; stems slender, many-branched, 4-angled. **Leaves** opposite; stipules absent; petioles 0–1mm long; leaf-blades simple, 7–33mm long, 2–14mm wide, oblong with entire margins. **Flowers** solitary, sessile in leaf axils; calyx tube green, 5–8mm long, tubular, 8–12-ribbed, glabrous; corolla 4–6-lobed, pink to purple, 3–4mm long; stamens 6; ovary superior, 2-celled. **Fruit** a capsule 3–4mm long, 2–3mm diam., ovate.

Distribution: *Pūkāmole* is native to South America and possibly Hawai'i; in the Hawaiian Islands it is found on six main islands (not Ni'ihau and Kaho'olawe). First collected in Hawai'i by the earliest European explorers in the late 1700s. It is common in open mesic disturbed habitats, such as pasturelands, windward coastal cliffs, wet forest margins, bare lava and along streams, from sea level to 2450m elevation. Introduced or ?native passive-invasive; FAC.

Note: In Hawai'i the root of *pūkāmole* was pounded and included in potions to relieve severe body aches and pains, and to treat boils or sores.

Melaleuca quinquenervia (Cav.) S.T.Blake
Broad-leaved paperbark, Australian paperbark   MYRTACEAE

Description: Tree 20–25m high, mostly glabrous; trunk erect with white to tan, spongy, paper-like bark. **Leaves** alternate, leathery, glandular-dotted, aromatic when crushed; stipules absent; petioles 3–8mm long, twisted; leaf-blades simple, 5–9cm long, 0.8–1.5cm wide, lanceolate, dull green or yellowish-green with 3–5 veins and entire margins. **Flowers** many, sessile, in terete spikes 3–10cm long; bracts minute; sepals 5, 1.2–1.5mm long, ovate; petals 5, cream, 2.5–3mm long, ovate; stamens many, cream, 10–15mm long, attached at the base in 5 bundles opposite the petals; ovary inferior, 3-celled. **Fruit** a capsule 3–4mm long, 4–5mm diam., globose, 3-valved.

Distribution: Broad-leaved paperbark is native to tropical Australia, New Guinea and New Caledonia, occurring in swamplands or sites where groundwater is close to the surface; in the Hawaiian Islands, where it is known as Australian paperbark, it is found on Kaua'i, O'ahu, Moloka'i, Maui and Hawai'i. First collected on Hawai'i in the 1920s when it was used for restoration of disturbed mesic forest, windbreaks and as a street tree and can also grow in standing water, from 30 to 890m elevation. Introduced aggressive-invasive; FAC.

Note: *Melaleuca quinquenervia* is a noxious weed in Florida. This species has been incorrectly identified in Hawai'i as *M. leucadendron* L. The widely used common name cajeput belongs to a different tree, *M. cajeputi* Powell.

120

Merremia umbellata (L.) Hallier f.
Hogvine   CONVOLVULACEAE

Description: Perennial vine 1–3m long, mostly glabrous with a milky sap; stems herbaceous, older parts becoming woody, terete or slightly grooved, twining or creeping, rooting at the nodes. **Leaves** alternate; stipules absent; petioles 1.5–10cm long; leaf-blades simple, 4–15cm long, 1–9cm wide, narrowly triangular to broadly ovate with cordate to obtuse base, entire margins and acuminate apex. **Flowers** few to many bisexual, on pedicels 1–3mm long, subtended by scale-like bracts, borne in axillary umbels on peduncles 1–7cm long; sepals 5, 5–8mm long, broadly elliptic to orbicular; corolla tubular, yellow, 2–3.5cm long; stamens 5; ovary superior, 4-celled. **Fruit** a capsule 10–12mm long, 6–8mm diam., ovoid to conical, splitting at the base by 4 valves, each valve lanceolate to narrowly ovate.

Distribution: Hogvine is native to the tropics of the Americas, tropical east Africa, and south and east Asia; in the Hawaiian Islands it is cultivated on most islands and documented on O'ahu in 1999 as a garden escape into lowland disturbed habitats, including coastal freshwater marsh habitats, from sea level to 30m elevation. Introduced aggressive-invasive; FACU.

Note: This species is a very aggressive weed in American Samoa and could become an environmental problem species in Hawai'i.

Mimosa pudica L. var. *unijuga* (Duchass. & Walp.) Griseb.
Sensitive plant   FABACEAE

Description: Perennial woody herb 5–
50cm high, 0.3–1.5m long, sparsely
hairy or glabrous; stems purple, bearing
curved spines. **Leaves** alternate; stipules
stiff spines; petioles 1.5–5cm long; leaf-
blades 2-pinnate; pinnae 2–6cm long
with 10–26 pairs of leaflets, sensitive
and closing when touched and at night;
leaflets 6–15mm long, 1.2–3mm wide,
linear. **Flowers** many bisexual, in spherical heads 8–10mm diam., on axillary
peduncles 1–4cm long; calyx 0–1mm
long; corolla 4-lobed, pink to red in upper part, pink to lavender below, 2–
2.5mm long; stamens 4; ovary superior,
1-celled. **Fruit** a pod 10–20mm long, 3–
5mm wide, flattened-linear, 2–5-
segmented, each segment 3–5mm long,

borne in clusters of 2–8 fruits.

Distribution: Sensitive plant is probably
originally from South America, now a
pantropical weed; in the Hawaiian Islands it is found on six main islands (not
Ni'ihau and Kaho'olawe). First collected
on O'ahu in the mid-1800s but likely
introduced much earlier, it now occupies
open, dry to wet, disturbed sites, especially lawns, from near sea level to
1300m elevation. Introduced aggressive-
invasive; FAC.

Note: This species is known by many
names, including shame plant, sleeping
grass and *pua hilahila*, and is poisonous
to cattle, especially after being cut and
dried.

Pandanus tectorius Parkinson ex Z
Hala, Tahitian screwpine
PANDANACEAE

Description: Small tree 3–10m high; trunk bearing wide-angled branches and supported by thick, rigid, prickly prop roots. **Leaves** closely spiralled; leaf-base sheathing; leaf-blades 80–180cm long, 4–8cm wide, linear-lanceolate with 1–4mm long scabrous prickles on underside midrib and margins. **Flowers** many, unisexual on separate plants; male flowers with many stamens subtended by 13–18 white, overlapping, fragrant, leaf-like bracts enclosing cream-colored spikes, 5–10cm long, borne on terminal branches 30–45cm long; female flowers 40–80 in globose heads 4–5cm diam. at flowering, expanding when ripening to 10–20cm long, 10–18cm diam. **Fruit** a drupaceous berry (called a phalange or key) 4–7cm long, 40–80 together, the inner fleshy end fibrous, yellow, orange or red when ripe, outer end woody, yellowish-orange.

Distribution: *Hala* is native to coastal southeast Asia, tropical Australia and the western Pacific; in the Hawaiian Islands it is known from seven main islands (not Kaho'olawe) in extensive groves in mesic coastal sites, as well as on slopes of coastal valleys, occasionally found in wetlands, from near sea level to 610m elevation. Native passive-invasive; FAC.

Note: The species native to Hawai'i has previously been incorrectly identified as *Pandanus odoratissimus* L.f., which is native to India, Sri Lanka and Malaysia, and extending eastward into the western Pacific. A younger name, *P. variegatus* Miq., was also used for this species. *Hala* is cultivated as a shade tree. The tough, pliable leaves are woven into mats, hats, pillows and thatch and a brown or black dye is extracted from the roots. The bracts, seeds and inner fleshy end of the fruit are edible. Fresh keys are used in lei and dried keys as brushes for painting kapa. The fragrant male inflorescence was used to scent oil.

Pluchea spp.
The marsh fleabanes
ASTERACEAE

Pluchea carolinensis (Jacq.) G.Don
Sourbush
Description: Shrub 1–4m high, densely hairy; stems many-branched, spreading. **Leaves** alternate, grayish-green; stipules absent; petioles 10–25mm long; leaf-blades simple, 4–18cm long, 2–8cm wide, elliptical to obovate with entire margins. **Flowers** rays none, 8–21 male and many female disk florets in heads 5–7mm diam., subtended by many involucral bracts in 4–5 rings, terminating large, flat-topped clusters; disk florets pinkish-lavender, 2–3mm long; stamens 5; ovary inferior, 1-celled. **Fruit** a nut 0.6–0.8mm long, 0.2–0.3mm wide, terete with a pale brown pappus.

Distribution: Sourbush is a native of tropical America, common in

mesic and wet forests; in the Hawaiian Islands it is found on Kure, Midway, French Frigate Shoals and all eight main islands. First reported from Oʻahu in 1931, it is now locally common in coastal wetlands, riparian and mesic habitats and particularly pastures, from sea level to 900m elevation. Introduced aggressive-invasive; FAC.

P. carolinensis

Note: *Pluchea symphytifolia* (Mill.) Gillis is a younger name; plants previously identified in Hawaiʻi as *P. odorata* (L.) Cass. are correctly identified as *P. carolinensis*.

Pluchea xfosbergii Cooperr. & Galang
Description: Shrub 0.5–1m high, sparsely hairy; stems low-spreading. **Leaves** dull green; petioles 5–10mm long; leaf-blades 2.5–15cm long, 1.2–5cm wide, obovate with dentate margins. **Flowers** in heads in flat-topped to hemispherical panicles; disk florets pink to purplish-pink. **Fruit** an aborted nut 0.5–1mm long with a ring of white pappus.

P. carolinensis

P. Xfosbergii

and many female disk florets in heads 5–6mm diam., subtended by many involucral bracts in 6–7 rings, terminating large hemispherical panicles; disk florets pink to purplish-pink, 3–4mm long; stamens 5; ovary inferior, 1-celled. **Fruit** a nut 0.8–1mm long, 0.2–0.3mm wide, terete with a ring of white pappus.

Distribution: Indian fleabane is a native of south Asia, now widespread in the tropics of Africa, Asia, Australia and the western Pacific, typically common in mesic and wet shrublands; in the Hawaiian Islands it is found on Midway, Laysan and all eight main islands. First reported on O'ahu in 1915, it is now locally common from coastal wetland and riparian habitats, from sea level to 450m elevation. Introduced aggressive-invasive; FAC.

Distribution: This hybrid is common in mesic and wet shrublands in the tropical Pacific region; in the Hawaiian Islands it is found on Midway, Kaua'i, O'ahu, Moloka'i and Maui. First reported on O'ahu in 1934, it is now locally common from coastal wetland and riparian habitats. Hybrid from introduced parents, non-invasive; FAC.

Note: A spontaneous sterile F1 hybrid between *Pluchea indica* and *P. carolinensis,* arising wherever these species occur together. The hybrid has leaves closer in form to *P. carolinensis*, and flower heads like those of *P. indica.*

Pluchea indica (L.) Less.
Indian fleabane

Description: Shrub 1–2m high, sparsely hairy; stems many-branched, spreading. **Leaves** alternate, lustrous green; stipules absent; petioles 0–5mm long; leaf-blades simple, 2.5–5cm long, 1.2–2cm wide, obovate with dentate margins towards the apex. **Flowers** rays none, 1–3 male

P. indica

125

Pritchardia martii (Gaudich.) H.Wendl.
Loulu hiwa

ARECACEAE

Description: Palm 3–16m high; trunk gray, solitary, erect, 15–25cm diam. **Leaves** apical, whorled; petioles 0.6–1.1m long; leaf-blades plicate, 0.8–1.1m long with pleated margins and silver-gray lower surface. **Flowers** many, sessile, on inflorescences with 1–3 flowering branches 15–20cm long, each branch strongly sinuate between the spirally arranged alternate flowers; calyx 4–6cm long, shallowly 3-lobed; petals 3; stamens 6; ovary superior, 3-celled. **Fruit** a brown to black drupe 4–5cm long, 2.8–4.5cm wide, spherical, narrowed toward both ends.

Distribution: *Loulu hiwa* is found on Oʻahu, now restricted to wet forest on slopes, ridges, precipices and cliffs, often following drainages, sometimes in mesic valleys or along streams, from 360 to 610m elevation. Endemic non-invasive; FAC.

Note: There are about 20 species of *loulu* in the Hawaiian Islands, several of which may have been associated with wetlands, for example, on Hawaiʻi *Pritchardia affinis* Becc. is associated with margins of anchialine pools and *P. lanigera* Becc. in boggy area of the Kohala Mountains and very wet windward slopes of Mauna Loa and Mauna Kea. Once widespread in lowland wetlands, these species of *loulu* have long been depleted by harvesting and seed predation. The wood of *loulu* was used to make spears and the unripe fruit was eaten. The leaves were used for thatching and are sometimes woven into hats and fans. Seasonally, Hawaiians built *heiau* (shrines) out of *loulu* leaves to appease fishing gods.

Photo: CP

Pterolepis glomerata (Rottb.) Miq.
False meadowbeauty   MELASTOMATACEAE

Description: Short-lived perennial herb 20–50cm high, stiff-hairy; stems erect, 4-angled. **Leaves** opposite and decussate; stipules absent; petioles 1–5mm long; leaf-blades simple, 14–45mm long, 6–16mm wide, ovate with 3 veins from leaf base and entire or minutely-toothed margins. **Flowers** 3–10, sessile in terminal clusters; involucral bracts 3.5–6mm long, ovate-lanceolate; sepals 4–7.5mm long, 1–2mm wide, triangular to ovate; petals 4, pink to white, 10–15mm long, 10–14mm wide, broadly ovate, caducous; stamens 8, larger anthers pink, 3–4mm long, smaller anthers yellow, 2.5–3.5mm long; ovary superior, 4-celled.

Fruit a capsule 4–6mm long, 2–5mm wide, ovoid to globose, enclosed by flower base.

Distribution: False meadowbeauty is native to tropical eastern South America; in the Hawaiian Islands it is found on Kaua'i, O'ahu, Moloka'i and Hawai'i. First collected on O'ahu in 1949, it is now common in mesic to wet, disturbed sites and along muddy trails, from 180 to 1220m elevation. Introduced aggressive-invasive; FAC.

Rhizophora mangle L.
Red mangrove, American mangrove RHIZOPHORACEAE

Description: Tree 3–10m high, glabrous throughout; prop roots arising from stems; trunk not buttressed. **Leaves** opposite and decussate, green; stipules lanceolate, reddish-green; petioles 1–2.5cm long; leaf-blades simple, 5–15cm long, 3–7cm wide, elliptic to obovate with entire margins. **Flowers** 2–3, in axillary clusters; peduncles 3–4cm long; pedicels 4–10mm long; sepals 4, 10–15mm long; corolla lobes pale yellow, 8–10mm long; stamens 4; ovary partially superior, 2-celled. **Fruit** a drupe 2–3cm long, 0.8–1.2cm wide, bullet-shaped with a viviparous seedling 10–25cm long.

Distribution: Red mangrove is native to tropical America, typically of coasts and saltwater riparian habitats; in the Hawaiian Islands it is found on six main islands (not Niʻihau and Kahoʻolawe). It was introduced to stabilize mudflats on Molokaʻi in 1902. Without intervention this species will take over fringing reefs and tidal strand, saltwater marshes and other maritime riparian habitats. Introduced aggressive-invasive; OBL.

Note: This is a landscape-altering species of reef-flats, fishponds, estuaries and streams.

Sphagneticola trilobata (L.) Pruski
Creeping ox-eye, wedelia

ASTERACEAE

Description: Perennial subshrub 10–20cm high, 0.5–2m long, stiff-hairy; stems decumbent, low-spreading, occasionally ascending, rooting adventitiously. **Leaves** opposite, dark green; stipules absent; petioles 0–1cm long, winged; leaf-blades simple but deeply lobed, 3–9cm long, 1.2–3.5cm wide, ovate-deltate with irregularly dentate to 3-lobed margins. **Flowers** 8–13 ray florets and many bisexual disk florets, in heads 15–20mm diam., subtended by few involucral bracts in 2–3 rings, terminating 3–10cm long peduncles; ray florets yellow, 6–15mm long; disk florets yellow, 4–5mm long; stamens 5; ovary inferior, 1-celled. **Fruit** a nut 4–5mm long, 2–3mm wide, angular-ellipsoid, warty with a ring of white connate, awned scales.

Distribution: Creeping ox-eye is native to the tropical Americas, typically common in mesic and wet forests; in the Hawaiian Islands, where it is known by its former generic name wedelia, it is a garden escape on Midway, Kaua'i, O'ahu, Maui and Hawai'i. First recorded on O'ahu in 1967, it currently spreads vegetatively, mostly in mesic and wet sites, from near sea level to 635m elevation. Introduced aggressive-invasive; FAC.

Note: The cultivar in Hawai'i spreads vegetatively, producing few mature fruit. Once the right pollinator arrives or a fertile strain develops, this species will become a very serious weed of all wetland habitats in the islands. It is spreading into remote coastal areas by being washed-up on beaches and into streams. *Wedelia* was recently split into several new genera, thus *W. trilobata* (L.) Hitchc. is a synonym.

Stachytarpheta jamaicensis (L.) Vahl
Jamaican vervain
VERBENACEAE

Description: Annual or perennial woody herb 0.6–1.2m high, sparsely hairy; stems ascending, many-branched. **Leaves** alternate or opposite, green; stipules absent; petioles 0.3–3.5cm long; leaf-blades 2–12cm long, 1.5–4cm wide, oblong to elliptic or ovate with serrate margins. **Flowers** many, bisexual, each subtended by triangular to obovate bracts, borne on terminal spikes 15–50cm long; calyx 4-lobed, 0.4–0.5mm long; corolla pale blue, 8–11mm long; stamens 4 (2 sterile); ovary inferior, 2-celled. **Fruit** a schizocarp 3–7mm long, 1.5–2mm wide, separating into 2 mericarps.

Distribution: Jamaican vervain is native to Central and tropical South America, now in the tropics worldwide; in the Hawaiian Islands it is found on Midway and seven main islands (not Niʻihau). First reported on Lānaʻi in 1913, it is common in wet to mesic and dry disturbed areas, from sea level to 490m elevation. Introduced aggressive-invasive; FACU.

Syzygium cumini (L.) Skeels
Java plum   MYRTACEAE

Description: Tree 6–20m high, glabrous; trunk with bark pale yellowish-brown, flaky. **Leaves** opposite; stipules absent; petioles 0.8–3.5cm long; leaf-blades simple, 7–19cm long, 2.5–11cm wide, lanceolate with 25–40 pairs of prominent veins and entire margins, glabrous. **Flowers** many, in compound axillary or terminal loose clusters 5–10cm long; peduncles 1–3cm long; bracts 1–1.5mm long; sepals 4, 3–4mm long; petals 4, white turning pink, 3–4mm long; stamens many, 4–6mm long, pink; ovary inferior, 3-celled. **Fruit** a glossy dark purple to black berry 1.2–3cm long, 0.8–1.4cm diam., oblong-ellipsoidal.

Distribution: Java plum is native to south and southeast Asia, now widely cultivated in the tropics; in the Hawaiian Islands it is found on six main islands (not Ni'ihau and Kaho'olawe). It was already established in Hawai'i by 1870, now primarily in valleys to disturbed mesic forest, especially along stream channels, from 40 to 1230m elevation. Introduced aggressive-invasive; FAC.

Note: Previously placed in the genus *Eugenia* as *E. cumini* (L.) Druce, and also known by the younger name *E. jambolana* Lam. Planted as a windbreak, but otherwise seldom intentionally grown.

131

Syzygium jambos (L.) Alston
Malabar plum, rose apple   MYRTACEAE

Description: Tree 6–15m high, glabrous; trunk with bark grayish-brown, smooth. **Leaves** opposite; petioles 0.5–1cm long; leaf-blades simple, 10–23cm long, 2.5–5cm wide, narrowly lanceolate with 10–20 pairs of prominent veins and entire margins. **Flowers** many, in terminal 1-branched close clusters 1–2cm long; peduncles 7–15mm long; bracts 0.8–1mm long; sepals 4, in pairs 4–8mm long, persistent; petals 4, white to greenish-white, 12–20mm long; stamens many, whitish-yellow, 10–50mm long; ovary inferior, 2-celled. **Fruit** a whitish-yellow to pinkish-yellow berry, 2–4cm diam., spherical.

Distribution: Malabar Plum or rose apple, is native to southeast Asia, but now pantropical; in the Hawaiian Islands it is found on six main islands (not Niʻihau and Kahoʻolawe). Brought to Hawaiʻi from Rio de Janeiro in 1825, it is now widespread in low elevation mesic to wet sites, primarily valleys and occasionally disturbed mesic forest, from 15 to 500m elevation. Introduced aggressive-invasive; FAC.

Note: Previously placed in the genus *Eugenia* and known by the name *E. jambos* L. Malabar plum is not often planted in Hawaiʻi today, but is readily encountered in wet forests. The fruit is eaten fresh or stewed, preserved, used in marmalades, jellies, confectionery and sauces or fermented into wine.

Terminalia catappa L.
Tropical almond, false kamani

COMBRETACEAE

Description: Tree 8–25m high, glabrous; trunk with branches conspicuously whorled in tiers around main trunk. **Leaves** alternate, in rosettes at branch tips; stipules absent; petioles 1–2cm long; leaf-blades simple, shiny dark green, 20–45cm long, 12–20cm wide, obovate with entire margins and obtuse apex. **Flowers** many, bisexual and unisexual, in 1–4 axillary spikes 10–25cm long; calyx 5-lobed, greenish-white; petals absent; stamens 10; ovary inferior, 1-celled. **Fruit** a green to red-tinged drupe 2–6cm long, 2–3cm wide, laterally compressed-ellipsoid.

Distribution: Tropical almond is native to southeast Asia but now widespread along pantropical coasts; in the Hawaiian Islands, where it is better known as false kamani, it is found on Kaua'i, O'ahu, Moloka'i, Maui and Hawai'i. It was introduced to O'ahu between 1851 and 1871 by Dr. William Hillebrand. It is prolific in coastal areas, especially along sandy or rocky shores and margins of anchialine ponds, but also inland in moist habitats, from sea level to 120m elevation. Introduced aggressive-invasive; FAC.

Note: Tropical almond is widely cultivated as an attractive, salt tolerant coastal shade tree. It is often conspicuous for a "fall foliage" effect twice each year due to older leaves turning red or yellow before they fall.

Thespesia populnea (L.) Sol. ex Correa
Milo, portia tree
MALVACEAE

Description: Tree 5–20m high, glabrous; trunk with thick, corrugated grey bark. **Leaves** alternate; stipules 8–10mm long, linear; petioles 3–20cm long; leaf-blades simple, shiny yellowish-green, 5–30cm long, ovate to triangular or cordate with entire margins and attenuate apex. **Flowers** solitary, axillary; pedicels 1–5cm long; floral bracts 3, 4–17mm long; calyx 8–12mm long, cup-like; corolla yellow (usually with a maroon spot at the base) fading to purplish-pink, 4–7cm long; stamens many, fused into a yellow column. **Fruit** a capsule 2–3.5cm long, 2.5–4.5cm diam., 5-angled globose.

Distribution: *Milo* is native to tropical Africa and Asia, now pantropical as a cultivated coastal shade tree; in the Hawaiian Islands it is found on six main islands (not Lāna'i and Kaho'olawe), in low-lying, protected coastal sites at the mouths of streams exposed to tidal influence, from sea level to 275m elevation. Introduced passive-invasive; FAC.

Note: A Polynesian introduction, the wood was used for calabashes and canoe hulls. *Milo* also yields a yellowish-green dye from the fruit, also medicine, oil and gum; the young leaves are edible. This species has been known by the younger name *Thespesia macrophylla* Blume. Also known as the Indian tulip tree.

Verbena litoralis Kunth
Seashore vervain, ōwī

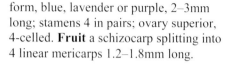

VERBENACEAE

Description: Perennial herb 0.4–1.5m high, glabrous or sparsely hairy; stems erect or ascending, woody at the base with few to many 4-angular branches. **Leaves** opposite and decussate; stipules absent; petioles 0–5mm long, winged; leaf-blades 3–10cm long, 1–3.5cm wide, lanceolate, scabrous with serrate margins. **Flowers** many, in terminal spikes 3–12cm long; peduncles and pedicels absent; calyx tubular, purple or green, 5-lobed, 1.5–2.3mm long; corolla salver-form, blue, lavender or purple, 2–3mm long; stamens 4 in pairs; ovary superior, 4-celled. **Fruit** a schizocarp splitting into 4 linear mericarps 1.2–1.8mm long.

Distribution: Seashore vervain, or ōwī as it is known in Hawai'i, is native to the American tropics, now widely naturalized; in the Hawaiian Islands it is found on Midway and all eight main islands. First reported from Hawai'i in 1837, it is now a common weed in wet to dry habitats, from sea level to 2200m elevation. Introduced passive-invasive; FACU.

Note: In Hawai'i *Verbena brasiliensis* Vell. was a misapplied name for this species. This species became an important medicinal plant immediately following its introduction.

Vigna luteola (Jacq.) Benth.
Hairypod cowpea

FABACEAE

Description: Perennial vine 10–20cm tall, up to 2m long, sparsely hairy; stems slender, trailing or twining, rooting at the nodes. **Leaves** alternate; stipules 3–4mm long, ovate-lanceolate; petioles 2–10cm long; leaf-blades trifoliate; leaflets 2.5–10cm long, 1.5–5cm wide, ovate to lanceolate with entire margins and acute to acuminate apex. **Flowers** several, 1.5–2.5cm long on pedicels 4–9mm long subtended by 1.5–2mm long bracts, borne on axillary racemes 6–45cm long; calyx 5-lobed, 3–4mm long, the lobes triangular, as long as the tube; petals 5, yellow to greenish, upper petal (standard) 1.3–2.5cm long, 1.2–2.6cm wide, lateral (wing) petals about same height as standard, 7mm wide, lower (keel) petals shorter than standard, 6mm wide; stamens 10 (1 distinct, the others joined into a tube); ovary superior, 1-celled. **Fruit** a pod 4–8cm long, 5–6.5mm wide, linear, variably pubescent.

Distribution: Hairypod cowpea is a widespread tropical lowland vine found throughout Africa, Asia and America in inland riparian and marsh habitats; in the Hawaiian Islands only collected from Oʻahu. First collected in 1999 from Kawai Nui Marsh, Oʻahu and subsequently in other windward Oʻahu coastal sites to the north, near sea level. Introduced passive-invasive; FAC.

Vigna marina (Burm.) Merr.
Mohihihi, notched cowpea

FABACEAE

Description: Short-lived perennial vine up to 3m long, sparsely to densely hairy; stems slender, creeping or climbing.
Leaves alternate; stipules 2–3mm long, ovate, caducous; petioles 5–10cm long; leaf-blades 1-pinnate, leaflets 3, 4–10cm long, 3–9cm wide, broadly to more narrowly ovate, the middle one the largest.
Flowers 10–20 bisexual, axillary or terminal; peduncles 4–11cm long (usually standing higher than the foliage); bracts 1.5–2mm long; pedicel 4.5–6mm long; calyx 3–4mm long; corolla bright yellow, 12–19mm long, upper petal (standard) broadly cordate-obcordate; stamens 5; ovary superior, 1-celled.
Fruit a pod 35–60mm long, 8–9mm wide, linear-inflated, slightly curved and constricted.

Distribution: *Mohihihi* is pantropical in coastal sites; in the Hawaiian Islands it is found on Kaua'i, O'ahu, Moloka'i, Maui and Hawai'i, on sandy beaches, sea cliffs or dry shrubby coastal slopes and in salt-water marshes, from sea level to 20m elevation. Native passive-invasive; FAC.

Note: *Mohihihi* has become an ornamental that is being promoted as a coastal site groundcover.

137

SECTION 4 — DICOT HERBS
Herbs with perianth in twos, fours or fives and mostly reticulate veins

This section treats plants without woody stems and flowers with their perianth parts (petals, sepals, tepals, or corolla and calyx lobes) usually in whorls of twos, fours or fives. The male (androecium) and female (gynoecium) may have the same number of flower parts, but may also be quite variable. Most dicotyledon leaf-blades have net-like (reticulate) veins. Some without leaf-blades have expanded petioles with longitudinal venation. In this field guide *Hydrocotyle* is included in the family Araliaceae following recent molecular analysis (previously Apiaceae).

Key to the common dicotyledonous herbs of Hawaii's wetlands

1 Leaves arising from a basal rosette, with 5–7 prominent longitudinal veins .... *Plantago major* Leaves borne on stems and branches; veins net-like (reticulate), or fewer than 5 veins if longitudinal or parallel 2

2(1) Lower stem leaves opposite or whorled .... 3 Lower stem leaves alternate 29

3(2) Leaf-blades divided at least halfway to the midvein .... *Bidens alba* Leaf-blades serrate, dentate or entire 4

4(3) Flowers in very compact clusters or heads .... 5 Flowers solitary or loosely clustered on stems 9

5(4) Leaf-blades sessile; flowers surrounded by a ring of bracts .... 6 Leaf-blades borne on a distinct petiole; flowers not surrounded by a ring of bracts 7

6(5) Leaf-blades elliptic-lanceolate with serrate margins; florets white .... *Eclipta prostrata* Leaf-blades ovate-deltate with irregularly dentate margins; florets yellow .... *Sphagneticola trilobata* (Section 3)

7(5) Florets borne in spikelets sessile in leaf-axils .... *Alternanthera sessilis* Florets borne in dense spikes or heads on long axillary or terminal peduncles .. 8

8(7) Florets yellow, 4–7mm long .... *Lipochaeta succulenta* (Section 3) Florets purplish-pink to white, 2–3mm long .... *Phyla nodiflora*

9(4) Stipules present .... 10 Stipules absent 13

10(9) Flowers one per leaf axil, sessile .... *Ludwigia palustris* Flowers more than 2 in axillary clusters 11

11(10) Leaf-blades linear, more than 10 times longer than wide .... *Spergularia marina*
Leaf-blades wider, less than 3 times longer than wide 12

12(11) Leaf-blades elliptic to oblong, 1–4mm wide; one main vein .. *Pilea microphylla*
Leaf-blades orbicular to reniform, 5–30mm wide; prominently 3–5-veined ....
.... *Drymaria cordata*

13(9) Leaves linear to lanceolate, more than four times longer then wide 14
Leaves ovate, obovate or elliptical, less than four times as long as wide 17

14(13) Plants more than 40cm high; leaf-blades with serrate margins ....
.... *Verbena litoralis* (Section 3)
Plants less than 40cm high; leaf-blades with entire margins 15

15(14) Flowers in sessile axillary clusters .... *Ammannia coccinea*
Flowers solitary on pedicels in leaf-axils 16

16(15) Leaves succulent; stems glabrous .... *Sesuvium portulacastrum*
Leaves not succulent; stems clothed with stiff red hairs ....
.... *Cuphea hyssopifolia* (Section 3)

17(13) Plants with glandular or stiff hairs on stems and leaves 18
Plants glabrous throughout or with few scattered hairs 19

18(17) Plants with glandular (sticky) hairs .... *Cuphea carthagenensis*
Plants with stiff hairs .... *Pterolepis glomerata* (Section 3)

19(17) Flowers many in terminal spikes 20
Flowers solitary or several in leaf axils 21

20(19) Leaf-blades entire; flowers yellow .... *Hypericum mutilum*
Leaf-blades serrate; flowers pale blue .... *Stachytarpheta jamaicensis* (Section 3)

21(19) Flowers on one side of a leafless spike .... *Asystasia gangetica*
Flowers axillary on leafy branches 22

22(21) Leaves succulent .... *Bacopa monnieri*
Leaves not succulent 23

23(22) Corolla rotate to campanulate (bell-shaped); fruit laterally compressed 24
Corolla bilabiate, tubular; fruit terete, not laterally compressed 26

24(23) Leaf margins irregularly dentate; capsules obovoid to subglobose ....
.... *Veronica plebeia*
Leaf margins entire to serrate; capsules obcordate 25

25(24) Pedicels less than 2mm long; corolla less than 1.5mm long .. *Veronica arvensis*
Pedicels 2–5mm long; corolla more than 2mm long .... *Veronica serpyllifolia*

26(23) Calyx 17–23mm long, completely enclosing the fruit .... *Torenia glabra*
Calyx 1–5mm long, not enclosing the fruit 27

27(26) Leaves hairy below; calyx lobed to the middle; capsules 3.5–5mm long ....
.... *Lindernia crustacea*
Leaves glabrous; calyx lobed almost to the base; capsules 4–13mm long 28

28(27) Corolla 8–13mm long .... *Lindernia antipoda*
Corolla 4–4.5mm long .... *Lindernia procumbens*

29(2) Leaf-blades, petioles, stipules or leaf-bases sheathing the stem 30
Leaves not sheathing the stem 36

30(29) Leaf-margins entire 31
Leaf-margins dentate to deeply lobed 32

31(30) Plants with glandular hairs throughout .... *Persicaria punctata*
Plants glabrous throughout .... *Persicaria glabra*

32(30) Leaf-blades orbicular to reniform .... *Centella asiatica*
Leaf-blades deeply lobed or pinnate 33

33(32) Flowers in compact heads, surrounded by bracts 34
Flowers in spreading terminal clusters 35

34(33) Disk florets white; ray florets absent .... *Erechtites hieracifolia*
Disk florets absent; ray florets yellow .... *Sonchus oleraceus*

36(33) Leaf-blades 1-pinnate with 3 leaflets .... *Cryptotaenia canadensis*
Leaf-blades 3–4-pinnate with many linear leaflets ....
.... *Cyclospermum leptophyllum*

36(29) Leaf-blades deeply lobed more than halfway to the midvein, or divided into
leaflets 37
Leaf-blades entire, dentate, serrate or shallowly lobed less than one quarter of
the distance to the midvein 43

37(36) Leaf-blades deeply lobed; flowers in dense heads surrounded by bracts ....
.... *Erechtites valerianifolia*
Leaf-blades divided into 3 or more leaflets; flowers not in dense heads 38

38(37) Leaflets irregularly lobed .... *Cardamine flexuosa*
Leaflets entire, dentate or serrate 39

39(38) Leaflets more than twice as long as wide 40
Leaflets almost as wide as long 41

40(39) Many flowers, in heads; petals very small with many long pink stamens ....
.... *Mimosa pudica* (Section 3)

Flowers 2 to several, well separated on stems; standard petal large, maroon or purple, stamens enclosed in flower .... *Macroptilium lathyroides*

41(39) Flowers purplish-pink; fruit flattened with 3–7 squarish segments ....
.... *Desmodium triflorum*
Flowers white to cream; fruit terete, not flattened or segmented 42

42(41) Leaflets broadly obovate to reniform; margins crenate .... *Rorippa sarmentosa*
Leaflets ovate to elliptic; margins entire to dentate .. *Nasturtium microphyllum*

43(36) Leaf-blades more than four times longer than wide 44
Leaf-blades less than four times longer than wide 46

44(43) Petioles present; stipules caducous; flowers solitary in leaf axils ....
.... *Ludwigia octovalvis*
Petiole absent; stipules absent; flowers in inflorescence clusters or heads 45

45(44) Flowers closely arranged along a curling spike ...... *Heliotropium curassavicum*
Flowers in heads .... *Conyza bonariensis*

46(45) Flowers in dense heads surrounded by bracts 47
Flowers in arranged in inflorescence clusters but not heads 48

47(46) Leaves with glandular hairs below; involucral bracts glabrous to sparsely hairy,
none glandular; florets lavender to white .... *Ageratum conyzoides*
Leaves without glandular hairs below; involucral bracts moderately to densely
hairy, some glandular; florets pale blue .... *Ageratum houstonianum*

48(46) Flowers pale blue, borne singly on a long spike ....
.... *Stachytarpheta jamaicensis* (Section 3)
Flowers red, pink to white, borne in axillary or terminal clusters 49

49(48) Leaf-blades lanceolate to sagittate-cordate; corolla tubular ... *Ipomoea aquatica*
Leaf-blades elliptic, orbicular to reniform; corolla of separate petals 50

50(49) Leaf-blades lanceolate to oblong-elliptic; petals more than 1cm long ....
.... *Impatiens walleriana*
Leaf-blades orbicular, globose or reniform; petals less than 5mm long 51

51(50) Petiole attached within the leaf-blade (peltate) .... *Hydrocotyle verticillata*
Petiole attached to edge of leaf-blade 52

52(51) Plants glabrous .... *Hydrocotyle sibthorpioides*
Plants hairy .... *Hydrocotyle bowlesioides*

Ageratum conyzoides L.
Billy-goat weed

ASTERACEAE

Description: Short-lived perennial herb 0.3–1.5m high, sparsely to densely hairy; stems erect with few branches. **Leaves** alternate, green; stipules absent; petioles 1–5cm long; leaf-blades simple, 3–10cm long, 3–7cm wide, ovate with crenate margins, glandular below. **Flowers** no ray florets and many disk florets, borne on 2–4mm diam. heads, subtended by involucral bracts without glandular hairs, terminating flat-topped cymes; disk florets lavender to white, 1.5–3mm long; stamens 5; ovary inferior, 1-celled. **Fruit** a nut 1–1.5mm long, 0.2–0.3mm diam., 5-angled, narrow ellipsoid, scabrous with a ring of awned scales.

Distribution: Billy-goat weed is native to tropical South America, now worldwide, typically common in disturbed mesic and wet forests; in the Hawaiian Islands it is found on all eight main islands. First reported on Hawai'i in 1871, it is now locally common in coastal wetlands, riparian and mesic habitats and particularly pastures and disturbed urban sites, from sea level to 1300m elevation. Introduced passive-invasive; FAC.

Note: Billy-goat weed is also known as tropical white-weed and locally as *maile hohono*. It is reported to be detrimental to the health of livestock.

Ageratum houstonianum Mill.
Bluemink

ASTERACEAE

Description: Short-lived perennial herb 0.3–1.5m high, densely hairy; stems erect with few branches. **Leaves** alternate, green; stipules absent; petioles 1–5cm long; leaf-blades simple, 3–10cm long, 3–7cm wide, ovate with crenate margins, without glandular hairs below. **Flowers** no ray florets and many disk florets, borne on 2–4mm diam. heads, subtended by involucral bracts with glandular hairs, terminating flat-topped cymes; disk florets pale blue, 1.5–3mm long; stamens 5; ovary inferior, 1-celled. **Fruit** a nut 1–1.5mm long, 0.2–0.3mm diam., 5-angled, narrow ellipsoid, scabrous with a ring of awned scales.

Distribution: Bluemink is native to tropical Central America, now worldwide, typically common in disturbed mesic and wet forests; in the Hawaiian Islands it is found on Kaua'i, O'ahu, Maui and Hawai'i. First reported on Hawai'i in 1871, it is now locally common in coastal wetlands and along trails and roadsides from 40 to 1300m elevation. Introduced passive-invasive; FACU.

Note: Bluemink has been known in recent times locally as *maile hohono*. It is reported to be detrimental to the health of livestock.

Alternanthera sessilis (L.) R.Br. ex DC.
Sessile joyweed

AMARANTHACEAE

Description: Perennial herb 5–20cm high, 0.1–1m long, glabrous to sparsely hairy; stems prostrate, rarely ascending, often adventitiously rooting at the nodes. **Leaves** opposite; stipules absent; petioles 1–5mm long; leaf-blades simple, 1–15cm long, 0.3–3cm wide, obovate to broadly elliptic with entire margins. **Flowers** many, in sessile clusters in leaf axils; involucral bracts shiny white, 0.7–1.5mm long; sepals 5, white, 2.5–3mm long; petals absent; stamens 5, 2 sterile; ovary superior, 1-celled. **Fruit** a utricle 2–2.3mm diam., globose, protruding from persistent sepals.

Distribution: Sessile joyweed is native to the tropical Americas and now widespread in the tropics and subtropics; in the Hawaiian Islands it is found on Kaua'i, O'ahu, Moloka'i, Maui and Hawai'i. First collected on O'ahu in 1935, it is common in lowland pasturelands, cultivated wetlands, poorly drained disturbed sites, stream banks and sometimes floating in water, from sea level to 350m elevation. Introduced passive-invasive; FAC.

Note: Although this is a federally-listed noxious weed, it is sold as an aquarium plant, especially the cultivars with bright red leaves.

Ammannia coccinea Rottb.
Valley redstem, scarlet toothcup
LYTHRACEAE

Description: Annual herb 10–30cm high, 10–50cm long, mostly glabrous; stems erect to ascending, usually 4-angled, spongy when growing in water. **Leaves** opposite; stipules and petioles absent; leaf-blades simple, 2–10cm long, 0.3–1.5cm wide, linear to lanceolate with short lobes at the base, entire margins and acute apex. **Flowers** 2–5, sub-sessile, clustered in leaf axils; calyx tube 2.5–5mm long; corolla purple to pink, 1–2mm long, deciduous; stamens 4–8; ovary superior, 2-celled. **Fruit** a capsule 3–4mm long, 2–3mm diam., ovoid, enclosed by the persistent crimson calyx.

Distribution: Valley redstem is native to the tropical Americas, now widespread; in the Hawaiian Islands it is found on Kaua'i, O'ahu and Maui. First collected on O'ahu in 1936, it is now common in wet sites, such as taro patches and freshwater marshes, from near sea level to 135m elevation. Introduced passive-invasive; OBL.

Note: Previously incorrectly identified in Hawai'i as *Ammannia auriculata* Willd.

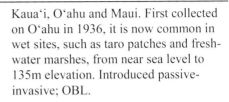

Asystasia gangetica (L.) T.Anderson
Chinese violet   ACANTHACEAE

Description: Perennial herb 20–60cm high, 0.5–2m long, sparsely hairy; stems decumbent or ascending, many-branched, nodes swollen, not rooting at the nodes. **Leaves** opposite; stipules absent; petioles 0.5–4.5cm long; leaf-blades simple, 2.5–13cm long, 2–7cm wide, ovate with entire margins. **Flowers** several, borne on pedicels 1–2mm long, subtended by 4 linear to triangular bracts 1–2mm long, on 1-sided spikes; calyx deeply divided into 5 linear lobes 5–7mm long; corolla pale blue to purple, pink or sometimes white or pale yellow, 3–3.5cm long, tubular, 5-lobed; stamens 4, in 2 pairs, included within corolla tube; ovary superior, 2-celled. **Fruit** a capsule 2–3cm long, narrow club-shaped, glandular-hairy with a beaked apex 3–4mm long.

Distribution: Chinese violet is native to south and southeast Asia and Africa, now widely distributed in the tropics and subtropics; in the Hawaiian Islands it is found on Midway, Kaua'i, O'ahu, Moloka'i, Maui and Hawai'i. First collected on O'ahu in 1925, it is now common in disturbed lowland habitats and urban areas, sometimes on saturated soils in freshwater marshes, from sea level to 700m elevation. Introduced passive-invasive; FACU.

Note: Chinese violet is commonly cultivated in gardens in Hawai'i and readily escapes.

Bacopa monnieri (L.) Wettst.
'Ae'ae, water hyssop

SCROPHULARIACEAE

Description: Aquatic perennial herb 5–10cm high, glabrous; stems prostrate, decumbent or floating, many-branched, rooting adventitiously. **Leaves** opposite; stipules absent; petioles 0–0.2cm long; leaf-blades 0.5–2cm long, 0.3–1cm wide, spathulate to obovate with entire margins. **Flowers** solitary, in leaf axils; pedicels 6–20mm; calyx 5-lobed, green, 4–6mm long, 2.5–5mm wide; corolla white to pale blue, 6–10mm long; stamens 4; ovary superior, 2-celled. **Fruit** a capsule 5–8mm long, 2–3mm wide, conical.

Distribution: *'Ae'ae* is native to subtropical and tropical regions worldwide, typically common in fresh to brackish marshes; in the Hawaiian Islands it is found on Midway and seven main islands (not Kaho'olawe). It is widespread in coastal wetlands, freshwater and brackish riparian habitats, rice fields and taro patches, from sea level to 230m elevation. Native passive-invasive; OBL.

Note: *'Ae'ae* is commonly used as a groundcover in horticulture and in wetland restoration projects.

Bidens alba (L.) DC. var. *radiata* (Sch.Bip.) Melchert
Romerillo, common beggars-tick   ASTERACEAE

Description: Short-lived perennial or annual herb 0.3–1.5m high, densely hairy; stems erect, often branching near ground. **Leaves** opposite, grayish-green; stipules absent; petioles 1–2cm long; leaf-blades simple to 1-pinnate, 5–15cm long, 0.5–2cm wide, oblanceolate or deeply divided into 1–3 leaflets with serrate margins. **Flowers** 5–8 ray florets and 25–70 disk florets, borne on 2.2–4.2cm diam. heads, subtended by many involucral bracts 2–5mm long, on peduncles 0.8–11cm long, terminating open clusters; ray floret petals white, 10–16mm long; disk florets yellow, 4–6mm long; stamens 5; ovary inferior, 1-celled. **Fruit** a nut 4–12mm long, 2–4mm wide, terete with a pappus of 2 awns.

Distribution: Romerillo is native to the tropical Americas, now worldwide, typically common in disturbed mesic and wet forests; in the Hawaiian Islands it is found on Kure, Midway and seven main islands (not Niʻihau). First collected on Oʻahu in 1958, it is now locally common in coastal wetlands, riparian and mesic habitats and particularly pastures and disturbed urban sites, from near sea level to 455m elevation. Introduced aggressive-invasive; FAC.

Note: Several different species are known by the name common beggars-tick. Other commonly used names for this species include Spanish needles and cobbler pegs.

148

Cardamine flexuosa With.
Woodland bittercress

BRASSICACEAE

Description: Short-lived perennial or annual herb 10–30cm high, sparsely hairy; stems ascending to weakly erect. **Leaves** alternate; stipules absent; petioles 1–3cm long; leaf-blades 1-pinnate; leaflets 3–11, irregularly ovate to reniform, 2–10mm long, 1.5–15mm wide, 3–5-lobed with a short mucro. **Flowers** 10–20, in terminal racemes 10–20cm long; pedicels 1–3mm long; sepals 4, 1–1.5mm long; petals 4, white, 2.5–3mm long; stamens 6; ovary superior, 2-celled. **Fruit** a capsule 1.5–2.5cm long, 1–2mm diam., compressed-terete, opening from the base and curling upward.

Distribution: Woodland bittercress is native to Eurasia, now worldwide; in the Hawaiian Islands it is found on six main islands (not Niʻihau and Kahoʻolawe). First collected in Hawaiʻi in 1840-41, it is now widespread in wet to seasonally wet lowland sites and disturbed sites in higher elevation wet forest, especially in gulches and streambeds, from near sea level to 2160m elevation. Introduced passive-invasive; FAC.

Note: This species has been known in Hawaiʻi by the younger synonym *Cardamine konaensis* H.St.John. It was previously incorrectly known as *C. hirsuta* L.

Centella asiatica (L.) Urb.
Indian pennywort, *gotu kola*

APIACEAE

Description: Low perennial herb 1.5–25cm high and to more than 1m long, glabrous; stems long-creeping with one to several branches, adventitiously rooting at nodes. **Leaves** alternate; stipules absent; petioles 3–30cm long, sheathing at the base; leaf-blades simple, succulent, 2–5cm long, 1.5–5cm wide, orbicular to reniform and palmately 5–9-veined with sinuate margins. **Flowers** 2–3, sessile in clusters, subtended by 2 ovate involucral bracts 2–4mm long, borne on 2–4 axillary peduncles 0.2–1.5cm long; sepals absent or almost so; petals white or purplish-rose, 0.5–1mm long; stamens 5; ovary inferior, 2-celled. **Fruit** a schizocarp breaking into 2 mericarps, 2–3mm long, 2–4mm diam., ovoid to orbicular, each mericarp 7–9-ribbed.

Distribution: Indian pennywort is native to south and southeast Asia, now worldwide; in the Hawaiian Islands, where it is known by its Chinese name *gotu kola,* it is found on six main islands (not Ni'ihau and Kaho'olawe). First recorded on Hawai'i before 1871, it is now common in moist, sunny to partially shaded, disturbed sites such as pastures, ditches and wetland margins, as well as upland bogs and wet forest, from sea level to 1700m elevation. Introduced passive-invasive; FAC.

Note: This species was previously known as *Hydrocotyle asiatica* L. There are many common names for this species, including Asiatic pennywort and spadeleaf. The fresh leaves are chewed, used as a tea, or as a salad vegetable.

Conyza bonariensis (L.) Cronquist
Flax-leaved fleabane   ASTERACEAE

Description: Annual herb 0.5–1.5m high, densely hairy; stems erect, often branching near ground. **Leaves** alternate, grayish-green; stipules absent; petioles absent; leaf-blades simple, 3–15cm long, 0.5–2cm wide, oblanceolate with serrate margins. **Flowers** many ray and disk florets, borne on 5–10mm diam. heads, subtended by many involucral bracts, terminating open panicles; ray floret petals pale yellow, 3–5mm long; disk florets pale yellow, 4–5mm long; stamens 5; ovary inferior, 1-celled. **Fruit** a nut 1–1.5mm long, 0.4–0.6mm wide, slightly compressed-ellipsoid with a ring of yellow to reddish-brown pappus.

Distribution: Flax-leaved fleabane is native to tropical America, now worldwide, typically common in disturbed mesic and wet forests; in the Hawaiian Islands it is found on Kure, Midway, French Frigate Shoals, Laysan and all eight main islands. First reported from Hawai'i in 1871, it is now locally common in coastal wetlands, riparian and mesic habitats and particularly pastures and disturbed urban sites, from sea level to 3000m elevation. Introduced passive-invasive; FAC.

Note: Also known as asthma-weed, hairy horseweed and locally as *ilioha.*

Cryptotaenia canadensis (L.) DC. var. *japonica* (Hassk.) Makino
Japanese honewort, *mitsuba*   APIACEAE

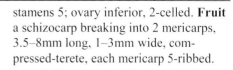

Description: Perennial herb 0.3–1.2m high, glabrous; stems erect, terete, many-branched, purplish-green. **Leaves** alternate; stipules absent; petioles 7–20cm long, oblong, sheathing; leaf-blades triangular to obovate in outline, divided into 3 leaflets; middle leaflet 2–9cm long, 2–10cm wide, diamond-shaped; lateral leaflets 1.5–8cm long, 1–6cm wide, ovate to obovate with serrate margins. **Flowers** 1–4, on 2–10 pedicels 2–35mm long in axillary and terminal 2–7-branched clusters 1–6cm long, subtended by an involucral bract (0–)4–10mm long, linear; sepals minute teeth; petals 5, white, 1–1.2mm long, 0.6–1mm wide;

stamens 5; ovary inferior, 2-celled. **Fruit** a schizocarp breaking into 2 mericarps, 3.5–8mm long, 1–3mm wide, compressed-terete, each mericarp 5-ribbed.

Distribution: Japanese honewort is native to cool moist woods in eastern Asia; in the Hawaiian Islands, where it is known by its Japanese name *mitsuba*, it is found on Kaua'i, O'ahu, Moloka'i, Maui and Hawai'i. First collected on O'ahu in 1925, it is now found in sites near waterfalls and along streams and trails, from near sea level to 900m elevation. Introduced passive-invasive; FAC.

Note: *Mitsuba* is widely cultivated as a culinary vegetable. Some botanists recognize this as a separate species, *Cryptotaenia japonica* Hassk., while others do not recognize it as a variety within *C. canadensis*.

Cuphea carthagenensis (Jacq.) J.F.Macbr.
Colombian waxweed   LYTHRACEAE

Description: Short-lived perennial or annual herb 1.5–5cm high, sticky-hairy; stems erect, often many-branched, green or red. **Leaves** opposite; stipules absent; petioles 0–2mm long; leaf-blades simple, 20–60mm long, 12–26mm wide, ovate-oblong with entire margins. **Flowers** solitary or several, in axillary or terminal clusters; pedicels 0–1mm long; calyx tube green, sometimes becoming red-dish-green, tubular, 4–7mm long, 12-ribbed and enlarged on one side at base, covered with sparse short-sticky hairs; corolla 6-lobed, magenta, pale pink or bluish, 1–1.5mm long; stamens 6–14; ovary superior, 1-celled. **Fruit** a capsule 3.5–5mm long, 3–4mm diam., ovoid.

Distribution: Colombian waxweed is native to South America, now wide-spread; in the Hawaiian Islands it is found on six main islands (not Ni'ihau and Kaho'olawe). First collected from Hawai'i in the mid-1800s, it is now common in mesic to wet disturbed sites, from 50 to 935m elevation. Introduced passive-invasive; FAC.

153

Cyclospermum leptophyllum (Pers.) Sprague ex Britton & P.Wilson
Marsh parsley   APIACEAE

Description: Annual herb 25–60cm high, glabrous; stems ascending to erect, many-branched, green. **Leaves** alternate; stipules absent; petioles 2–11cm long, sheathing at the base; leaf-blades broadly ovate to orbicular in outline, 4–12cm long, 4–10cm wide, 3–4-pinnate; ultimate leaflets linear, 10–15mm long. **Flowers** 5–23, in axillary and terminal compound clusters, on pedicels 0–4mm long, subtended by 2–5 ovate involucral bracts 1–2mm long; sepals 0–1mm long; petals 5, white or greenish-white, 1–2mm long; stamens 5; ovary inferior, 2-celled. **Fruit** a schizocarp breaking into 2 mericarps, 1.5–2mm long, 1.2–3mm diam., compressed-ellipsoid, each meri-carp 4–6-ribbed.

Distribution: Marsh parsley is native to South America, now nearly worldwide; in the Hawaiian Islands it is found on Kure, Midway and six main islands (not Niʻihau and Kahoʻolawe). First collected on Oʻahu in 1911, it now occurs in disturbed mesic to seasonally wet sites, from sea level to 1700m elevation. Introduced passive-invasive; FAC.

Note: This species is less widely known as fir-leaved celery. *Ciclospermum* is an alternative spelling of this genus. *Apium tenuifolium* (Moench.) Thell. is a younger synonym.

Desmodium triflorum (L.) DC.
Creeping tick-trefoil   FABACEAE

Description: Perennial herb 2–5cm high, 2–50cm long, glabrous; stems prostrate, slender, many-branched. **Leaves** alternate; stipules acuminate, 3–4mm long; petioles 2–7mm long; leaf-blades 1-pinnate; leaflets 3, 0.3–1.2cm long, 0.3–1.1cm wide, obovate or cordate with entire margins; upper surface glabrous, lower surface with short white hairs on midrib. **Flowers** 1–5, clustered in leaf axils; pedicels 3–8mm long; calyx 1–2mm long; corolla 3–4mm long, purplish-pink; stamens 5; ovary superior, 1-celled. **Fruit** a pod 6–17mm long, 2–3mm wide, flattened-linear, 3–7-segmented, each segment squarish, 2–2.5mm long/wide.

Distribution: Creeping tick-trefoil is native to tropical and subtropical Africa and Asia, now worldwide; in the Hawaiian Islands it is found on seven main islands (not Niʻihau). First collected on Oʻahu in 1864–65, it is now in dry to wet, disturbed lowland areas, dry slopes and lava flows, lawns, pastures, wastelands and roadsides, from near sea level to 440m elevation. Introduced passive-invasive; FAC.

Note: Also known as threeflower beggarweed.

Drymaria cordata (L.) Willd. ex Roem. & Schult. var. *pacifica* M.Mizush.
Whitesnow   CARYOPHYLLACEAE

Description: Annual herb 1–3cm high and 60–90cm long, mostly glabrous with some sticky hairs; stems prostrate, spreading, sometimes weakly erect, rooting at the nodes. **Leaves** opposite; stipules 0.5–1mm long, membranous with linear extensions; petioles 2–15mm long; leaf-blades simple, 5–25mm long, 5–30mm wide, orbicular to reniform, prominently 3–5-veined with entire margins. **Flowers** 3–10, clustered in leaf axils; peduncles 2–15mm long; bracts lanceolate; pedicels 3–5mm long; sepals green, 2–4mm long, lanceolate to ovate; petals 3–5, white, deeply divided (appearing as 6–10), 2–3mm long; stamens 2–5; ovary superior, 1-celled. **Fruit** a capsule 1.5–3mm long, 2–3mm wide, ovoid, green, splitting by 3 valves.

Distribution: Whitesnow is native to Central and tropical South America in damp shaded sites near streams; in the Hawaiian Islands it is found on Kaua'i, O'ahu, Moloka'i, Maui and Hawai'i. First recorded from Kaua'i in 1895, it is now common in shady, moist sites and disturbed, muddy forest openings, from 10 to 1280m elevation. Introduced passive-invasive; FAC.

Note: The local Hawaiian name *pipili* means "sticky, viscid", in reference to the glandular hairs on the sepals. This species is a noxious weed and is poisonous to livestock.

Eclipta prostrata (L) L.
False daisy
ASTERACEAE

Description: Annual herb 0.3–1m high, densely stiff-hairy; stems many-branched, decumbent or ascending, rooting at nodes. **Leaves** opposite, green; stipules absent; petioles absent; leaf-blades simple, 2–10cm long, 0.4–2.5cm wide, elliptic-lanceolate with serrate margins. **Flowers** 30–50 ray florets and 20–40 disk florets, in heads 4–6mm diam., subtended by 12–20 involucral bracts in 2 whorls, borne on short axillary peduncles; involucral bracts 7–10; ray floret petals white, 0.8–1mm long; disk florets white, 1.5–1.8mm long; stamens 4; ovary inferior, 1-celled. **Fruit** a nut 2–2.5mm long, 0.3–0.5mm wide, rhombic-ellipsoid, warty, without a ring of pappus.

Distribution: False daisy is native to the tropical Americas, Africa and Asia, typically common in disturbed mesic and wet forests; in the Hawaiian Islands it is found on seven main islands (not Kaho'olawe). First reported from Hawai'i in 1871, it is now locally common in coastal wetlands, riparian and mesic habitats and particularly pastures and disturbed urban sites, from sea level to 150m elevation. Introduced passive-invasive; FACW.

Note: Previously known in Hawai'i by the younger name, *Eclipta alba* (L.) Hassk.

Erechtites spp.
Fireweed

ASTERACEAE

Erechtites hieracifolia (L.) Raf. ex DC.
Fireweed

Diagnosis: This species differs from *E. valerianifolia* (see below) by its leaves with stem-clasping petioles 0–2cm long; leaf-blades simple, 4–20cm long, 0.5–4cm wide, lanceolate-elliptic to obovate with dentate to irregularly lobed margins; disk floret pappus white; corolla white to greenish-yellow, 0.4–0.5mm long.

Distribution: Fireweed is native to temperate and tropical America; in the Hawaiian Islands it is found on six main islands (not Ni'ihau and Kaho'olawe). First reported from Hawai'i in 1871, it occurs in coastal wetlands, riparian and moist habitats, pastures and urban sites, from near sea level to 1370m elevation. Introduced passive-invasive; FAC.

Note: Also known as American burnweed.

Erechtites valerianifolia (Wolf) DC.
Tropical burnweed

Description: Annual herb 0.5–2.5m high, glabrous to densely hairy; stems erect with few branches, striate. **Leaves** alternate, grayish-green; stipules absent; petioles 0–8cm long, winged; leaf-blades deeply pinnately lobed, 4–20cm long, 2–10cm wide, lanceolate to narrow ovate with dentate or serrate

margins. **Flowers** ray florets none and disk florets 40–60, in heads 5–8mm diam., subtended by 12–16 involucral bracts in a single ring, terminating pyramidal clusters; disk florets yellow to pale purple, 0.4–0.5mm long; stamens 5; ovary inferior, 1-celled. **Fruit** a nut 0.8–1mm long, 0.2–0.3mm diam., ellipsoid with a ring of pink to pale purple pappus.

Distribution: Tropical burnweed is native to tropical Central and South America, now common in disturbed mesic and wet forests; in the Hawaiian Islands it is found on seven main islands (not Ni'ihau). First reported on Lāna'i in 1916, it occurs in coastal wetlands, riparian and mesic habitats, and particularly pastures and urban sites, from near sea level to 1670m elevation. Introduced passive-invasive; FAC.

E. valerianifolia   *E. valerianifolia*

158

Heliotropium curassavicum L.
Kīpūkai, seaside heliotrope
BORAGINACEAE

Description: Succulent herb 10–45cm long, glabrous, glaucous; stems prostrate or becoming erect at the ends. **Leaves** alternate, bluish-gray; stipules and petioles absent; leaf-blades simple, 2–5cm long, 0.3–0.9cm wide, oblanceolate with entire margins. **Flowers** many, sessile, arranged along terminal or axillary curling spikes, 2–10cm long, sweetly scented; calyx 1–2mm long; petals white with a yellow or green center, 5-lobed, tubular, 1.2–4mm long; stamens 5; ovary superior, 4-celled. **Fruit** a schizocarp breaking into 4 mericarps, 1.5–2mm long, 1.5–2.5mm wide, globose.

Distribution: *Kīpūkai* is found along seacoasts, in marshy areas and salt flats of tropical North America to South America, Oceania and Australia; in the Hawaiian Islands it is found on Laysan, French Frigate Shoals, Nihoa and all eight main islands in a variety of wet or dry coastal habitats, including sand dunes, sea cliffs, salt marshes and mudflats, from sea level to 200m elevation. Native passive-invasive; FAC.

Note: In Hawai‘i this species was dried and brewed for use as a tonic tea and medicinally used as an ointment for weeping sores. *Nena* is another Hawaiian common name for this species.

Hydrocotyle spp.
Marshpennyworts

ARALIACEAE

Hydrocotyle bowlesioides Mathias & Constance

Large-leaved marshpennywort

Description: Perennial herb 5–25cm high, stiff-hairy; stems slender, creeping. **Leaves** alternate; stipules small; petioles 1–12cm long, attached at leaf-blade margin; leaf-blades simple, 1–2cm long, 1.5–3cm wide, angular-reniform with 5 shallowly lobed margins. **Flowers** 2–10, sessile, subtended by a linear involucral bract (0–)4–10mm long, borne on peduncles 2–12mm long in globose clusters; sepals 5 minute teeth; petals 5, white, c.1mm long; stamens 5; ovary inferior, 2-celled. **Fruit** a schizocarp breaking into 2 mericarps, 0.6–1mm long, 1–1.5mm wide, compressed-terete to ellipsoid, each mericarp 5-ribbed.

Distribution: Large-leaved marshpennywort is native to Central America; in the Hawaiian Islands it is found on Kaua'i, O'ahu, Lāna'i, Maui and Hawai'i. First collected on O'ahu in 1943, it is now

common in moist disturbed sites such as pastures, ditches and wetland margins, as well as upland bogs and wet forest, from near sea level to 2050m elevation. Introduced passive-invasive; FAC.

Hydrocotyle sibthorpioides Lam.
Lawn marshpennywort

Description: Perennial strongly aromatic herb 5–25cm high, glabrous; stems slender, prostrate, creeping, many-branched, rooting at nodes, not swollen. **Leaves** alternate; stipules small; petioles 0.5–6cm long, attached at leaf-blade margin; leaf-blades simple, 0.5–1.5cm long, 0.8–2.5cm wide, suborbicular to reniform with shallowly 5–7-lobed margins. **Flowers** 3–10, sessile, in single axillary globose clusters, subtended by an ovate-lanceolate involucral bract 1–1.5mm long, borne on pedicels 5–35mm long; sepals minute teeth; petals 5, greenish-white, 1–1.2mm long with yellow glands; stamens 5; ovary inferior, 2-celled. **Fruit** a schizocarp breaking into

H. sibthorpioides

H. sibthorpioides

2 mericarps, 1–1.5mm diam., compressed-globose, each mericarp 5-ribbed.

Distribution: Lawn marshpennywort is native to tropical Asia, now widespread through cultivation; in the Hawaiian Islands it is found on Kaua'i, O'ahu, Maui and Hawai'i. First collected on O'ahu in 1932, it is generally common in lawns and other moist, disturbed sites, near sea level to 1700m elevation. Introduced passive-invasive; FAC.

Hydrocotyle verticillata Thunb.
***Pohe*, whorled marshpennywort**

Description: Perennial herb 5–20cm high, glabrous; stems slender, creeping, rooting at the nodes. **Leaves** alternate; stipules small; petioles 0.5–26cm long, attached in middle of leaf-blades (peltate); leaf-blades simple, 0.5–6cm wide, orbicular with 8–13 wavy-lobed margins. **Flowers** 2–7, sessile on branched axillary spikes 1.5–17cm long; sepals 5 minute teeth; petals 5, white,

0.7–1mm long; stamens 5; ovary inferior, 2-celled. **Fruit** a schizocarp breaking into 2 mericarps, 1–3mm long, 2–4mm wide, compressed-ellipsoid, each mericarp 5-ribbed.

Distribution: *Pohe* is native to North America and possibly Hawai'i; in the Hawaiian Islands it is found on six main islands (not Ni'ihau and Kaho'olawe). First collected from Hawai'i before 1871, now common in wet sites in wet forest, pond and stream margins, muddy sites and bogs, from near sea level to 1600m elevation. Introduced or ?native passive-invasive; OBL.

Note: Used medicinally by Hawaiians in combination with other plant materials "for mothers who are weakened because of giving birth to a large number of children" and "for when one's face becomes red, thin and kind of bumpy" (Chun 1994).

H. verticillata

H. verticillata

Hypericum mutilum L. ssp. *mutilum*
Dwarf St. John's wort   CLUSIACEAE

Description: Perennial herb 5–25cm high, glabrous; stems slender, erect or ascending, mostly branching in the upper part. **Leaves** opposite; petioles absent; leaf-blades simple, 7–30mm long, 4–10mm wide, ovate to oblanceolate with entire margins. **Flowers** many, in axillary and terminal clusters; sepals 5, green, 3–3.5mm long; petals 5, yellow, 2–3.5mm long, caducous; stamens 8–9; ovary superior, 3-celled. **Fruit** a capsule 3–5mm long, 2–3mm diam., oblong-ovoid.

Distribution: Dwarf St. John's wort is native to North America, now a world-wide weed; in the Hawaiian Islands it is found on Kaua'i, Moloka'i, Maui and Hawai'i. First collected on Hawai'i in 1943, it now occurs in poorly drained disturbed sites and forest trails, from 350 to 1770m elevation. Introduced passive-invasive; FACW.

Impatiens walleriana Hook.f.
Busy Lizzie

BALSAMINACEAE

Description: Perennial herb 0.3–1m tall, glabrous; stems green, fleshy, weak, rooting at nodes. **Leaves** alternate or uppermost opposite; stipules absent; petioles 3–6cm long with 1–3 glands; leaf-blades simple, green or reddish-green, 3–12cm long, 2.5–5.5cm wide, lanceolate to oblong-elliptic with scalloped or dentate margins and acute apex. **Flowers** 1–5, in axillary or terminal racemes, on peduncles 3.5–5cm long; pedicels 1.5–3cm long; sepals 3, green, 1 petal-like with a spur 3–4.5cm long; petals 5, red, pink, orange, purple or white, uppermost petal flat or helmet-like, adjacent petals joined into 2 pairs; stamens 5, joined into a short tube; ovary superior, 5-celled. **Fruit** a capsule 1.5–2.5mm long, spindle-shaped, 5-valved, explosively coiling open to release seeds.

Distribution: Busy-Lizzie is native to eastern tropical Africa and cultivated worldwide; in the Hawaiian Islands it is found on six main islands (not Ni'ihau and Kaho'olawe). First collected on O'ahu in 1939, it is now often found in moist, shady, disturbed habitats in valleys and along rocky stream channels, from near sea level to 1200m elevation. Introduced passive-invasive; FACU.

Note: The species name is alternately spelled *wallerana*. Busy Lizzie (or Lizzy) is commonly cultivated as a bedding plant, a situation from which it readily escapes. Younger names for this species include *Impatiens holstii* Engl. & Warb. and *I. sultanii* Hook.f.

Ipomoea aquatica Forssk.
Swamp morning glory, *ung-choi*

CONVOLVULACEAE

Description: Annual herbaceous vine 4m or more long, glabrous, exuding a milky sap when cut; stems terete, hollow or spongy, floating on water or prostrate on soil, rooting at the nodes. **Leaves** alternate; stipules absent; petioles 3–14cm long; leaf-blades simple, 4–12cm long, 1–4.5cm wide, lanceolate to sagittate-cordate with 2-lobed entire margins. **Flowers** 1–5, in axillary clusters; peduncles 2–9cm long; bracts 1.5–2mm long; pedicels 2–7cm long; sepals 5, 6–7mm long; corolla tubular, pale purple with a deep purple throat or rarely white, 4–5cm long; stamens 5; ovary superior, 2-celled. **Fruit** a brown capsule 8–10mm long, ovoid to globose.

Distribution: Swamp morning glory is native to southeast Asia, now widely distributed in the tropics; in the Hawaiian Islands, where it goes by its Chinese name *ung-choi*, it is found on O'ahu, Maui and Hawai'i. An introduction by Chinese immigrants prior to 1871, it is now found in streams, ponds, roadside ditches and taro patches, from near sea level to 25m elevation. Introduced aggressive-invasive; OBL.

Note: This species has been previously incorrectly called *Ipomoea reptans* in Hawai'i. In Asia the young leaves and stems are eaten boiled, steamed or stir-fried or added to soups, stews and curries. The leaves have high protein content and are rich in vitamin A.

Lindernia spp.
False pimpernel
SCROPHULARIACEAE

Lindernia antipoda (L.) Alston
Sparrow false pimpernel

Description: Perennial herb 5–20cm high, glabrous throughout; stems erect or decumbent, branching at the base, rooting adventitiously at lower nodes. **Leaves** opposite; stipules absent; petioles absent; leaf-blades 1–5cm long, 0.6–1cm wide, elliptic to obovate with entire to serrate margins. **Flowers** solitary in leaf axils; pedicels 2–17mm long; calyx deeply 5-lobed, green, 3–5mm long; corolla pale violet to pale bluish-white, 8–13mm long; stamens 4 (2 sterile); ovary superior, 2-celled. **Fruit** a capsule 5–14mm long, 1–1.5mm wide, linear-terete.

Distribution: Sparrow false pimpernel is native to tropical south and southeast Asia in freshwater to brackish marshes; in the Hawaiian Islands it is found on Maui and Hawaiʻi. First reported on Hawaiʻi in 1987, it is now locally common in coastal wetlands and freshwater riparian habitats and taro patches, from sea level to 200m elevation. Introduced passive-invasive; FACW.

Lindernia crustacea (L.) F.Muell.
Malaysian false pimpernel

Diagnosis: This species differs from *L. antipoda* by being hairy (upper leaf surface glabrous); petioles 0.1–0.6cm long; leaf-blades 0.5–1.5cm long, ovate to cordate with serrate margins; calyx 5-lobed to middle, 2–4mm long; corolla purplish-blue to pale blue (pale yellow towards base), 5–8mm long; capsule 3.5–5mm long, obovoid, warty.

Distribution: Malaysian false pimpernel is native to tropical south and southeast Asia in marshes; in the Hawaiian Islands it is found on Oʻahu, Maui and Hawaiʻi. First reported on Hawaiʻi in 1987, it is locally common in coastal wetlands, streams banks and taro patches, from sea level to 200m elevation. Introduced passive-invasive; FACW.

Lindernia procumbens (Krock.) Philcox
Prostrate false pimpernel

Diagnosis: This glabrous species differs from *L. antipoda* by leaf-blades 1–2.5cm long, elliptic to oblong with entire to dentate margins; pedicels 12–20mm long; calyx deeply 5-lobed, 3–4mm long; corolla pink to purple, 4–4.5mm long; stamens 4 (all fertile); capsule 3–4mm long, ovoid.

Distribution: Prostrate false pimpernel is native to south and southeast Asia; in the Hawaiian Islands it is found on Kauaʻi where it was first collected in 1985. It is locally common in coastal wetlands and riparian habitats and taro patches, from sea level to 85m elevation. Introduced passive-invasive; FACW.

L. antipoda

Ludwigia octovalvis (Jacq.) P.H.Raven
Kāmole, primrose willow   ONAGRACEAE

Description: Perennial herb 0.5–4m high, glabrous to densely hairy throughout; stems erect to spreading, many-branched. **Leaves** alternate; stipules 0.5–1mm long, caducous; petioles 0.1–1cm long; leaf-blades simple, 1–14cm long, 0.5–4cm wide, linear to narrow ovate with entire margins. **Flowers** solitary, sessile, axillary; sepals 4, green, 6–13mm long; corolla lobes yellow, 6–16mm long; stamens 8; ovary inferior, 1-celled. **Fruit** a capsule 17–45mm long, 2–3mm diam., 8-ribbed, terete.

Distribution: *Kamole* is of unknown origin, now distributed worldwide; in the Hawaiian Islands it is found on six main islands (not Niʻihau and Kahoʻolawe). First collected in 1794, it is suspected to have been a stowaway during Polynesian migration. It is widespread in wetlands, riparian areas, cultivated lands and wet forests, from sea level to 1000m elevation. Introduced or ?native aggressive-invasive; OBL.

Note: Also known by many other names, including Mexican primrose-willow.

Ludwigia palustris (L.) Elliott
Water purslane

ONAGRACEAE

Description: Perennial herb 10–50cm long, glabrous throughout; stems prostrate to ascending, many-branched, rooting adventitiously. **Leaves** opposite; stipules 0.5–1mm long, caducous; petioles 0.1–1cm long; leaf-blades simple, 1–4cm long, 0.4–2cm wide (submerged leaves larger), elliptic to ovate with entire margins. **Flowers** solitary, sessile, axillary; sepals 4, green, 1–2mm long; corolla absent; stamens 4; ovary inferior, 1-celled. **Fruit** a green capsule 2–5mm long, 1.5–2mm diam., 4-sided-oblong.

Distribution: Water purslane is native to temperate and tropical America, Africa and Eurasia; it is typically common in riparian areas, rice fields, taro patches and wetlands; in the Hawaiian Islands it is found on Kaua'i, O'ahu, Moloka'i, Maui and Hawai'i. First recorded from O'ahu in 1934, it is now widespread in cultivated land, wetlands and wet forests, from sea level to 1200m elevation. Introduced passive-invasive; OBL.

Note: Also known by many vernacular names, including marsh purslane and marsh seedbox.

Macroptilium lathyroides (L.) Urb.
Wild bushbean

FABACEAE

Description: Erect annual or biennial herb 0.6–1.5m tall, finely pubescent; stems branching, longitudinally grooved, sometimes trailing or twining. **Leaves** alternate; stipules 5–6mm long, lanceolate; petioles 1–5cm long; leaf-blades trifoliate; leaflets 2.5–8cm long, 1–3.5cm wide, narrow elliptic to narrow ovate with entire margins and acute leaf-tip, lower surface sparsely long-hairy. **Flowers** 2 to several, subsessile on axillary racemes 10–50cm long; calyx 4–7mm long, ribbed, shallowly 5-lobed; petals 5, 12–15mm long, upper petal (standard) maroon to purple, lateral (wing) and lower (keel) petals tinged green, red or white; stamens 10 (1 separate, the others joined into a tube); ovary superior, 1-celled.

Fruit a pod 5.5–10cm long, 2.5–3.5mm wide, linear, reddish-brown, strongly twisted upon opening, surface long-hairy.

Distribution: Wild bushbean is native to the tropical Americas, now widely cultivated and naturalized in the tropics and subtropics; in the Hawaiian Islands it is found on all eight main islands. First collected on Oʻahu in 1864–65, it is now common in pastures and disturbed lowland sites, including freshwater marsh habitats, from sea level to 610m elevation. Introduced passive-invasive; FACU.

Nasturtium microphyllum Boenn. ex Rchb.
Watercress

BRASSICACEAE

Description: Aquatic perennial herb 10–20cm high, 10–60cm long, glabrous; stems floating, prostrate or ascending, hollow, rooting at the nodes. **Leaves** alternate, stipules absent; petioles 1–4cm long; leaf-blades 1-pinnate; leaflets 3–9, 1.5–4cm long, 0.5–2cm wide, ovate to elliptic with entire to dentate margins. **Flowers** few, in terminal racemes, on pedicels 11–20mm long; sepals 4, 1–2mm long; petals 4, white, 3–4mm long; stamens 4; ovary superior, 2-celled. **Fruit** a capsule 1.5–2.5cm long, 1–2mm diam., terete.

Distribution: Watercress is native to western Europe, but now widely culti-vated; in the Hawaiian Islands it is found on Kaua'i, O'ahu, Maui and Hawai'i. First collected on Kaua'i in 1917, it is common in taro patches, along streams and springs, and in seasonally wet areas, from near sea level to 1220m elevation. Introduced passive-invasive; OBL.

Note: This species has been misidenti-fied as *Nasturtium officinale* R.Br., the primary commercially grown species of watercress, which differs in having smaller flowers and shorter fruit (1–2cm long). This species has also been known as *Rorippa microphylla* (Boenn. ex Rchb.) A.Löve & D.Löve. Watercress is a salad vegetable, eaten raw for its pep-pery flavor or cooked as greens. It is also known by the Hawaiian name *lēkō*.

Persicaria spp.
Knotweed, smartweed   POLYGONACEAE

Persicaria glabra (Willd.) M.Gómez
Knotweed

Diagnosis: Differing from *P. punctata* (below) by being glabrous throughout, leaves with stipules 10–30mm long, not ciliate, petioles 0.5–2cm long, leaf-blades 10–28cm long, 2–6cm wide; sepals pinkish-white; stamens 6–8; and nut 2–3mm long.

Distribution: Knotweed is native to tropical America, Africa and Asia; in the Hawaiian Islands it is found on Kaua'i, O'ahu, Moloka'i, Maui and Hawai'i. First recorded on O'ahu in 1840, it is widespread in wetlands and wet forests, from sea level to 1400m elevation. Introduced passive-invasive; OBL.

Note: Knotweed has been given the Hawaiian name *kamole*; the same name is also applied to *Ludwigia octovalvis*. This species has been previously known as *Polygonum glabrum* Willd.

Persicaria punctata (Elliott) Small
Water smartweed

Description: Perennial herb 0.3–1m high, glandular-hairy; stems reddish-green, occasionally-branched, ascending to decumbent with rhizomes, rooting adventitiously. **Leaves** alternate; stipules forming a tubular leaf-base 9–18mm long with bristles 1.5–6.5mm long; petioles 0.3–1cm long; leaf-blades simple, 6–15cm long, 0.2–2cm wide, lanceolate with entire margins. **Flowers** 2–4 in open racemes 5–10cm long; sepals 5, greenish-white, 2–

2.5mm long; petals absent; stamens 5; ovary superior, 1-celled. **Fruit** a glossy dark brown to black nut 1.8–3mm long, 1.5–2mm wide, trigonous to compressed-ovoid with persistent perianth.

Distribution: Water smartweed is native to subtropical and tropical America, now worldwide; in the Hawaiian Islands it is found on Maui and Hawai'i. First recorded on Hawai'i in 1909, it is widespread in wetlands and wet forests, from sea level to 1900m elevation. Introduced passive-invasive; OBL.

Note: This species has been previously known as *Polygonum punctatum* Elliott.

P. punctata

P. punctata

Phyla nodiflora (L.) Greene
Spatulate-leaved fogfruit

VERBENACEAE

Description: Perennial herb up to 10cm high, 40–60cm long, sparsely hairy; stems prostrate, many-branched, rooting adventitiously at nodes. **Leaves** opposite, green; stipules absent; petioles 4–6mm long; leaf-blades 1.5–4cm long, 0.5–2cm wide, spathulate to narrow obovate with margins dentate above the middle. **Flowers** 25–100, in globose to terete heads 1–2.5cm long, 0.8–1cm diam., subtended by triangular to obovate bracts, borne on axillary spikes 2.5–8cm long; calyx 4-lobed, green, 1.2–1.5mm long, 0.5–0.8mm wide; corolla purplish-pink to white, 2–3mm long; stamens 4; ovary inferior, 2-celled. **Fruit** a schizocarp separating into 2 mericarps, 1.5–1.9mm long, 1–1.2mm wide, compressed-obovoid.

Distribution: Spatulate-leaved fogfruit is native to tropical Central and South America, now a worldwide ornamental groundcover; in the Hawaiian Islands it is found on Midway, O'ahu, Moloka'i and Maui. First collected from cultivation on O'ahu in 1967, it is now naturalized in disturbed areas behind beaches and wet to mesic sandy areas, from sea level to 50m elevation. Introduced passive-invasive; FAC.

Note: This plant goes by many names , including turkey tangle fogfruit, frogfruit [*sic*] and carpet-grass.

171

Pilea microphylla (L.) Liebm.
Artillery plant

URTICACEAE

Description: Short-lived perennial herb 10–50cm high, glabrous; stems succulent, prostrate, many-branched, rooting adventitiously. **Leaves** opposite, unequal; stipules connate, 0–1mm long; petioles 1–4mm long; leaf-blades simple, 2–10mm long, 1–4mm wide, elliptic to oblong with entire margins. **Flowers** several, unisexual, in axillary clusters; peduncles 1–6mm long; pedicels absent; calyx 4-lobed, greenish-white, 0.6–1mm long; corolla absent; stamens 4; ovary superior, 1-celled. **Fruit** a greenish-white nut 0.5–1mm long, 0.2–0.3mm wide, compressed-ellipsoid.

Distribution: Artillery plant is native to the American tropics, typically common in wet habitats; in the Hawaiian Islands it is found on Midway, Kauaʻi, Oʻahu, Lānaʻi, Maui and Hawaiʻi. First recorded on Oʻahu in 1925, it is now locally common in seasonal wetlands habitats, from sea level to 520m elevation. Introduced passive-invasive; FAC.

Note: Also know as rock weed.

Plantago major L.
Common plantain, *laukahi*

PLANTAGINACEAE

Description: Perennial herb 6–40cm high, sparsely hairy; stems (scapes) erect from a taproot. **Leaves** in a basal rosette; leaf-base sheathing; petiole simple, 3–40cm long, 2–15cm wide, ovate to broadly elliptic with 5–7 longitudinal veins and wavy, dentate margins. **Flowers** many, densely arranged on axillary spikes 2.5–25cm long; each floret subtended by an elliptic bract 2.5–3mm long; sepals 4, 2–2.5mm long, ovate; corolla salverform with 4 lanceolate lobes 1.2–1.6mm long; stamens 4; ovary superior, 2-celled. **Fruit** a gray capsule 1.5–3mm long, 1–2mm diam., ellipsoid.

Distribution: Common plantain is native to Europe and north and central Asia, now a cosmopolitan weed; in the Hawaiian Islands it is found on Midway and six main islands (not Niʻihau and Kahoʻolawe). First collected on Oʻahu in 1864–1865, it is common in pastures and disturbed mesic and wet forests, from sea level to 1250m elevation. Introduced passive-invasive; FACU.

Note: Leaves used in a poultice for boils and in a tea for the treatment of diabetes.

Rorippa sarmentosa (G.Forst. ex DC.) J.F.Macbr.
Pā'ihi, longrunner

BRASSICACEAE

Description: Perennial herb 10–60cm high, glabrous; stems solid (not hollow), prostrate to weakly erect, rooting at the nodes. **Leaves** mostly basal; stipules absent; petioles to 6cm long; leaf-blades 1-pinnate; leaflets 3–7, 0.7–3cm long, 0.4–2.8cm wide, broadly ovate to reniform with crenate margins, the terminal leaflet much larger than laterals. **Flowers** few, on pedicels 4–8mm long, borne on terminal racemes 10–30cm long; sepals 4, c.1mm long; petals 4, white to cream, tinged purple, 1–1.5mm long. **Fruit** a capsule 1.5–3cm long, 1–2mm diam., terete.

Distribution: *Pa'ihi* is possibly native to the south Pacific region, now widely distributed throughout the Pacific by Polynesian migrations; in the Hawaiian Islands it is found on Kaua'i, O'ahu, Moloka'i, Maui and Hawai'i along streams in moist gulches or disturbed muddy sites, from sea level to 900m elevation. Introduced or ?native passive-invasive; FACW.

Note: Polynesians used the stems of this species to make a black dye; the plant was also used in a medicinal recipe for chest pains. This species has also been known as *Nasturtium sarmentosum* (G.Forst. ex DC.) Schinz & Guillaumin.

174

Sesuvium portulacastrum (L.) L.
'*Ākulikuli*, sea purslane   AIZOACEAE

Description: Succulent perennial herb 5–12cm high, 0.5–2m long, glabrous; stems prostrate, many-branched, red to green, adventitiously rooting at the nodes. **Leaves** opposite; stipules absent; petioles 0–3mm long, sheathing; leaf-blades simple, 1–6cm long, 0.2–1.5cm wide, terete or laterally flattened, green (older leaves often yellow or red) with entire margins and rounded to acute apex. **Flowers** solitary in leaf axils; pedicels 2–12mm long; sepals 5, green on outside, pinkish-purple to white within, 4–10mm long, 3–6mm wide; petals absent; stamens 5, pinkish-purple; ovary superior, 3-celled. **Fruit** a capsule 4–7mm long, 4–5mm diam., ovoid to globose, opening at the top.

Distribution: '*Akulikuli* is pantropical, widely distributed along seacoasts; in the Hawaiian Islands it is found on Pearl and Hermes, Lisianski, Laysan, Necker and all eight main islands, in a variety of exposed coastal habitats, including rocky or sandy shorelines exposed to saltwater or salt spray, saltwater or brackish marshes, muddy margins of saline ponds and sea cliffs, from sea level to 20m elevation. Native passive-invasive; FAC.

Note: One of the most salt-tolerant of coastal plants, '*ākulikuli* is used as a groundcover for saline soils, salt-sprayed coasts and xeriscape gardens.

Sonchus oleraceus L.
Common sowthistle

ASTERACEAE

Description: Annual herb 0.1–2m high, glabrous; stems erect with few branches and a milky sap. **Leaves** alternate; stipules absent; petioles absent, clasping; leaf-blades pinnatifid, 6–30cm long, 1–15cm wide, lanceolate to spathulate with earlobes at the base, dentate margins and acute apex. **Flowers** ray florets many and disk florets none, borne on 5–8mm diam. heads, subtended by many involucral bracts, terminating few branches forming open cymes; corolla 11–12mm long, yellow; stamens 5; ovary inferior, 1-celled. **Fruit** a nut 2.5–3mm long, 0.6– 0.8mm diam., 6–10-angled, narrow ellipsoid, rugulose with a persistent ring of pappus.

Distribution: Common sowthistle is native to Europe, now a cosmopolitan weed, typically common in disturbed mesic and wet forests; in the Hawaiian Islands it is found on Kure, Midway, Pearl and Hermes, French Frigate Shoals and all eight main islands. Reported from Hawai'i before 1871, it is now locally common in coastal wetlands, riparian and mesic habitats and particularly pastures and disturbed urban sites, from sea level to 2430m elevation. Introduced passive-invasive; FACU.

Note: This species also has the Hawaiian name *pualele*.

Spergularia marina (L.) Griseb.
Lesser sea spurrey
CARYOPHYLLACEAE

Description: Annual or biennial herb 10–30cm high, 5–30cm long, glabrous or sticky-hairy; stems erect to prostrate, sometimes many-branched. **Leaves** opposite or appearing whorled, fleshy; stipules 2–4mm long, sheathing-triangular; petioles 0–1mm long; leaf-blades simple, 5–40mm long, 0.5–1.5mm wide, linear with entire margins. **Flowers** 3–8, on terminal or axillary clusters; peduncles 2–5mm long; bracts 0–1mm long; pedicels 1–2mm long; sepals green, 2.5–5mm long, ovate; petals 5, white or pink, 2–4mm long, ovate; stamens 2–5; ovary superior, 1-celled. **Fruit** a green capsule 3.5–6mm long, 3–5mm wide, ovoid, splitting by 3 valves.

Distribution: Lesser sea spurrey is native to Eurasia and now worldwide, particularly in saltmarshes; in the Hawaiian Islands it is found on Kure, Midway, French Frigate Shoals, Kaua'i, O'ahu, Moloka'i and Maui. First collected on O'ahu in 1909, it is now found throughout coastal and low elevation saline areas and mudflats, from sea level to 450m elevation. Introduced passive-invasive; FAC.

Note: The recent Hawaiian name for this species is *mimi 'īlio*, which means "dog urine", apparently referring to its unpleasant scent when rubbed. A less-widely used common name for this species is the saltmarsh sand spurrey.

Torenia glabra Osbeck
Wishbone flower, *nani-o-Ola'a*

SCROPHULARIACEAE

Description: Annual herb 5–20cm high, 10–40cm long, glabrous or sparsely hairy (upper leaf surface scabrous); stems prostrate, many-branched at the base, rooting adventitiously. **Leaves** opposite, light green; stipules absent; petioles 2–15mm long; leaf-blades 1–2.5cm long, 0.8–2cm wide, ovate with serrate margins. **Flowers** solitary, axillary or several in terminal clusters; pedicels 1–2.5cm long; calyx tubular, green, 10–13mm long; corolla violet or purple, 20–25mm long; stamens 4 in pairs, the upper pair with basal appendages; ovary superior, 2-celled. **Fruit** a capsule 10–

13mm long, 3–3.5mm wide, terete.

Distribution: This wishbone flower is native to east Asia, typically common in mesic forests; in the Hawaiian Islands, where it is locally known as *nani-o-Ola'a*, it is found only on Hawai'i, where it is a garden escape. First collected in 1977, it is now locally common between Hilo and Volcano in wet habitats from 75 to 1100m elevation. Introduced passive-invasive; FACW.

Note: In Hawai'i this species has been confused as *Torenia asiatica* L. A third species, *T. fournieri* E.Fourn., is also grown in Hawai'i. All three species are widely cultivated for use in floral *lei* throughout the islands.

Veronica spp.
Speedwell

SCROPHULARIACEAE

Veronica arvensis L.
Corn speedwell

Diagnosis: This species, with smaller flowers than *V. serpyllifolia*, differs from *V. plebeia* by having erect or decumbent habit; petioles to 3mm long; leaf-blades 0.5–2cm long, 0.3–1.3cm wide, ovate with serrate margins. **Flowers** solitary, in axillary racemes; pedicels 0.5–2mm long; calyx 3–5mm long; corolla blue to violet, 1–1.5mm long; capsule 2.5–3.5mm long, compressed-globose.

Distribution: Corn speedwell is native to temperate Eurasia, now common worldwide; in the Hawaiian Islands it is found on Moloka'i, Maui and Hawai'i. First reported on Hawai'i in 1909, it is now locally common in seasonal wetlands habitats, from 430 to 2000m elevation. Introduced passive-invasive; FAC.

Veronica plebeia R.Br.
Common speedwell

Description: Annual herb 10–50cm high, hairy throughout; stems procumbent, many-branched at the base, rooting adventitiously at nodes. **Leaves** opposite; stipules absent; petioles 0.3–1.5cm long; leaf-blades 0.8–5cm long, 0.6–2.3cm wide, ovate to deltate with serrate margins. **Flowers** 6–14 in axillary racemes; pedicels 5–15mm long; calyx 4-lobed, green, 3–4mm long; corolla blue, 3–3.6mm long; stamens 2; ovary superior, 2-celled. **Fruit** a capsule 3–3.6mm diam., compressed-globose.

Distribution: Common speedwell is native to temperate Australia, typically common in wet habitats and now widely naturalized; in the Hawaiian Islands it is found on Maui and Hawai'i. First reported on Hawai'i in 1909, it is now locally common in seasonal wetlands habitats, from 860 to 2500m elevation. Introduced passive-invasive; FACW.

Veronica serpyllifolia L.
Thyme-leaved speedwell

Diagnosis: This larger-flowered species differs from *V. plebeia* by its petioles 0–0.6cm long; leaf-blades 0.7–2cm long, 0.4–1.3cm wide, elliptic to ovate with crenulate to entire margins; pedicels 2–5mm long; calyx 2.5–3.5mm long; corolla pale blue to white, 2–3mm long; stamens 2; ovary superior, 2-celled; capsule 2.3–2.7mm long, 3.5–4.5mm wide, compressed-globose.

Distribution: Thyme-leaved speedwell is native to Europe, typically common in wet habitats and now widely naturalized; in the Hawaiian Islands it is found on Kaua'i, Lāna'i, Maui and Hawai'i. First reported on Hawai'i in 1926, it is now locally common in seasonal wetland habitats, from 820 to 3000m elevation. Introduced passive-invasive; FAC.

V. plebeia

SECTION 5 — MONOCOT HERBS
Herbs with perianth in threes; flowers not in spikelets

This section treats a diverse group of monocots with perianth parts (petals, sepals and tepals) in threes, as well as the stamens and carpels. The leaf-blade venation may be reticulate or parallel. The flowers are arranged in several types of inflorescences (e.g., cymes, spadices and spikes), but never the spikelets of the grasses and sedges. The spadix has a single large inflorescence bract, called a spathe, which protects the entire inflorescence as it is developing. In *Hedychium* four of the stamens are infertile and petal-like. These are called labella (*sing.* labellum, not to be confused with the labellum of the orchids, which is a petal).

Key to the monocot herbs of Hawaii's wetlands

1   Plants with linear, simple leaf-blades more than 10 times longer than wide 2
    Plants with narrowly elliptical to sagittate leaf-blades less than 10 times longer than wide 6

2(1) Flowers with yellow to white petals 5mm or longer, and sepals light brown ... 3
    Flowers with brown to dark brown scale-like tepals less than 5mm long 4

3(2) Leaves 1.5–4(–6)mm wide; floral clusters 4–8mm diam. .... *Xyris complanata*
    Leaves 5–10mm wide; floral clusters 8–15mm diam. .... *Xyris platylepis*

4(2) Flowers borne singly or in clusters, never in dense spikes .... *Juncus* spp.
    Flowers borne in dense spikes 5

5(4) Male flowers in spikes below and separated from female spike; female and male flowers with scale-like tepals .... *Typha domingensis*
    Male flowers below but usually contiguous with the female spike; female flowers without tepals; male flowers with hair-like tepals .... *Typha latifolia*

6(1) Flowers arranged on a dense stem (spadix) protected by a single large bract (spathe); petals and sepals absent 7
    Flowers not arranged on a spadix protected by a spathe; petals and sepals present, often showy 9

7(8) Leaf-blades with the petiole attached within the leaf-blade (peltate) ....
    .... *Colocasia esculenta*
    Leaf-blades with the petiole attached at the edge of the leaf-blade 8

8(7) Leaf apex pointing upwards .... *Alocasia macrorrhizos*
    Leaf apex pointing downwards .... *Xanthosoma robustum*

9(6) Leaves with long petioles 10
Leaves lacking petioles 12

10(9) Leaf-blades deeply lobed, palmate .... *Tacca leontopetaloides*
Leaf-blades simple entire, sagittate 11

11(10) Leaf-base sheathing .... *Monochoria vaginalis*
Leaf-base not sheathing .... *Sagittaria latifolia*

12(9) Stems 2–4mm diam.; flowers blue .... *Commelina diffusa*
Stems 1–3cm diam.; flowers white or yellow 13

13(12) Flowers well-spaced in an erect spike; stamens bright orange, longer than the
labella .... *Hedychium gardnerianum*
Flowers closely spaced in an ascending spike; stamens white or yellow, shorter
than, or as long as, the labella 14

14(13) Flowers white; labella-base abruptly tapering .... *Hedychium coronarium*
Flowers yellow; labella-base gradually tapering .... *Hedychium flavescens*

Alocasia macrorrhizos (L.) G.Don
Giant taro, *'ape*   ARACEAE

Description: Perennial herb 1–5m high, glabrous; rhizome stout, erect, up to 20cm diam., tuberous, exuding a milky sap when cut. **Leaves** basal, whorled; petioles 75–130cm long, sheathed in the lower half; leaf-blades simple, sagittate with the basal lobes 12–40cm long and terminal lobe 25–120cm long, 20–90cm wide, upper surface shiny dark green. **Flowers** many, unisexual, sessile in compact terete spikes (spadix) 11–32cm long, subtended by a bract (spathe) 13–35cm long, 4–6cm wide, oblong, white to cream, terminal on 2 to several 20–45cm long peduncles in leaf axils; perianth absent; stamens 3–8; ovary superior, 1-celled. **Fruit** a scarlet berry 8–10mm long, 5–8mm diam., ovoid.

Distribution: Giant taro is native to south Asia, now found throughout southeast Asia, eastward to Polynesia and widely cultivated; in the Hawaiian Islands it is found on Kaua'i, O'ahu, Moloka'i, Maui and Hawai'i. Introduced by the Polynesian settlers, it now occurs in low elevation mesic valleys, primarily along streams or in other wet to moist sites, from near sea level to 460m elevation. Introduced passive-invasive; FAC.

Note: Sometimes grown as an accent plant in gardens. The starchy rhizome (corm) is used in the same way as taro, but toxic calcium oxalate crystals require that the stem be thoroughly cooked. The rhizome was also used to treat burns and cuts. A liquid made from the peeled stem is used as a purgative for stomachaches. The leaves were used as a wrap to induce sweating and thereby reduce fever.

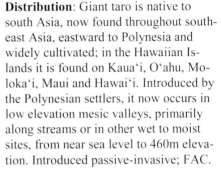

Colocasia esculenta (L.) Schott
Taro, *kalo* ARACEAE

Description: Perennial herb 0.5–1.5m high; rhizome stout, erect, up to 15cm diam., tuberous, exuding a pink or cream milky sap when cut. **Leaves** basal; petioles 40–180cm long, sheathed in lower half, green, green dappled purple or purple, fading to pink near the base; leaf-blades simple, peltate, 25–45cm long, 12–32cm wide, long-cordate with main lobe facing downward, 3–4 times longer than 2 basal lobes, with veins on upper surface green, on lower surface dark purple to yellow. **Flowers** many, unisexual, sessile in compact terete spikes (spadix) 6–14cm long, subtended by a yellow bract (spathe) 15–40cm long, borne terminally on 2–7 peduncles 15–50cm long; perianth absent; stamens 3–6; ovary superior, 1-celled. **Fruit** a red berry 3–5mm diam., ovoid.

Distribution: Taro is native to south Asia, now widely cultivated throughout the tropics for its edible rhizome (corm); in the Hawaiian Islands, where it is known as *kalo,* it is found on seven main islands (not Kahoʻolawe). Introduced by the Polynesian settlers and cultivated in wetlands as a staple, it occurs in poorly drained disturbed sites, marshes and along streams, from near sea level to 600m elevation. Introduced passive-invasive; OBL.

Note: Taro is the single most important starch staple in the Pacific; its cultivation continues on a small scale in Hawaiʻi. As many as 300 varieties were once farmed locally, mainly for the production of *poi*. Taro is also used in religious rituals, as medicine, for gluing *kapa* pieces together and as a red dye. The cut petioles were used to stop wounds from bleeding; and the leaf is rubbed onto insect bites to prevent swelling and pain.

Commelina diffusa Burm.f.
Climbing dayflower, *honohono*

COMMELINACEAE

Description: Annual herb 5–10cm high, up to 1m long, mostly glabrous; stems prostrate to ascending, 2–4mm diam., rooting at the nodes. **Leaves** alternate; petioles sheathing, 1–2cm long; leaf-blades simple, 3.5–11cm long, 0.8–2cm wide, narrowly to broadly lanceolate, entire with a few white hairs along the margin. **Flowers** 3–5 bisexual and 1–4 male, borne axillary or terminal on pedicels 2–5mm long, subtended by a leaf-like bract (spathe) 1.5–2cm long, lanceolate, borne terminally on peduncles 1.5–2cm long; sepals 3, 3–4mm long; petals 3, blue, 4–6mm long, the upper 2 reniform, the lower smaller, pouched; stamens 3; ovary superior, 2–3-celled. **Fruit** a green capsule 3–6mm long, 3–5mm diam., trigonous-narrow ellipsoid.

Distribution: Climbing dayflower is native to tropical Africa and Asia and now widely dispersed; in the Hawaiian Islands, where it is also known as *honohono*, it is found on Midway and six main islands (not Ni'ihau and Kaho'olawe). First recorded from the island of Hawai'i in 1837, it is now common in mesic valleys to disturbed mesic and wet forest, freshwater wetlands and other disturbed sites, from near sea level to 1220m elevation. Introduced aggressive-invasive; FACW.

Note: Sometimes eaten raw or cooked, and used as cattle feed. The flowers open after sunrise and close by midday.

Hedychium spp.
Garland-lilies

ZINGIBERACEAE

Hedychium coronarium J.König
White ginger, white garland-lily

Description: Perennial herb 1–3m high, glabrous; stems ascending, 1–3cm diam., arising from rhizomes, fragrant when cut. **Leaves** cauline; petioles absent; ligule membranous, 1.7–3mm long, 2-lobed; leaf-blades simple, 25–60cm long, 4–11cm wide, lanceolate. **Flowers** many, bisexual, in cluster of 3–6 flowers, subtended by bracts 3.5–5.5cm long in erect terminal spikes 7–20cm long, 4–8cm wide; calyx 2.5–4cm long, tubular; corolla tube white, 7–9cm long with 3 narrow, linear lobes 3–5cm long; stamens 5 (1 fertile, 4 petal-like labella); ovary superior, 3-celled. **Fruit** a capsule 2–3cm long, 1–1.5cm wide, narrow ellipsiod.

Distribution: White ginger is native to south Asia, now widely cultivated in the tropics; in the Hawaiian Islands it is found on Oʻahu, Molokaʻi, Lānaʻi, Maui and Hawaiʻi. First collected on Lānaʻi in 1913, it is now common in mesic forest and moist habitats along streams, from near sea level to 1160m elevation. Introduced aggressive-invasive; FAC.

Note: *Hedychium coronarium* is widely cultivated and the flowers are used in the commercial lei industry and as the basis for perfumes and cosmetics. Locally known as *ʻawapuhi keʻokeʻo.*

Hedychium flavescens N.Carey ex Roscoe   **Yellow ginger**

Diagnosis: This species differs from *H. coronarium* by light yellow flowers and smaller labella, 2.5–4cm wide, that tapers gradually rather than abruptly at the base.

H. coronarium

H. flavescens

Distribution: Yellow ginger is native to south Asia, now widely cultivated in the tropics; in the Hawaiian Islands it is found on six main islands (not Niʻihau and Kahoʻolawe). First recorded from Lānaʻi in 1913, it is now common in mesic forest and moist habitats along streams, from 15 to 1260m elevation. Introduced aggressive invasive; FAC.

Note: Originally misidentified in Hawaiʻi as *Hedychium flavum* Roxb. It reproduces vegetatively, as it is not known to produce fruit in the wild.

Hedychium gardnerianum Ker Gawl.
Kahili ginger

Description: Perennial herb 1–2m high, glabrous; stems ascending, 1–3cm diam., arising from horizontal underground rhizomes. **Leaves** cauline, horizontal; petioles 1–2cm long; ligules membranous, 1.5–3mm long, entire or 2-lobed; leaf-blades simple, 20–45cm long, 10–15cm wide, ovate to elliptic with entire margins. **Flowers** many, bisexual, in widely spaced pairs subtended by leafy bracts 3–5cm long, borne in erect, terminal, terete spikes 16–45cm long; calyx 3–3.5cm long, tubular; corolla tube 5–5.5cm long with 3 greenish-yellow lobes 3.5–5cm long, narrow, linear; stamens 5 (1 fertile, the other 4 petal-like labella); ovary superior, 3-celled. **Fruit** a fleshy orange capsule 10–15mm long, 6–12mm diam., ellipsoid.

Distribution: Kahili ginger is native to south Asia and widely cultivated in the tropics; in the Hawaiian Islands it is found on Kauaʻi, Oʻahu, Lānaʻi, Maui and Hawaiʻi. First collected on Hawaiʻi around 1940, it is now common in wet forests, along streams and wetland margins, near sea level to 1700m elevation. Introduced aggressive-invasive; FACW.

H. gardnerianum

Juncus spp.
Rushes   JUNCACEAE

Juncus and other members of the family Juncaceae are typically plants of temperate and tropical highlands. There are seven species of *Juncus* recorded for the Hawaiian Islands, all associated with higher elevation wetland habitats, but some reaching down into lowland agricultural areas and wetlands impacted by invasive species and other human modifications.

These plants are readily recognizable from grasses and sedges. Their fruit are few to many-seeded capsules, compared with the single-seeded nuts of grasses and sedges. The flowers of *Juncus* have a perianth of six chaffy tepals, surrounded by floral bracts.

Key to species of *Juncus* of Hawaii's wetlands

1   Leaves sheaths only, without blades; lowest bract of the inflorescence stem-like, erect, appearing to be a continuation of the stem, causing the inflorescence to appear lateral 2
      Leaves with leaf-blades present; lowest bract of the inflorescence leaf-like, oblique, causing the inflorescence to appear terminal 3

2(1) Pith of stems solid; tepals equaling or longer than the capsule .... *J. effusus*
      Pith of stems not solid; tepals shorter than the capsule .... *J. polyanthemos*

3(1) Leaf-sheaths with lobed ligules 4
      Leaf-sheaths without lobed ligules 5

4(3) Leaf-blades without cross-walls; stamens 6 .... *J. tenuis*
      Leaf-blades with faint cross-walls; stamens 3 .... *J. acuminatus*

5(3) Leaf-blades with incomplete cross-walls; capsules 1-celled .... *J. ensifolius*
      Leaf-blades without cross-walls; capsules 3-celled 6

6(5) Floral bracts absent; perennial .... *J. planifolius*
      Floral bracts present; annual .... *J. bufonius*

Juncus acuminatus Michx.
Sharp-fruited rush

JUNCACEAE

Description: Perennial herb 0.2–1m high, glabrous; culms erect, 1–3mm diam., terete, densely tufted, on short rhizomes. **Leaves** mostly basal; leaf-sheaths open on one side with membranous margins; ligules with rounded lobes, 1–5mm long; leaf-blades flattened below and terete above, 8–40cm long, 1–4mm wide, linear with faint complete cross-walls. **Flowers** 5–30 bisexual, in 3–50 dense clusters 5–10mm diam., subtended by a leaf-like bract 3–9cm long, terminating many spreading branches; floral bracts 2; tepals greenish-brown, 3–5mm long, lanceolate with a small mucro; stamens 3; ovary superior, 1-celled. **Fruit** a pale yellow capsule 3–5mm long, ellipsoid to ovoid with many brown seeds.

Distribution: Sharp-fruited rush is probably native to Eurasia, Africa and North America; in the Hawaiian Islands it is found on Maui and Hawai'i. First recorded on Maui in 1910, it is now common along roadsides, trails, disturbed boggy sites and grasslands, from 1000 to 1500m elevation. Introduced passive-invasive; OBL.

Note: The flowers and leaves are often enlarged or deformed by parasitic infestation.

Photo: RM

Juncus bufonius L.
Toad rush, common rush   JUNCACEAE

Description: Annual herb 5–40cm high, glabrous; culms erect or ascending, weak, reddish-brown, 0.4–1mm diam., terete with 0–2 scales (cataphylls), tufted on short branched rhizomes. **Leaves** basal and cauline; leaf-sheaths open on one side with membranous margins; ligules lacking lobes; leaf-blades strongly flattened, 3–15cm long, 0.3–1.2mm wide, linear without cross-walls, and with slightly rolled margins. **Flowers** 1–4, bisexual, in open clusters subtended by a leaf-like bract appearing as a continuation of the stem, 3–17cm long, borne on ascending, branched stems 4–20cm long; floral bracts 2, membranous; tepals 3–8mm long, green with white membranous margins and acute apex, the inner ones obtuse; stamens 3 (rarely 4–6); ovary superior, 3-celled. **Fruit** a yellowish to reddish-brown capsule 3–5mm long, 1–1.7mm diam., ellipsoid with many brown seeds.

Distribution: Toad rush is probably native to temperate regions of Eurasia, Africa and North America; in the Hawaiian Islands it is found on Kaua'i, O'ahu, Moloka'i, Maui and Hawai'i. First recorded on Maui in 1910, it is now common along roadsides, trails and in disturbed boggy sites and grasslands, from 1000 to 1500m elevation. Introduced passive-invasive; FACW.

189

Juncus effusus L.
Bog rush
JUNCACEAE

Description: Perennial herb 0.4–1.3m high, glabrous; culms erect, solid, 1–4mm diam., terete with 35–65 striations, densely tufted on short-creeping rhizomes. **Leaves** basal; leaf-sheaths scale-like, dark reddish-brown to purple, 2–3cm long; ligules and leaf-blades absent. **Flowers** many, bisexual, in loose clusters at the ends of short branches, subtended by an erect bract appearing to be a continuation of stem, 5–28cm long; floral bracts 3, membranous, 0.3–0.7mm long; tepals rigid, yellowish-green to pale brown, 1–2.5mm long, lanceolate with acuminate apex; stamens 3(–6); ovary superior, 3-celled. **Fruit** a golden brown capsule 1.5–3mm long, trigonous-narrow ellipsoid with many amber-colored seeds.

Distribution: Bog rush is native to temperate and mountainous areas in Eurasia, Africa, Australasia and the Americas; in the Hawaiian Islands it is found on O'ahu, Moloka'i, Maui and Hawai'i. Probably introduced to Hawai'i about 1900 from Japan as a source of matting material, it was cultivated and is now naturalized along margins of streams and ponds, in open boggy sites and wet areas, from 1000 to 2000m elevation. Introduced aggressive-invasive; OBL.

Note: Bog rush is one of the most widely distributed and variable species in the genus. In Hawai'i the pith was used as a wick for oil lamps and candles, and also medicinally as a diuretic and tranquilizer. It is the plant used for making beach mats.

Juncus ensifolius Wikstr.
Dwarf rush

JUNCACEAE

Description: Perennial herb 20–60cm high, glabrous; culms erect, 2–6mm diam., flattened with 0–2 straw-colored scales (cataphylls), arising singly on long-creeping rhizomes. **Leaves** basal and cauline; leaf-sheaths open on one side with membranous margins; ligules lacking lobes; leaf-blades flattened below and terete towards apex, 7–15cm long, 2–5mm wide, linear with incomplete cross-walls. **Flowers** 3–12, bisexual, in 4–12 dense, rounded clusters 1–14cm long, subtended by a stem-like, erect bract 1–5cm long, terminating short, erect or ascending branches; floral bracts absent; tepals dark reddish-brown to black, 2–4mm long, lanceolate with an acute apex; stamens 3; ovary superior, 1-celled. **Fruit** a dark glossy brown capsule 2.4–3.5mm long, trigonous-obovoid with many rusty orange seeds.

Distribution: Dwarf rush is native to temperate western North America; in the Hawaiian Islands it is found on Maui and Hawai'i. First recorded on Hawai'i in 1911, now relatively common in marshy areas, from 100 to 1500m elevation. Introduced passive-invasive; FACW.

Juncus planifolius R.Br.
Broadleaf rush

JUNCACEAE

Description: Perennial herb 10–60cm high, glabrous; culms erect, 1– 2mm diam., terete to somewhat flattened, tufted on short-creeping rhizomes. **Leaves** basal; leaf-sheaths pinkish-pale brown, open on one side with membranous margins; ligules lacking lobes; leaf-blades flat, 10–40cm long, 1.5–11mm wide, without cross-walls. **Flowers** many, bisexual, 5–30 in loose clusters, subtended by a stem-like bract 2–10cm long, terminating slender unbranched stems; floral bracts absent; tepals dark brown, 1.8–2.5mm long, with inrolled margins and rounded apex; stamens 3; ovary superior, 3-celled. **Fruit** a red-brown capsule 2–3mm long, trigonous-obovoid with many pale brown seeds.

Distribution: Broadleaf rush is native to South America and Australasia in temperate and cooler high elevations; in the Hawaiian Islands it is found on six main islands (not Niʻihau and Kahoʻolawe). First recorded on Hawaiʻi in 1930, it is now common in moist to wet disturbed places such as in depressions along margins of forests and bogs, from 850 to 1300m elevation. Introduced aggressive-invasive; FACW.

Juncus polyanthemos Buchenau
Manyflower rush

JUNCACEAE

Description: Perennial herb 0.4–1.3m high, glaucous; culms erect, 2–4.5mm diam., terete with 40–100 striations, dark brown at base, pith interrupted, densely tufted on short-creeping rhizomes. **Leaves** basal; leaf-sheaths (cataphylls) dark brown, 3–25cm long; ligules and leaf-blades absent. **Flowers** many, bisexual, solitary in very loose, many-branched clusters 8–12cm long, subtended by an erect, terete, stem-like bract 10–40cm long; floral bracts 2; tepals pale brown with membranous margins, 1.7–2.3mm long; stamens 3; ovary superior, 3-celled. **Fruit** a golden brown capsule 2–2.6mm long, 1–1.5mm diam., trigonous-obovoid with many rusty brown seeds.

Distribution: Manyflower rush is native to Australia; in the Hawaiian Islands it is found on Maui and Hawai‘i. First recorded on Hawai‘i in 1953, it now occurs in muddy disturbed sites, from 700 to 1280m elevation. Introduced passive-invasive; OBL.

Note: Very similar to *Juncus effusus*, differing in that the pith in the culm is interrupted instead of solid; the flower parts are equal to or shorter than the capsule instead of being definitely shorter; and the culms and leaf bases are dark brown instead of being reddish-brown or purple.

193

Juncus tenuis Willd.
Slender rush
JUNCACEAE

Description: Perennial herb 10–60cm high, glabrous; culms erect, 0.6–1.5mm diam., terete, loosely tufted on short, densely branched rhizomes. **Leaves** basal; leaf-sheaths open on one side with membranous margins; ligules rounded projections 1–6mm long; leaf-blades 7–30cm long, 0.5–1.8mm wide, flattened toward stem, without cross-walls. **Flowers** 5–40, bisexual, solitary or rarely in lax clusters 1–7cm long, subtended by 2–3 leaf-like bracts 5–20cm long, terminating erect unbranched stems; floral bracts 2, membranous, acute; tepals straw-brown, 3–4.5mm long, lanceolate, inner ones equal or slightly smaller, margin white, membranous, apex long-tapered to a sharp point; stamens 6; ovary superior, 1-celled. **Fruit** a light brown capsule 3.3–4.7mm long, 1.3–1.7mm diam., trigonous-ovoid with many yellowish-brown seeds.

Distribution: Slender rush is native to Eurasia, the Americas and Australia; in the Hawaiian Islands it is found on Kaua'i, Moloka'i, Maui and Hawai'i. First recorded on Hawai'i in 1915, it is now common in wet disturbed places such as along trails and in grasslands and pastures, from 700 to 2000m elevation. Introduced passive-invasive; FAC.

Note: A very variable species with many described varieties.

Monochoria vaginalis (Burm.f.) C.Presl
Cordate pickerel weed

PONTEDERIACEAE

Description: Emergent freshwater perennial herb 10–25cm high, glabrous; stems tufted, long-creeping stolons 1–2cm diam., rooting in mud. **Leaves** mostly basal, whorled; leaf-base sheathing; petioles 7–30cm long, not inflated; leaf-blades simple, 5–10cm long, 1.5–5cm wide, linear to cordate with entire margins. **Flowers** 3–20, bisexual, on 10–40cm long spikes; pedicels 3–6mm long; perianth limbs purplish-blue, 8–12mm long, oblong; stamens 6 (1 larger); ovary superior, 3-celled. **Fruit** a green capsule 8–10mm long, 2–3mm diam., ellipsoid.

Distribution: Cordate pickerel weed is native to southeast Asia, now a worldwide weed; in the Hawaiian Islands it is found on Kaua'i, O'ahu and Hawai'i. First recorded on O'ahu in 1934, it is locally abundant in coastal wetlands, freshwater ponds and ditches and taro patches, from near sea level to 120m elevation. Introduced passive-invasive; OBL.

Note: *Monochoria vaginalis* is a declared noxious weed in the United States.

Sagittaria latifolia Willd.
Watapo, common arrowhead

ALISMATACEAE

Description: Aquatic perennial herb 0.2–2m high, glabrous, exuding a milky sap when cut; rhizome stout, erect, bearing tuberous stolons. **Leaves** basal, alternate; petioles 20–70cm long, trigonous; leaf-blades simple, 3–30cm long, 2–20cm wide, sagittate (linear when submerged) with basal lobes as long as the terminal one. **Flowers** 6–20, bisexual and unisexual, the males above females, in 2–7 3-flowered clusters, each subtended by 2–3 bracts 0.5–1.5cm long, on a 15–90cm long emergent stem; sepals 5–10mm long, ovate; petals 3, white, 1–2cm long, broadly ovate; stamens many; ovary superior, 3-celled. **Fruit** a nut 2.5–4mm long, 1.5–2mm wide, compressed-ovoid with a wing 0.5–1.5mm wide.

Distribution: *Watapo* or common arrowhead is native to temperate and tropical North America and tropical South America; in the Hawaiian Islands it is found on Kaua'i, O'ahu, Maui and Hawai'i. First known on O'ahu prior to 1871, it is now common in wetlands, slow streams and taro patches, from sea level to 50m elevation. Introduced passive-invasive; OBL.

Note: Previously incorrectly identified as *Sagittaria sagittifolius* L. in Hawai'i. Common arrowhead is cultivated as an ornamental in fishponds and water gardens. The stolons, in Chinese called *chee koo*, are high in starch and protein.

Tacca leontopetaloides (L.) Kuntze
Pia, batflower

TACCACEAE

Description: Perennial herb 1–2m high, glabrous; stems deep-rooted in sandy soil with elongate tubers 15–50mm long, 10–80mm diam. **Leaves** palmately divided; leaf-base sheathing, 2–25cm long; petioles 15–120cm long, hollow; leaf-blades simple, broadly obovate, 30–70cm long, 1.5–5cm wide, with deeply dissected margins. **Flowers** 2–40, bisexual, on 20–170cm long scapes, surrounded by many long cataphylls (slender bracts); pedicels 30–60mm long; perianth tube 1.5–5mm long, lobes greenish-yellow to purple, 4–7mm long; stamens 6. **Fruit** a orange berry 15–30mm long, 15–25mm diam., ellipsoid.

Distribution: *Pia* is native to Africa, east Asia and northern Australia and transported as survival food of Melanesian and Polynesians, cultivated throughout the Pacific; in the Hawaiian Islands it is found on Kaua'i, O'ahu, Moloka'i, Maui and Hawai'i. Rarely now in cultivation, it is occasionally found in periodically submerged habitats and valley floors, from near sea level to 290m elevation. Introduced non-invasive; FAC.

Note: *Pia* produces a starch, which was grated and washed multiple times to remove bitterness. It was used as famine food and a thickener with coconut milk. It is also known as Polynesian arrowroot and Indian arrowroot, but is unrelated to commercial arrowroot. *Tacca hawaiiensis* H.Limpr. was a younger name used in Hawai'i for this species.

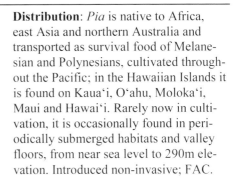

Typha domingensis Pers.
Southern cattail

TYPHACEAE

Description: Perennial emergent aquatic herb 2.5–4m high, glabrous; culms erect, 3–4mm diam., arising from 1.5–3m long creeping rhizomes, deep-rooted in sandy soil. **Leaves** alternate, mostly basal; leaf-base strongly sheathing, 1–10cm long; leaf-blades simple, 2.5–4m long, 0.6–1.8cm wide, linear, hollow with longitudinal and lateral partitions and rough margins. **Flowers** many, unisexual, females above males on the same culm in separate spikes 10–20cm long; floral bracts bristle-like; tepals linear, scale-like in females and males, 5–12mm long; stamens usually 3; ovary superior, 3-celled. **Fruit** a brown capsule 0.8–1.1mm long, 0.8–1mm diam., ellipsoid.

Distribution: Southern cattail is a native of Europe and the Americas; in the Hawaiian Islands it is known from the Pearl Harbor area on Oʻahu. First recorded in 1939, it is an uncommon species of coastal marshes, from sea level to 25m elevation. Introduced passive-invasive; OBL.

Typha latifolia L.
Common cattail

TYPHACEAE

Description: Perennial emergent aquatic herb 0.8–1.2m high, glabrous; culms erect, arising from 1.5–3m long-creeping rhizomes, deep-rooted in sandy soil. **Leaves** alternate, mostly basal; leaf-base strongly sheathing, up to 1.2m long; leaf-blades simple, 0.3–1m long, 0.8–2.5cm wide, linear, hollow with longitudinal and lateral partitions and rough margins. **Flowers** many, unisexual, females above males on the same culm in contiguous, terete spikes 20–30cm long; floral bracts bristle-like; tepals absent in females, and simple hairs in males, 5–12mm long, lobes pale greenish; stamens usually 3; ovary superior, 3-celled. **Fruit** a brown capsule 1.2–1.6mm long, 0.8–1.2mm diam., ellipsoid.

Distribution: The common cattail is a native of northern Africa, Eurasia and North America; in the Hawaiian Islands it is known from Kaua'i, O'ahu, Moloka'i and Hawai'i. First recorded on O'ahu in 1979, it is an uncommon species of coastal marshes, from sea level to 25m elevation. Introduced aggressive-invasive; OBL.

Xanthosoma robustum Schott
Capote, *'ape*

ARACEAE

Description: Perennial herb 1.8–2.5m high, glaucous; stems short, up to 15cm diam. with plantlets at base; sap milky. **Leaves** basal; petioles 0.9–1.8m long, green, sheathed towards the base; leaf-blades simple, 0.9–1.3m long, 0.7–0.9m wide, ovate to sagittate with entire margins and apex pointing downward. **Flowers** many, unisexual, sessile in compact terete spikes (spadix) 10–28cm long, subtended by a large bract (spathe) 12–30cm long, green to pinkish-creamy white, terminal on 2–6 peduncles 15–30cm long, in leaf axils; perianth absent; stamens 2; ovary superior, 1-celled. **Fruit** not seen in Hawai'i.

Distribution: Capote is native to Central America; in the Hawaiian Islands, where it is generally known as *'ape*, it is found on Kaua'i, O'ahu, Maui and Hawai'i. It was deliberately introduced to Hawai'i in the 1920s and first collected as a garden escape on O'ahu in 1935, and it is now common in mesic roadside swales, moist forest margins, disturbed sites near urban and rural agricultural fields and along stream banks and in ponds, from near sea level to 100m elevation. Introduced passive-invasive; FAC.

Note: Capote is occasionally used in ornamental landscapes. Thinly sliced sections of the peeled petioles are used as a topping in hot soups sold in local Vietnamese restaurants. It has also been known in Hawai'i by the younger name *Xanthosoma roseum* Schott.

Xyris spp.
Yelloweyed grasses

XYRIDACEAE

Xyris complanata R.Br.
Yelloweyed grass

Description: Perennial herb 10–60cm high, glabrous; culms laterally flattened, 1–3mm diam., tufted, lacking rhizomes. **Leaves** basal, ascending to erect; leaf-sheaths 3–7cm long; leaf-blades stiff, 10–60cm long, 1.5–4(–6)mm wide, linear, twisted with scabrous margins. **Flowers** many, bisexual, subtended by overlapping triangular bracts, the lower bracts 2–4mm long, upper bracts 5–6mm long, forming ovoid to terete spikes 5–25mm long, 4–8mm diam., borne terminally on unbranched culms 10–60cm long; sepals 3–5mm long; petals 3, yellow or white, 5–6mm long; stamens 3; ovary superior, 1-celled. **Fruit** a globose capsule not yet seen in Hawai‘i.

Distribution: This species of yellow-eyed grass is native to southeast Asia and Australia, primarily in wet habitats; in the Hawaiian Islands it is found on Kaua‘i and Hawai‘i. First collected on Hawai‘i in 1963, it now occurs in wet muddy areas and on lava, from 500 to 1370m elevation. Introduced passive-invasive; FACW.

Note: The long-stalked cone-like heads have been sold locally in dry bouquets since the 1950s.

Xyris platylepis Chapm.
Broad-scale yelloweyed grass

Description: Perennial herb 0.5–1.1m high, glabrous; culms laterally flattened, 1–3mm diam., tufted, lacking rhizomes. **Leaves** basal, ascending to erect; leaf-sheaths 3–7cm long; leaf-blades soft, 10–50cm long, 5–10mm wide, linear, twisted with smooth margins. **Flowers** many, bisexual, subtended by overlapping, elliptic-obovate bracts 5–7mm long, forming ellipsoid to ovoid spikes 15–40mm long, 8–15mm diam., borne terminally on unbranched culms 0.5–1.1m long; sepals 5–6mm long; petals 3, yellow or white, 5–6mm long; stamens 3; ovary superior, 1-celled. **Fruit** a globose capsule.

Distribution: Broad-scale yelloweyed grass is native to southeastern North America; in the Hawaiian Islands it is only found on Hawai‘i. First collected in 1951, it now occurs as a garden escape in wet muddy areas and on lava, from 500 to 1370m elevation. Introduced passive-invasive; FACW.

Photo: DL

SECTION 6 — SEDGES
Herbs with one floral bract and solid trigonous stems

The sedges have flowering stems (culms) that are mostly trigonous (3-sided), hence the saying "sedges have edges". In most genera the culms (inflorescence stems) are solid, the exception for genera treated here being *Cladium*. Most leaves are basal, in threes and may be reduced to leaf-sheaths only (scales or cataphylls). The complete floret (flower) consists of a trilocular superior ovary and three or six stamens surrounded by a perianth of six bristles (tepals). In *Carex* the perianth of the female floret is fused into a sac-like structure called the perigynium (literally: around the carpel), and absent in the male floret. Usually below the floret is one floral bract (sometimes called a scale or glume—but not equivalent to the glume of grasses). The floral bracts may be laterally compressed (keeled) and in two rows (spikelets flattened), or not at all laterally compressed and spirally arranged. These bracts are mostly without awns.

Key to the sedges of Hawaii's wetlands

1   Florets unisexual, female or male; nut surrounded by a sac-like structure
         (perigynium) 2
       Florets bisexual and male only; nut not enclosed in a perigynium 3

2(1)   Spikes loosely arranged on upper part of culm; perigynium base notched, edges
         not winged .... ***Carex echinata***
       Spikes crowded apically on culms; perigynium base wedge-shaped; edges
         winged .... ***Carex longii***

3(1)   Culms hollow, often branched at lower nodes; nut more or less terete, surface
         somewhat spongy .... ***Cladium jamaicense***
       Culms solid, unbranched; nut triangular or elliptic in cross-section, surface
         leathery 4

4(3)   Floral bracts keeled, conspicuously arranged in 2 rows, usually flattened 5
       Floral bracts not keeled, spirally arranged or in more than 2 rows, usually not
         flattened 7

5(4)   Floral bracts 5 or more; styles 3-fid; nuts trigonous .... ***Cyperus*** spp.
       Floral bracts 1–3; styles 2-fid; nuts laterally compressed 6

6(5)   Spikelets pale green, becoming yellow with age; floral bracts without wings .....
         .... ***Kyllinga brevifolia***
       Spikelets white, becoming brownish-white with age; floral bracts with broad
         wings, toothed along edge .... ***Kyllinga nemoralis***

7(4)   Perianth absent .... ***Fimbristylis*** spp.
       Perianth present as 1–7 bristles 8

8(7)   Style-base continuous with nut, breaking off at base of style 9
       Style-base not continuous with nut, but spongy and thickened, breaking off
       above its persistent base 13

9(8)   Culms with nodes, leafy; inflorescence appearing to be at tip of stem (apex of
       culm or terminal), subtended by 2 or more leaf-like bracts ....
       .... ***Bolboschoenus maritimus***
       Culms with no nodes above their bases; leaves reduced to short, bladeless
       sheaths; inflorescence appearing to be produced along side of culm 10

10(9)   Inflorescences compound with clusters of 1–4 spikelets on elongate branches;
       lowest bract of the inflorescence shorter than or equaling the inflorescence .. 11
       Inflorescences simple, head-like or a cluster of 3–25 spikelets; lowest bract of
       the inflorescence erect, usually longer than the inflorescence 12

11(10) Culms light to dark green, trigonous, at least just below the inflorescence; bris-
       tles subtending the florets spreading, feathery .... ***Schoenoplectus californicus***
       Culms dull green, terete along entire length; bristles subtending the florets with
       short, stiff, backward-pointing hairs .... ***Schoenoplectus tabernaemontani***

12(10) Culms strongly trigonous, stout, (2–)3–8mm diam. ....
       .... ***Schoenoplectus mucronatus***
       Culms terete or 6-angled, slender, 1–4mm diam. ...... ***Schoenoplectus juncoides***

13(8) Inflorescence a single spikelet at tip of stem; floral bracts spirally arranged,
       overlapping, all but basal few subtending a bisexual floret ...... ***Eleocharis*** spp.
       Inflorescence branched or a head of 3–6 spikelets; floral bracts 5–8 (20–30 in *R.*
       radicans), the middle 3–6 subtending florets, 1–4 of them bisexual 14

14(13) Inflorescence a single head of 3–6 spikelets at apex of stem ....
       .... ***Rhynchospora radicans***
       Inflorescence bearing 1–5 small, simple to several times divided partial panicles
       15

15(14) Spikelets 7–8mm long; nuts 2–2.3mm long (not including persistent style base) .
       .... ***Rhynchospora chinensis***
       Spikelets 3–5mm long; nuts 1–1.6mm long (not including persistent style base)
       16

16(15) Culms 20–70cm high, 0.5–0.8mm wide at base; rhizomes absent; leaves 0.8–
       2.5mm wide .... ***Rhynchospora rugosa***
       Culms 60–120cm high, 1.8–3mm wide at base; rhizome short-creeping; leaves
       3–7mm wide .... ***Rhynchospora caduca***

Bolboschoenus maritimus (L.) Palla ssp. *paludosus* (A.Nelson) T.Koyama
Kaluhā, saltmarsh bulrush   CYPERACEAE

Description: Perennial herb 0.5–1.5m high, glabrous; culms erect, 1–8mm diam., sharply trigonous, smooth. **Leaves** basal and cauline, erect; leaf-sheath brown 5–17cm long; ligules absent; leaf-blades keeled, 8–30cm long, 3–12mm wide, linear with scabrous midvein and margins, tapering to an acuminate apex. **Flowers** 25–40, bisexual, borne on 2–20 sessile, ovoid to lanceolate spikelets 10–40mm long, 7–10mm wide, in a single dense cluster 1–3cm long, terminating culm or a simple umbel of 1–4 unequal branches 4–10cm long, subtended by 1–5 leaf-like bracts 3–30cm long, 1–6mm wide; floral bracts 25–40, spirally loosely imbricate, membranous, 5–7mm long, 2–3mm wide, hairy, faintly 1-veined, narrowly ovate-acute with a 1–2mm long mucro; perianth 2–6 coppery bristles 2–4mm long, not persistent; stamens 3. **Fruit** a pale brown to brown nut 3–4mm long, compressed-ovoid, smooth.

Distribution: *Kaluhā* is native to warm temperate and subtropical North America; in the Hawaiian Islands it is found on six main islands (not Lānaʻi and Kahoʻolawe), where it occurs in saline and fresh water, on mudflats and in coastal wetlands, from sea level to 6m elevation. Native non-invasive; OBL.

Note: *Bolboschoenus maritimus* ssp. *paludosus* has previously been known as *Scirpus paludosus* A.Nelson. Subspecies *maritimus* may not occur in Hawaiʻi. It has trifid styles and trigonous nuts. *Bolboschoenus maritimus* and a closely related species, *B. robustus* (Pursh) Soják, are both known as saltmarsh bulrush.

Carex echinata Murray
Star sedge
CYPERACEAE

Description: Perennial herb 0.1–0.9m high, glabrous; culms erect, 1–3mm diam., trigonous, densely tufted on stout rhizomes. **Leaves** basal and cauline, erect; leaf-sheaths brown, tightly surrounding the stem base, inner band membranous, 1.8–2.5cm long; ligules 0.6–4.5mm long, obtuse to acute; leaf-blades keeled, 5–40cm long, 0.7–4mm wide, linear with an acute apex. **Flowers** 1 unisexual per spikelet in 2–8 spikes, the terminal ones male and female lateral spikes 3–12mm long, 3–5mm diam., subtended by bracts 1–2cm long; floral bracts spirally arranged, membranous, 1–4mm long, 0.7–2.3mm wide, ovate with an acute apex and mucro; perigynium 1.5–4.8mm long, ovoid with a trigonous beaked apex; stamens 2; ovary bearing 2 stigmas. **Fruit** a stalked, enclosed nut 1.3–2.1mm long, 0.8–1.6mm wide, compressed-ovoid, smooth, enclosed within the perigynium and falling together.

Distribution: Star sedge is native to Eurasia and Polynesia; in the Hawaiian Islands it is found on Kaua'i, Maui and Hawai'i, where it occurs in bogs, along streams, pond margins and other wet sites, from 300 to 2225m elevation. Native non-invasive; OBL.

Note: Younger names for this plant in earlier Hawaiian literature include *Carex svenonis* Skottsb., *C. svenonis* var. *alakaiensis* Skottsb. and *C. hawaiiensis* H.St.John.

Photo: ANBG

Carex longii Mack.
Long's sedge   CYPERACEAE

Description: Perennial herb 0.2–1.2m high, glabrous; culms erect, 1–3mm diam., sharply trigonous, scabrous, tufted on short rhizomes. **Leaves** basal, erect; leaf-sheaths pale green, papery, tightly surrounding the stem, prominently veined; ligules 2–6mm long; leaf-blades flat, green, 8–30cm long, 2–4mm wide, linear. **Flowers** 1 male or female per spikelet in 2–11 clusters of ellipsoid spikes 7–11cm long, 5–8mm wide, subtended by bracts 0.5–3cm long; floral bracts membranous, silvery greenish-brown, 2–4mm long, lanceolate with an obtuse apex; anthers 2; perigynium 3–4mm long, obovoid; ovary superior, bearing 2 stigmas. **Fruit** a nut 3–4.5mm long, 1.7–2.5mm wide, compressed-obovate, closely appressed in a membranous pale brown perigynium, with prominent veins, margins narrowly winged and beak somewhat flattened, 0.8–1mm long, 2-toothed.

Distribution: Long's sedge is native to the temperate and tropical Americas, now also naturalized in New Zealand; in the Hawaiian Islands it is found on Maui and Hawai'i. First collected on Hawai'i in 1956, it is now becoming widespread in wetlands, from 1200 to 4600m elevation. Introduced passive-invasive; FAC.

Note: Previously misidentified in Hawai'i as *Carex ovalis* Gooden.

Cladium jamaicense Crantz
'Uki, saw-grass

CYPERACEAE

Description: Perennial herb 1–3m high, glabrous; culms erect, hollow, 5–10mm diam., trigonous, tufted on long, thick horizontal rhizomes. **Leaves** cauline, erect; leaf-sheaths loose, 2–5cm long; ligules absent; leaf-blades stiff, flat to keeled, 60–90cm long, 5–20mm wide, linear with scabrous margins tapering to a trigonous apex mucro. **Flowers** 2–3 male and 2 bisexual, in reddish-brown spikelets 2–3mm long, 1–2mm diam., ellipsoid, borne in 4–12 loose clusters 4–9mm diam., subtended by sheathing leaf-like bracts 1–5cm long, terminating 30–90cm long culms; floral bracts 5–8, spirally arranged, reddish-brown to dark brown, 2–3mm long, 1–2mm diam., obovate, 1-veined with an obtuse apex and short mucro; stamens 2; ovary superior with 3 stigmas. **Fruit** a sessile, glossy, brown drupe 1.8–2mm long, 0.8–1mm diam., globose to ovoid with irregular vertical lines.

Distribution: *'Uki* is native to subtropical and tropical Eurasia and the Americas and many Pacific Islands; in the Hawaiian Islands it is found on Kaua'i, O'ahu, Moloka'i, Maui and Hawai'i in wet sites, such as marshes, seeps, along streams and in fresh to brackish wetlands, from sea level to 640m elevation. Native passive-invasive; OBL.

Note: *Cladium jamaicense* is important as the dominant species in much of the Florida Everglades; it provides food and shelter to waterbirds and other animals. Previously known in Hawai'i by the younger name *Cladium leptostachyum* Nees & Meyen.

Cyperus spp.
Flatsedges

CYPERACEAE

Cyperus is by far the largest genus of sedges found in the Hawaiian Islands with 28 species, 15 of which are common in wetlands. The generic concept of *Cyperus* used here includes the sometimes segregated genera of *Mariscus*, *Pycreus* and *Torulinium*, and excludes *Kyllinga*. *Cyperus* species can be recognized by their floral bracts being two-ranked, all of which have bisexual florets that lack a perianth (bristles). *Kyllinga* is excluded because it has floral bracts that lack florets (empty or sterile).

Key to the common species of *Cyperus* in Hawaii's wetlands

1	Spikelet stem not jointed, not breaking apart at maturity 2	
	Spikelet stem jointed and breaking apart at maturity 4	
2(1)	Nut laterally compressed (elliptic in cross-section), borne with edge next to spikelet stem 3	
	Nut trigonous (triangular in cross-section) or with one side flattened, borne with face next to spikelet stem 6	
3(2)	Spikelet lanceolate, 1–2mm wide; floral bract pale yellow to reddish-brown .... ***C. polystachyos***	
	Spikelet elliptic, 2–2.6mm wide; floral bract dark purple to brownish-black .... ***C. sanguinolentus***	
4(1)	Spikelet stem jointed at base and between florets, breaking into segments with wings that become corky and clasp the nut .... ***C. odoratus***	
	Spikelet stem jointed only at base, not breaking into segments, lacking wings . 5	
5(4)	Spikelets flattened, 5–7-flowered, 4.5–6mm long; floral bracts spreading, the apex of the first at most reaching the base of the last .... ***C. javanicus***	
	Spikelets linear, 3–4-flowered, 6–10mm long; floral bracts erect, the apex of the first overlapping the base of the last .... ***C. meyenianus***	
6(2)	Spikelets arranged singly along an elongate spike exposing the stem 7	
	Spikelets arranged in digitate clusters with the stem concealed 8	
7(6)	Spikelet stem winged; leaf-sheaths only without blades .... ***C. papyrus***	
	Spikelet stem not winged; leaves with elongate blades .... ***C. pilosus***	
8(6)	Leaf-blades absent; leaf-sheaths only 9	
	Leaves with elongate blades 10	
9(8)	Leaf-like bracts subtending the inflorescence longer than the inflorescence, 15–27cm long, 3–20mm wide .... ***C. involucratus***	

Leaf-like bracts subtending the inflorescence shorter than the inflorescence, 0.5–12cm long, 1–4mm wide .... *C. prolifer*

10(8) Floral bracts 3–3.5mm long, awned; nut 1–1.5mm long .... *C. trachysanthos*
Floral bracts less than 1.5mm long, awnless or with a very short awn; nut 0.5–1mm long 11

11(10) Bracts subtending the inflorescence 2–3, the longer erect 3–12cm long, and appearing continuous with the stem with the inflorescence on side of stem ....
.... *C. laevigatus*
Bracts subtending the inflorescence 1–8, spreading, up to 50cm long; inflorescence terminal on stem 12

12(11) Spikelets 6–12-flowered with a pointed apex; nut dark brown or black, 1.2–1.4mm long .... *C. eragrostis*
Spikelets 8–28-flowered with a rounded apex; nut yellow, 2–15mm long 13

13(12) Spikelets many, densely congested, 2–6mm long; floral bracts ovate, awnless; annual plants with fibrous roots .... *C. difformis*
Spikelets 1–15, not congested, 5–15mm long; floral bracts oblong to obovate, awned; short-lived perennial often with elongate rhizomes .... *C. halpan*

Cyperus difformis L.
Smallflower umbrella sedge

CYPERACEAE

Description: Annual herb 0.2–0.6m high, glabrous; culms erect or ascending, soft, 1.2–2.5mm diam., trigonous. **Leaves** basal, erect; leaf-sheaths yellowish-brown, 1–9cm long; leaf-blades linear, flat, 7–22cm long, 2–4mm wide, gradually tapering to an acute apex. **Flowers** 8–28, borne on many flattened, lanceolate spikelets 2–6mm long, 0.8–1.2mm wide, in densely congested clusters 5–17mm diam., terminating simple or partially compound umbels consisting of 2–4 unequal primary branches 1–4cm long, subtended by 2–4 leaf-like, erect to more or less horizontal bracts 2–22cm long; secondary branches 0–1cm long;

floral bracts laxly imbricate, dark green tinged purplish-brown, 0.6–0.8mm long, 0.6–0.8mm wide, faintly 3-veined, ovate with obtuse apex and mucro; stamens 1–2. **Fruit** a sessile yellowish-pale brown nut 0.6–0.8mm long, 0.3–0.4mm wide, trigonous-obovoid to ellipsoid, finely reticulate.

Distribution: Smallflower umbrella sedge was probably native to Africa, Eurasia and Australia but is now distributed worldwide, particularly in rice-growing areas; in the Hawaiian Islands it is found on Kaua'i, O'ahu and Maui. First recorded on O'ahu in 1895, probably accidentally introduced with rice cultivation, it is now locally common in coastal wetlands and areas disturbed by agriculture, from sea level to 50m elevation. Introduced passive-invasive; OBL.

Note: Also known as variable flatsedge.

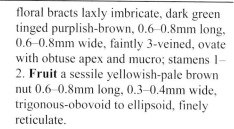

Cyperus eragrostis L.
Tall flatsedge

CYPERACEAE

Description: Perennial herb 30–90cm high, glabrous; culms 1–2mm diam., trigonous to terete, on tufted short rhizomes. Leaves basal; leaf-sheath 1.5–2.5mm long; leaf-blades flat or keeled, 10–50cm long, 5–12mm wide, linear. **Flowers** 20–70, in laterally compressed spikelets 5–20mm long, 2.2–3mm wide, oblong, 20–70 borne in globose heads 10–40mm diam., terminating 3–10 branches 2.5–12cm long, subtended by 4–8 horizontal to ascending leaf-like bracts 30–50cm long; floral bracts off-white to golden-brown, 2–2.3mm long, ovate-deltate, basally keeled, without lateral veins; stamen 1; ovary superior with styles 1–1.2mm long. **Fruit** a stalked black or dark brown nut 1.2–1.4mm long, 0.5–0.6mm diam., broadly ellipsoid, minutely pitted.

Distribution: Tall flatsedge is native to tropical and temperate South America, now widely distributed; in the Hawaiian Islands it is found on Hawai'i, where it was first recorded in 1999. It is now locally common in the upper Hamakua area around 1430m elevation. Introduced passive-invasive; OBL.

Cyperus halpan L.
Sharp-edge sedge

CYPERACEAE

Description: Perennial herb 0.2–1m high, glabrous; culms erect, soft, 1–4mm diam., trigonous, on short to long rhizomes. **Leaves** basal; leaf-sheaths brown tinged purplish- or reddish-brown, 2–10cm long; leaf-blades usually absent or linear, flat to keeled, 10–30cm long, 2–5mm wide, gradually tapering to an acute apex. **Flowers** 10–28, borne on 1–15 flattened, linear-lanceolate spikelets 3–18mm long, 1–1.6mm wide, in loose digitate clusters 5–10mm diam., terminating simple or partially compound umbels of 5–15 unequal primary branches 5–10(–20)cm long, each bearing a few secondary branches to 6.5cm long, subtended by 1–3 leaf-like, ascending flat bracts 0.5–18cm long; floral bracts closely imbricate, pale brown, often tinged reddish, greenish or purplish-brown, 1–1.9mm long, 0.8–1mm wide, faintly 3-veined, oblong to obovate with mucronate apex; stamens 3. **Fruit** a stalked white or reddish-brown nut 0.5–0.7mm long, 0.3–0.5mm wide, trigonous-ellipsoid, warty.

Distribution: Sharp-edge sedge is native to the wet tropics and subtropics worldwide; in the Hawaiian Islands it is found on Kaua'i, Moloka'i, Maui and Hawai'i. First recorded on Kaua'i in 1957, it is now widespread in wet disturbed areas, such as bogs, wet forests and open muddy areas, from sea level to 1700m elevation. Introduced passive-invasive; FACW.

Note: In many floras the species epithet is incorrectly spelled *haspan*.

Cyperus involucratus Roxb.
Umbrella sedge

CYPERACEAE

Description: Perennial herb 0.3–1.5m high, glabrous; culms erect, 2–5mm diam., trigonous, scabrous, on short stiff rhizomes. **Leaves** basal; leaf-sheaths pale green to yellowish-brown, 10–20cm long; leaf-blades absent. **Flowers** 6–30, borne on 6–30 flattened, ovoid to linear-lanceolate spikelets 3–25mm long, 1.5–3mm wide, in dense clusters terminating compound umbels consisting of 14–22 unequal primary branches 5–20cm long, subtended by 4–22 leaf-like horizontal or ascending bracts 15–27cm long, 3–20mm wide, each bearing 4–10 secondary branches 0.3–4cm long, tertiary branches 0.3–2.5cm long; floral bracts closely imbricate, pale green tinged reddish-brown, 1.6–2.4mm long, 1–1.7mm wide, prominent keel 3–5-veined, deltate-ovate with acute apex; stamens 3.

Fruit a subsessile brown nut 0.6–0.8mm long, 0.4–0.6mm wide, trigonous-ellipsoid, minutely pitted.

Distribution: Umbrella sedge is native to tropical Africa, now cultivated world-wide; in the Hawaiian Islands it is found on Midway, Kaua'i, O'ahu, Maui and Hawai'i. Probably introduced about 1900, it is a recent garden escape into wet disturbed sites along streams, from sea level to 460m elevation. Introduced aggressive-invasive; FACW.

Note: The identity of *C. involucratus* has been long confused with *C. alternifolius* L., a species endemic to Madagascar and Réunion. Consequently many common names, including umbrella-plant and *pu'uka'a haole* are now applied to both species.

Cyperus javanicus Houtt.
'Ahu'awa, Java sedge

CYPERACEAE

Description: Perennial herb 0.4–1.1m high, glaucous; culms erect, stiff, 3–5mm diam., trigonous, scabrous, on short rhizomes. **Leaves** basal, ascending; leaf-sheaths dark-brown or purplish-brown, 5–16cm long; leaf-blades linear, folded below the middle, flat or with rolled margins above, scabrous, 0.1–1.2m long, 8–12mm wide, glaucous. **Flowers** 5–7, borne on many flattened, lanceolate spikelets 4.5–6mm long, 1.8–2mm wide, in deflexed spikes 1.5–3cm long, terminating in partially compound umbels of 6–10 unequal primary branches up to 12cm long, subtended by 5–6 leaf-like bracts, the lower ones much longer than the inflorescence, sometimes bearing 3–6 secondary branches; floral bracts brown tinged reddish-brown, 2.8–3mm long, 2–2.5mm wide, broadly ovate with many veins and rounded apex; stamens 3. **Fruit** a sessile blackish-brown nut 1.2–1.5mm long, 0.7–0.9mm wide, trigonous-ovoid, minutely pitted.

Distribution: *'Ahu'awa* is native to tropical Africa, Asia and Polynesia; in the Hawaiian Islands it is found on Midway and seven main islands (not Kaho'olawe). It is a common species in marshes, taro patches, streams, ditches, disturbed areas, coastal sites and wet cliffs, from sea level to 180m elevation. Native non-invasive; FACW.

Note: In floras that recognize *Mariscus* as a segregate genus, this species is known as *M. javanicus* (Houtt.) Merr. & C.R.Metcalfe. Early Hawaiians used the pounded fiber from the culms to strain *'awa*.

Cyperus laevigatus L.
Makaloa, smooth flatsedge
CYPERACEAE

Description: Perennial herb 0.2–1m high, glabrous; culms smooth, stout, 0.5–5mm diam., terete to trigonous, in a single row on short to long-creeping rhizomes. **Leaves** basal; leaf-sheaths reddish-brown, 3–20mm long; leaf-blades absent, a short awn only or 3–30mm long. **Flowers** 12–24, borne on 3–30 flattened, lanceolate spikelets 7–12mm long, 1.6–3mm wide, in dense clusters terminating culms subtended by 2–3 leaf-like bracts, 1 bract erect, appearing as a continuation of the culm, 3–12cm long, 0.5–3mm wide, shorter bracts more or less horizontal, 0.3–4.5cm long, 0.2–1mm wide; floral bracts closely imbricate, red-flecked pale yellowish-brown, 1.5–3mm long, 1.3–2mm wide, 3–4-veined, slightly keeled, broadly ovate with rounded or pointed apex; stamens 2. **Fruit** a sessile, grayish-brown nut 1.2–1.8mm long, 0.7–1.2mm, compressed-ovoid, smooth or pitted.

Distribution: *Makaloa* is widespread in warm temperate and subtropical regions worldwide; in the Hawaiian Islands it is found on Laysan, Ni'ihau, O'ahu, Moloka'i, Maui and Hawai'i. It is a common coastal species found on edges of freshwater, brackish or salt ponds, mudflats and other sandy coastal areas, from sea level to 10m elevation. Native non-invasive; OBL.

Note: The name *Juncellus laevigatus* (L.) C.B.Clarke is used for this species in some floras. The culms were woven into hats and the finest Ni'ihau mats.

215

Cyperus meyenianus Kunth
Meyen's flatsedge   CYPERACEAE

Description: Perennial herb 20–50cm high, glabrous; culms erect, smooth, 1–3mm diam., trigonous, tufted on very short rhizomes. **Leaves** basal, ascending; leaf-sheaths reddish or purplish-brown, 1–4cm long; leaf-blades flat, 30–60cm long, 3–8mm wide, linear. **Flowers** 3–4, borne on many linear to lanceolate spikelets 6–10mm long, 0.8–1mm wide, in terete spikes 1.5–3cm long, 1–2cm diam., terminating partially compound umbels consisting of 4–12 unequal primary branches to 10cm long, subtended by 5–10 leaf-like bracts, bearing 3–5 secondary branches; floral bracts widely spaced but overlapping, pale yellowish-brown, 3–3.7mm long, smooth, 1–1.5mm wide, oblong to elliptic, 9-veined and minutely pointed apex; stamens 3.

Fruit a sessile brown nut 2–2.5mm long, 0.7–0.8mm wide, trigonous-oblong, smooth.

Distribution: Meyen's flatsedge is native to tropical Central and South America; in the Hawaiian Islands it is found on Kaua'i, O'ahu, Moloka'i and Hawai'i. First recorded from Kaua'i in 1922, it is now locally common from wetlands and disturbed sites in mesic to wet forests, especially along trails, from 30 to 1200m elevation. Introduced passive-invasive; FACW.

Note: In floras that recognize *Mariscus* as a segregate genus, this species is known as *M. meyenianus* (Kunth) Nees.

Cyperus odoratus L.
Pu'uka'a, rusty flatsedge

CYPERACEAE

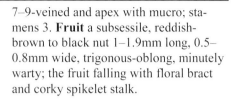

Description: Annual or short-lived perennial herb 0.3–1.4m high, glabrous; culms erect, smooth, 7–17mm diam., trigonous, tufted on short rhizomes. **Leaves** basal; leaf-sheaths reddish or purplish-brown, 30–60cm long; leaf-blades flat, 5–60cm long, 6–18mm wide, linear. **Flowers** 10–25, borne on 10–60 spreading to reflexed, terete spikelets 10–25mm long, 1–2.5mm wide, in dense terete spikes 1–4cm long, 0.8–3.5cm diam., terminating compound umbels consisting of 10–12 unequal primary branches 6–30cm long, subtended by 4–10 leaf-like bracts 3–55cm long, 1–17mm wide, each bearing 3–8 secondary branches 2–8cm long, third-order branches (when present) 0–2cm long; floral bracts laxly imbricate, red-flecked pale reddish to yellowish-brown, 2–3.5mm long, 1.2–1.8mm wide, obovate, 7–9-veined and apex with mucro; stamens 3. **Fruit** a subsessile, reddish-brown to black nut 1–1.9mm long, 0.5–0.8mm wide, trigonous-oblong, minutely warty; the fruit falling with floral bract and corky spikelet stalk.

Distribution: *Pu'uka'a* is native to tropical Asia, Micronesia, Polynesia, Central and South America and now worldwide; in the Hawaiian Islands it is found on Kaua'i, O'ahu, Moloka'i, Maui and Hawai'i, where it occurs in on margins of ponds, streams and taro patches, from sea level to 60m elevation. Native non-invasive; FACW.

Note: In floras that recognize *Torulinium* as a segregate genus, this species is known as *T. odoratum* ssp. *auriculatum* (Nees & Meyen ex Kunth) T.Koyama (*Cyperus auriculatus* Nees & Meyen ex Kunth). This subspecies is characterized by floral bracts 3–3.5mm long and is a larger and stouter plant than ssp. *odoratum*, however, the features separating the two subspecies may not be reliable.

Photo: KD

Photo: KD

217

Cyperus papyrus L.
Papyrus   CYPERACEAE

Description: Perennial herb 3–5m high, glabrous; culms erect, 15–45mm diam., trigonous to terete, arising from long stiff rhizomes. **Leaves** basal; leaf-sheaths 10–30cm long, brown; leaf-blades mostly absent, rarely 1–3cm long. **Flowers** 6–20, borne on 6–30 linear, 4-sided spikelets 6–10mm long, 0.8–1mm wide, in terete spikes 1.2–2cm long, 0.6–1cm diam., terminating compound umbels consisting of many arching, 10–30cm long, unequal primary branches, subtended by 4–10 mostly erect, keeled leaf-like bracts 3–8cm long, each branch bearing 3–8 secondary branches 8–20cm long, subtended by 2–5 leaf-like bracts 1.5–4cm long; floral bracts loosely imbricate, reddish-brown, 1.8–2.2mm long, 1.2–1.5mm wide, ovate-elliptic, 5-veined, weakly keeled with a rounded apex; stamens 3. **Fruit** a sessile light brown nut 0.8–1mm long, 0.3–0.4mm wide, compressed-ellipsoid, minutely pitted.

Distribution: Papyrus is native to eastern tropical Africa and Madagascar and now widely cultivated and naturalized in other parts of the world; in the Hawaiian Islands it is cultivated in water gardens and now naturalized on Kauaʻi, Oʻahu and Hawaiʻi. First recorded in cultivation in 1910, it is a recent garden escape into permanent coastal wetlands, from sea level to 30m elevation. Introduced aggressive-invasive; OBL.

Note: Also known in Hawaiʻi as *kaluha* and *papulo* and elsewhere as Egyptian paper-reed and bulrush.

Cyperus pilosus Vahl
Fuzzy flatsedge

CYPERACEAE

Description: Annual or short-lived perennial herb 0.3–0.9m high, glabrous; culms erect, 5–8mm diam., acutely trigonous, on creeping stolons to 3–5cm long, covered with brown leaf-sheaths. **Leaves** basal, erect; leaf-sheaths pale green to pale brown, to 25cm long; leaf-blades linear, flat, 10–35cm long, 3–10mm wide. **Flowers** 8–25, borne on linear-lanceolate, hairy spikelets 6–15mm long, 1.5–2.5mm wide, in 1–6 triangular spikes 2–3cm long, 1–2cm wide, terminating compound umbels of 3–10 unequal primary branches 1–16cm long, each bearing 2–5 secondary branches 0.5–2cm long, subtended by 3–5 leaf-like, ascending, flat bracts 5–35cm long; floral bracts laxly imbricate, reddish-brown flecked pale yellowish-brown, 1.8–2.2mm long, 1.2–1.6mm wide, deltoid-ovate, distinctly 5- or 7-veined with acute apex; stamens 3. **Fruit** a sessile dark brown nut 1–1.2mm long, 0.5–0.7mm wide, trigonous-ovoid to ellipsoid, minutely pitted.

Distribution: Fuzzy flatsedge is native to the wet tropics of south and east Asia; in the Hawaiian Islands it is only found on Kaua'i, where it was first collected in 1916, probably introduced accidentally with rice cultivation, from near sea level to 120m elevation. Introduced passive-invasive; FACW.

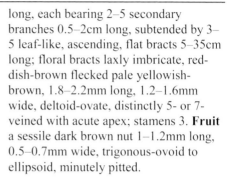

Cyperus polystachyos Rottb.
Manyspike flatsedge

CYPERACEAE

Description: Annual or perennial herb 25–90cm high, glabrous; culms erect, stiff, 1–2.5mm diam., terete to trigonous, tufted on short rhizomes. **Leaves** basal, erect; leaf-sheaths yellow to reddish-brown, to 15cm long; leaf-blades flat to keeled, 20–60cm long, 1–4mm wide, linear, scabrous towards acute apex. **Flowers** 8–40, borne on many strongly compressed, lanceolate spikelets 5–25mm long, 1–2mm wide, in lax to dense spikes 2–5cm diam., terminating simple or partially compound umbels consisting of 1–12 unequal primary branches 0.5–6cm long, subtended by 3–7 horizontal to ascending, keeled leaf-like bracts 5–30cm long; floral bracts pale yellow to reddish-brown, 1.5–2.4mm long, 1–1.4mm wide, oblong-ovate, 3-veined, strongly keeled with an acute pointed apex; stamens 2. **Fruit** a sessile reddish-brown nut 0.8–1.2mm long, 0.3–0.6mm wide, compressed-oblong, minutely warty.

Distribution: Manyspike flatsedge is native to tropical and subtropical regions of the world; in the Hawaiian Islands it is found on Midway and seven main islands (not Kahoʻolawe). It grows in dry and wet soils, particularly in open disturbed mesic coastal sites and wet forests, from sea level to 1420m elevation. Native passive-invasive; FACW.

Note: Two subspecies native to Hawaiʻi are ssp. *holosericeus* (Link) T.Koyama with lax 8–26-flowered inflorescences and yellowish-brown floral bracts, and ssp. *polystachyos* with inflorescences forming 10–40-flowered head-like clusters and pale to dark reddish-brown floral bracts. Also known as *Pycreus polystachyos* (Rottb.) P.Beauv.

Cyperus prolifer Lam.
Dwarf papyrus

CYPERACEAE

Description: Perennial herb 0.3–1.1m high, glabrous; culms erect to decumbent, 2–6mm diam., terete to trigonous, on stout creeping rhizome, also rooting adventitiously. **Leaves** basal, ascending; leaf-sheaths reddish-brown to dark purple, 1–12cm; leaf-blades absent. **Flowers** 7–25, borne on 1–30 quadrangular, linear to ovoid, reddish-brown spikelets 3–17mm long, 1–1.5mm wide, in dense clusters terminating compound umbels consisting of 50–250 unequal primary branches 4–16cm long, subtended by a single horizontal or reflexed, reddish-brown bract 0.5–1cm long; each bearing secondary branches 0.5–5cm long, subtended by 2–3 nearly horizontal, flat, linear bracts 4–12cm long, 1–4mm wide; floral bracts reddish-brown, 1.2–1.7mm long, 0.7–0.9mm wide, ovate, 1–3-veined with minutely pointed obtuse apex; stamens 3. **Fruit** a stalked brown nut 0.4–0.5mm long, 0.2–0.3mm wide, obovoid, minutely reticulate.

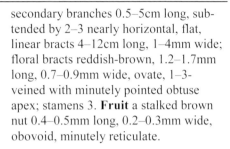

Distribution: Dwarf papyrus is native to southeastern Africa, and has long been cultivated worldwide as an ornamental in fish ponds and water gardens; in the Hawaiian Islands it is at least sparingly naturalized in the Kanaele Bog, Kaua‘i, at 620 to 630m elevation. Introduced passive-invasive; OBL.

Note: *Cyperus isocladus* Kunth is a younger name previously used for this species in Hawai‘i.

Cyperus sanguinolentus Vahl
Bloodscale sedge   CYPERACEAE

Description: Short-lived perennial or annual herb 20–60cm high, glabrous; culms erect, 0.3–2mm diam., trigonous to terete, arising from short-creeping rhizomes. **Leaves** basal; leaf-sheaths 1–2cm long, pale brown; leaf-blades 7–40cm long, 1–2mm wide, linear, keeled, narrowing to an acute apex. **Flowers** 6–32, borne on 3–20 compressed, oblong-elliptic spikelets 6–18mm long, 2–2.6mm wide, in dense clusters 1–2cm diam., terminating (mostly) simple umbels of 2–5 unequal branches 1–5cm long, subtended by 2–4 more or less ascending, leaf-like bracts 1–8cm long, 0.5–2mm wide; floral bracts closely imbricate, dark purple to brownish-black, 1.9–2.7mm long, 1.8–2.3mm wide, ovate, 3-veined, 2-keeled with obtuse apex; stamens 3. **Fruit** a subsessile dark brown nut 1–1.4mm long, 0.4–0.8mm wide, compressed-obovoid, minutely pitted.

Distribution: Bloodscale sedge is native to subtropical Africa and Asia; in the Hawaiian Islands it is found only on Hawaiʻi, where it was first recorded in 1949. It grows in wetland habitats in Kona from 800 to 1000m elevation. Introduced passive-invasive; FACW.

Note: *Cyperus polystachyos* has been also been known as *Pycreus sanguinolentus* (Vahl) Nees.

Cyperus trachysanthos Hook. & Arn.
Pu'uka'a   CYPERACEAE

Description: Perennial herb 20–50cm high, glabrous; culms erect, viscous, 1–4mm diam., trigonous, arising from short stout rhizomes. **Leaves** basal, erect; leaf-sheaths yellowish-brown, 1.5–10cm long; leaf-blades glaucous, 10–35cm long, 2.5–3.5mm wide, gradually tapering to a long, acuminate apex. **Flowers** 8–20, borne on flattened, ovate–lanceolate spikelets 8–12mm long, 3–5mm wide, in dense clusters terminating simple umbels of 1–5 unequal branches 4–9cm long, each bearing 2–6 clusters of spikelets, subtended by 3–5 leaf-like bracts longer than the inflorescence; floral bracts pale yellowish to pale reddish-brown, 3–3.5mm long, broadly ovate, 1-veined and minutely pointed apex; stamens 3. **Fruit** a sessile dark brown nut 1–1.5mm long, 0.5–0.7mm wide, trigonous-ovoid, minutely pitted.

Distribution: *Pu'uka'a* is only found on the Hawaiian Islands of Ni'ihau, Kaua'i, O'ahu, Moloka'i and historically from Lāna'i, where it occurs in seasonally wet sites such as margins of ponds and wet slopes, from sea level to 160m elevation. Endemic non-invasive; FACW.

Note: Listed by federal law and the State of Hawai'i as an endangered species.

223

Eleocharis spp.
Spikerushes CYPERACEAE

Eleocharis is represented by six species in the Hawaiian Islands, all found in wetlands. The genus can be recognized by its inflorescence being a single terminal spikelet with floral bracts spirally arranged, all bearing florets with perianth bristles. The species can be generally determined by their fruit colors and they have distinctive persistent style-bases and surface architecture (see below). The species in Hawai'i are called *kohekohe.*

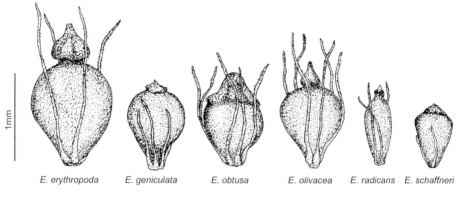

1mm

E. erythropoda   *E. geniculata*   *E. obtusa*   *E. olivacea*   *E. radicans*   *E. schaffneri*

Key to the species of *Eleocharis* in Hawaii's wetlands

1   Plants with horizontal surface stems (stolons); nuts yellow 2
    Plants without stolons; nuts black, brown or olive 3

2(1) Nut laterally compressed, 0.9–1.6mm long; style-base spongy .. ***E. erythropoda***
    Nut narrowly obovoid, 0.6–0.9mm long; style-base not spongy ..... ***E. radicans***

3(1) Apex of leaf-sheath firm, oblique 4
    Apex of leaf-sheath thin and transparent, straight or nearly so 5

4(3) Nut brown; style-base trigonous, nearly as wide as apex of nut .... ***E. obtusa***
    Nut black; style-base conical, about one third as wide as apex of nut ....
    .... ***E. geniculata***

5(3) Spikelets 3–4mm long; nut 0.5–0.7mm long, obconical; style-base low and
    broad .... ***E. schaffneri***
    Spikelets 3–9mm long; nut 0.5–1.1mm long, the surface minutely pitted; style-
    base elongated and narrow .... ***E. olivacea***

Eleocharis erythropoda Steud.
Bald spikerush

CYPERACEAE

Description: Perennial herb 20–80cm high, glabrous; culms erect, slender, 0.3–1.5mm diam., terete with 8–12 ridges, densely tufted on slender brown stolons. **Leaves** basal; leaf-sheaths membranous, 2–9cm long, reddish-brown stripes at base, truncate; ligules and leaf-blades absent. **Flowers** 15–50, each subtended by a pale reddish-brown floral bract 2–3.5mm long, 1.2–1.3mm wide, lanceolate-elliptic with an obtuse apex, borne on a single narrowly ovoid to terete terminal spikelet 3–18mm long, 2–4mm wide; perianth of 4 slender bristles 1.2–1.8mm long, or absent; stamens 3. **Fruit** a sessile, glossy, dark yellow nut 0.9–1.6mm long, 0.7–1.2mm wide, compressed-obovoid, smooth.

Distribution: Bald spikerush is native to temperate North America; in the Hawaiian Islands it is found on Niʻihau, Oʻahu and Kahoʻolawe. First recorded from Oʻahu in 1916, it is now found sporadically growing along margins of marshes and ponds, from sea level to 250m elevation. Introduced or ?native non-invasive; OBL.

Note: The species was previously known in Hawaiʻi as *Eleocharis calva* Torr., an invalid name because it had been previously used for a different species.

Photo: GF

Photo: GF

Eleocharis geniculata (L.) Roem. & Schult.
Bent spikerush
CYPERACEAE

Description: Annual herb 20–50cm high, glaucous; culms erect, slender, 0.2–1mm diam., terete with 5–6 ribs, densely tufted, lacking rhizomes. **Leaves** basal; leaf-sheaths reddish-brown 0.5–3cm long with 5 veins, membranous margins and dry, truncate, oblique apex; ligules and leaf-blades absent. **Flowers** 15–125, borne on a single ovoid to globose terminal spikelet 1–9mm long, 1–4mm wide, subtended by a bract 2–3mm long; floral bracts spirally overlapping, membranous, reddish-brown 0.8–3mm long, 0.6–2.3mm wide, ovate with green midvein and rounded apex; perianth of 4–8 bristles (or absent) 0.6–1mm long; stamens 1–3. **Fruit** a sessile, glossy, black nut 0.5–1.1mm long, 0.3–0.7mm wide, compressed-obovoid, smooth or very finely reticulate.

Distribution: Bent spikerush is native to the tropics worldwide; in the Hawaiian Islands it is found on Kaua'i, O'ahu, Moloka'i and Maui. First collected on O'ahu in 1909, it is now locally common growing in moist soil, marshy places, salt marshes, taro paddies and seeps, from sea level to 760m elevation. Introduced passive-invasive; OBL.

Note: A very variable species in the Hawaiian Islands.

Eleocharis obtusa (Willd.) Schult.
Blunt spikerush

CYPERACEAE

Description: Annual herb 20–50cm high, glabrous; culms erect, slender, 0.2–2mm diam., densely tufted on very short rhizomes. **Leaves** basal; leaf-sheaths 1–6cm long, purplish-brown at base, oblique apex with mucro; ligules and leaf-blades absent. **Flowers** 15–200, bisexual, borne on a single ovoid to terete terminal spikelet 2–13mm long, 2–5mm wide; floral bract orange-brown to tan, 1.7–2.5mm long, 0.9–1.1mm wide, ovate with green midvein and rounded apex; perianth 5–7 stout, scabrous bristles (or absent) 0.9–1.7mm long; stamens (2–)3. **Fruit** a sessile, glossy brown nut 0.9–1.3mm long, 0.7–0.9mm wide, compressed-obovoid, smooth.

Distribution: Blunt spikerush is native to temperate North America; in the Hawaiian Islands it is found on Kauaʻi,

Oʻahu, Molokaʻi, Maui and Hawaiʻi, where it is found growing in bogs, ponds, along streams and other wet places, from 390 to 1900m elevation. Native non-invasive; OBL.

Note: *Eleocharis obtusa* is sometimes treated as the same species as *E. ovata* (Roth) Roem. & Schult., although the latter species differs in its mostly 2-branched styles, mostly 2 stamens and narrower tubercles. Robust plants with floral bracts 2.5mm long and nuts 1.2–1.3mm long (*E. obtusa* var. *gigantea* (C.B.Clarke) Fernald) are rare.

Other *Eleocharis* spp.
Spikerushes

CYPERACEAE

Eleocharis olivacea Torr.
Bright green spikerush

Description: Perennial herb 10–30cm high, glabrous; culms erect, slender, soft, spongy, 0.5–1mm wide, slightly flattened, tufted or scattered on slender stolons. **Leaves** basal; leaf-sheaths membranous; ligules and leaf-blades absent. **Flowers** 30–65 on terminal spikelets 3–9mm long, 1.5–2.2mm wide, ellipsoid; floral bracts brown, 1.5–3mm long, 0.4–1.6mm wide, obovate; perianth (0–)3–6 rough bristles 1–2mm long; stamens 3. **Fruit** a yellow-brown nut 0.5–1.1mm long, 0.4–0.8mm wide, compressed-obovoid, very finely reticulate; style-base elongate and narrow.

Distribution: Bright green spikerush is native to temperate eastern North America; in the Hawaiian Islands it is found on Hawai‘i, where it was discovered in 1980 on the banks of the Wailuku River at 1200m elevation. Introduced passive-invasive; OBL.

Note: Sometime placed as a variety of *Eleocharis flavescens* (Poir.) Urb.

Eleocharis radicans (Poir.) Kunth
Rooted spikerush

Description: Perennial herb 3–12cm high; culms erect, soft, slender, spongy, 0.3–1mm diam., terete with c.10 ribs, on slender rhizomes. **Leaves** basal; leaf-sheaths 0.5–2cm long, membranous, disintegrating early; ligules and leaf-blades absent. **Flowers** 5–15 on terminal spikelets 2–4mm long, 1–1.5mm wide, ovoid with acute apex; floral bracts greenish-white, 1.5–2.5cm long, 0.6–

0.8mm wide, lanceolate to ovate, faintly 3–5-veined with an acute to rounded apex; perianth 4 very slender, rough bristles; stamens 3. **Fruit** a sessile yellow to brown nut 0.6–0.9mm long, 0.3–0.4mm wide, narrowly obovoid, reticulate; style-base short and narrow.

Distribution: Rooted spikerush is native to tropical North America; in the Hawaiian Islands it is found on Kaua‘i, O‘ahu, Maui and Hawai‘i. First collected on Kaua‘i in 1917, it is now growing in marshes, taro patches and along streams, from 20 to 1220m elevation. Introduced passive-invasive; OBL.

Eleocharis schaffneri Boeck.
Schaffner's spikerush

Description: Annual herb 3–5cm high; culms slender, spreading, bristly, 0.6–0.8mm wide with many ribs, tufted on rhizome. **Leaves** basal; leaf-sheaths membranous; ligules and leaf-blades absent. **Flowers** many, on terminal spikelets 3–4mm long, 2mm wide; floral bracts light red or bronze, 1.5–1.7mm long, 0.7–0.8mm wide, ovate with rounded or acute apex; perianth 6–7 rough bristles 0.3–0.5mm long; stamens 3. **Fruit** a olive-green nut 0.5–0.7mm long, compressed-obconical with longitudinal striations; style-base low and broad.

Distribution: Schaffner's spikerush is native to Central America; in the Hawaiian Islands it is found on Kaua‘i, where it was discovered in 1989 on the Hanalei National Wildlife Refuge, 10m elevation. Introduced passive-invasive; OBL.

Fimbristylis spp.
Fimbries   CYPERACEAE

Fimbristylis is a genus of about 200 species, mostly from the wet tropics and subtropics of southeast Asia and Australia. They are typical components of wetlands. The generic name refers to the thread-like styles of some of these plants, although this morphology is not confined to this genus. *Fimbristylis* species can be recognized by their floral bracts being spirally arranged (not keeled or flattened), all of which have bisexual florets that lack a perianth (bristles).

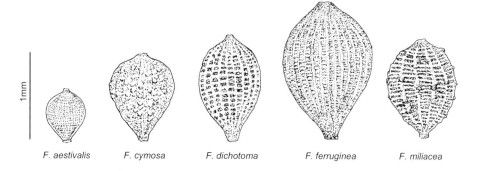

F. aestivalis   F. cymosa   F. dichotoma   F. ferruginea   F. miliacea

Key to the species of *Fimbristylis* in Hawaii's wetlands

1   Styles thread-like, not or scarcely flattened, the margins smooth or with scattered long hairs, not fringed; spikelets 2–6mm long 2
    Styles strongly flattened, the margins conspicuously fringed; spikelets 4–14mm long 4

2(1) Upper leaves at base of culm reduced to bladeless sheaths; leaves laterally compressed; spikelets spherical or nearly so .... ***F. miliacea***
    Upper leaves at base of culm with blades; leaves not laterally compressed; spikelets oval, elliptic or terete 3

3(2) Leaf-blades 1–4mm wide, rigid, apex blunt .... ***F. cymosa***
    Leaf-blades 0.3–1mm wide, apex gradually tapering to a point .... ***F. aestivalis***

4(1) Floral bract hairless; nut coarsely reticulate with usually 5–12 rows of rectangular cells .... ***F. dichotoma***
    Floral bract with dense, short, silvery, appressed hairs at least at tips; nut finely reticulate with usually 25–35 rows of square cells .... ***F. ferruginea***

Fimbristylis aestivalis (Retz.) Vahl
Summer fimbry

CYPERACEAE

Description: Annual herb 3–20cm high, coarse-hairy; culms compressed, angular, 0.3–0.5mm diam., densely tufted from very short rhizomes. **Leaves** basal; leaf-sheath 5–15mm long, yellowish-brown; ligules absent; leaf-blades linear, 1.5–4cm long, 0.3–1mm wide, tapering to a point. **Flowers** 8–15, in a single ovate spikelet 2.5–7mm long, 1–1.5mm wide with an acute apex, terminating compound umbels consisting of 3–7 lax primary branches 0.5–2.7cm long, subtended by 1–4 leaf-like bracts, shorter or slightly longer than the inflorescence; floral bracts spirally arranged, membranous, yellowish-brown to pale reddish-brown, 1–1.5mm long, ovate, green medially 3-veined, and apex with a minute projection; stamens 2; ovary with styles not flattened, not fringed but base with fine hairs; stigmas 2. **Fruit** a short-stalked, glossy, yellow nut 0.5–0.7mm long, 0.4–0.5mm diam., compressed-obovoid to ellipsoid, smooth or faintly pitted.

Distribution: Summer fimbry is widely distributed but primarily in warm areas, especially in tropical Asia; in the Hawaiian Islands it is found on Kaua'i and Hawai'i, first recorded from Hanalei Valley, Kaua'i in 1977, now found along roadside ditches, from sea level to 30m elevation. Introduced passive-invasive; FACW.

Fimbristylis cymosa R.Br.
Mau'u 'aki'aki, tropical fimbry

CYPERACEAE

Description: Perennial herb 5–60cm high, glabrous; culms erect, stiff, trigonous, 0.3–2mm diam., deeply grooved, grayish-green, densely tufted on short rhizomes. **Leaves** basal, spreading to ascending; leaf-sheaths pale to dark brown, lustrous, 1–2.5cm long with membranous margins, persistent; ligules absent; leaf-blades flat or weakly rolled, 10–30cm long, 1–4mm wide, linear with scabrous margins and an obtuse, pointed apex. **Flowers** many, in spikelets 3–6mm long, 1.5–2.5mm wide with an obtuse apex, in brown heads or clusters of 2–5 terminating simple or compound umbels up to 4cm long, 5–7cm wide, or heads 0.7–2cm diam., consisting of 10 or more spikes, subtended by 1–3 leaf-like bracts more than 2cm long; floral bracts 1–2mm long, 1–1.2mm wide, ovate with 3–5 veins and obtuse or notched apex; stamens 2–3; ovary with 2–3 stigmas. **Fruit** a grayish-brown to dark brown nut 0.7–1mm long, 0.4–0.5mm diam., weakly trigonous or compressed-obovoid, smooth.

Distribution: *Mau'u 'aki'aki* is native to salt marshes and mangrove swamps across the Pacific basin; in the Hawaiian Islands it is found on Kure, Midway, Laysan, French Frigate Shoals and seven main islands (not Kaho'olawe) commonly on sandy beaches, in cracks or soil pockets in lava or limestone and among rocks, from sea level to 60m elevation. Native passive-invasive; FAC.

Note: Two subspecies of *Fimbristylis cymosa* are native to Hawai'i: ssp. *spathacea* (Roth) T.Koyama has inflorescence branches 2–5cm long, and clusters of 2–5 spikelets and 2 stigmas; ssp. *umbellato-capitata* (Hillebr.) T.Koyama has an inflorescence contracted into a single head 0.7–2cm diam. or on branches 1–2cm long, and 3 stigmas.

Fimbristylis dichotoma (L.) Vahl
Forked fimbry

CYPERACEAE

Description: Short-lived perennial herb 10–80cm high, glabrous; culms erect, trigonous, 0.5–1.5mm diam., base thickened but not bulbous, tufted with very short rhizomes or absent. **Leaves** basal, spreading to ascending; leaf-sheaths 1–4mm long, sometimes hairy, pale to reddish-brown; ligules a ring of hairs; leaf-blades flat to weakly rolled, 10–40cm long, 2–3mm wide, linear with a blunt apex. **Flowers** many, in pale reddish-brown solitary spikelets or clusters of 2–3, 4–8mm long, 2.5–3mm wide, ovate with an acute apex, terminating compound, dense or open, ascending umbels 2–10cm long, 1–5cm wide with 2–5 branches 1–6cm long, the lateral ones longer, subtended by 2–5 leaf-like bracts, lower ones usually longer than the inflorescence; floral bracts spirally arranged, yellowish-brown, 2–3mm long, ovate with 1–3-veins and acute, pointed apex; stamens 2; styles strongly flattened, fringed; stigmas 2. **Fruit** a short-stalked yellow to white nut 0.8–1.2mm long, 0.7–1mm diam., compressed-obovoid with ribs forming rectangles.

Distribution: Forked fimbry is distributed in temperate to tropical regions worldwide; in the Hawaiian Islands it is found on Kaua‘i, O‘ahu, Moloka‘i, Maui and Hawai‘i, primarily in open, moist areas in mesic or wet forests, on lava flows, bogs, grassy areas and along trails and roads, from 10 to 2730m elevation. Native passive-invasive; FAC.

Note: This is one of the most widespread and weedy species of *Fimbristylis* and has many races and forms.

Fimbristylis ferruginea (L.) Vahl
West Indian fimbry

CYPERACEAE

Description: Perennial herb up to 1m high, glabrous; culms terete, becoming flattened near apex, 1.5–3mm diam., weakly many-ribbed, arising from short, stout rhizomes. **Leaves** basal, erect; leaf-sheaths pale green, back conspicuously veined; ligules a 0.3–0.4mm wide fringe of pale, appressed hairs; leaf-blades flat to weakly rolled, light green to brown, 5–40cm long, 1–2mm wide, linear with scabrous margins and acute apex. **Flowers** in 1–12 spikelets 0.6–1.2cm long, 3–5mm wide, ovate, on mostly simple branches subtended by 2–6 leaf-like bracts 1–7cm long, 0.8–1.4mm wide with scabrous margins; floral bracts spirally arranged, pale reddish-brown, 3.5– 4mm long, 2–3mm wide, obovate, 1(–3)-veined with an apical mucro; stamens 2. **Fruit** a short-stalked pale brown nut 1.5–1.7mm long, 1.1–1.2mm wide, compressed-obovoid, finely reticulate.

Distribution: West Indian fimbry has a pantropical distribution; in the Hawaiian Islands it is found only on Oʻahu, where it was first collected in 1981, now growing in wetlands, along edges of marshes and in wildlife refuges, from near sea level to 730m elevation. Introduced passive-invasive; OBL.

Fimbristylis miliacea (L.) Vahl
Grass-like fimbry   CYPERACEAE

Description: Annual herb 15–70cm high, glabrous; culms light green, 1–3mm wide, flattened or somewhat 4-angled toward base, tufted, lacking rhizomes. **Leaves** mostly cauline, erect; sheaths keeled; ligules absent; leaf-blades flat, rigid, 15–40cm long, 1–2mm wide, linear with scabrous margins and acute apex. **Flowers** many, in solitary to dense clusters of dark red-brown spikelets 1.5–5mm long, 1.5–3mm wide, ovate to globose, terminating 3–7 un-equal branches, the longer outer ones spreading, 1–5cm long, scabrous, sub-tended by 2–4 bristly leaf-like bracts, one half to one third the length of the inflorescence branches; floral bracts pale to reddish-brown, 0.8–1mm diam., ovate to circular with midvein rarely pointed; stigmas 1–2; ovary bearing 3-fid styles. **Fruit** a pale or yellowish-brown nut 0.6–1mm long, 0.3–0.5mm wide, trigonous-obovoid with 4–7 rows of rectangular pits and mostly warty.

Distribution: Grass-like fimbry probably originated from southeast Asia, now a weed worldwide; in the Hawaiian Islands it is found on Kaua'i, Maui and Hawai'i. First collected on Kaua'i in 1977, it occurs in taro patches, reservoirs and streams, from near sea level to 120m elevation. Introduced passive-invasive; OBL.

Kyllinga brevifolia Rottb.
Shortleaf spikesedge

CYPERACEAE

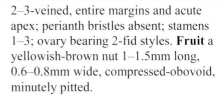

Description: Perennial herb 5–30cm high, glabrous; culms erect, dark green, smooth, sharply trigonous, 0.5–1.5mm diam., tufted along a slender, horizontal, long-creeping rhizome 1–2mm diam. **Leaves** mostly basal; leaf-sheaths 1–6.5cm long, gray-brown, membranous, dry; leaf-blades herbaceous, flat, 2–21cm long, 1.5–3.5mm wide, linear with scabrous midvein and margins, and acute apex. **Flowers** 1–2, male above bisexual, in many flattened green spikelets 2.5–3.5mm long, 0.8–1mm wide, clustered in single or several terminal heads 5–10mm diam., subtended by 2–3 spreading, leaf-like bracts 3–8cm long; floral bracts keeled, pale green, 2–2.5mm long with 2–3-veined, entire margins and acute apex; perianth bristles absent; stamens 1–3; ovary bearing 2-fid styles. **Fruit** a yellowish-brown nut 1–1.5mm long, 0.6–0.8mm wide, compressed-obovoid, minutely pitted.

Distribution: Shortleaf spikesedge is a pantropical species of unknown origin; in the Hawaiian Islands it is found on six main islands (not Niʻihau and Kahoʻolawe). First collected on Oʻahu in 1864–65, it is generally common growing in disturbed areas such as lawns, roadsides, pastures and along trails in mesic to wet forest, from 20 to 1220m elevation. Introduced passive-invasive; FAC.

Note: *Kyllinga* is often treated as a subgenus of *Cyperus*, viz., *C. brevifolius* (Rottb.) Hassk. Previously misidentified in Hawaiʻi as *Kyllinga monocephala* Rottb.

Kyllinga nemoralis (J.R.Forst. & G.Forst.) Dandy ex Hutch. & Dalziel
Whitehead spikesedge   CYPERACEAE

Description: Perennial herb 10–45cm high, glabrous; culms erect, dark green, smooth, sharply trigonous, 0.5–1.5mm diam., tufted along a slender, horizontal, long-creeping rhizome 1–2mm diam. **Leaves** mostly basal; leaf-sheaths 1–6.5cm long, brown to purplish-brown, membranous, dry; leaf-blades herbaceous, flat, 5–25cm long, 2–5mm wide, linear with scabrous midvein and margins, and acute apex. **Flowers** 1–2, male above bisexual, in many flattened white spikelets 2.5–3.5mm long, 0.8–1mm wide, clustered in single or several terminal heads 5–10mm long, 5–7mm diam., subtended by 3–4 spreading, leaf-like bracts 5–30cm long; floral bracts white, keeled, 1–1.5mm long with 3–4-veined, entire margins and acute apex; perianth bristles absent; stamens 1–3; ovary bearing 2-fid styles. **Fruit** a brown nut 1.2–1.5mm long, 0.6–0.8mm wide, compressed-obovoid, minutely pitted.

Distribution: Whitehead spikesedge is a pantropical species of unknown origin; in the Hawaiian Islands it is found on six main islands (not Niʻihau and Kahoʻolawe). First collected on Oʻahu in 1929, it commonly occurs in wet pastures and roadsides, from sea level to 200m elevation. Introduced passive-invasive; FAC.

Note: *Kyllinga* is treated by some botanists as a subgenus of *Cyperus*, and it has also been known by the synonym, *C. kyllinga* Endl.

236

Rhynchospora caduca Elliott
Anglestem beakrush

CYPERACEAE

Description: Perennial herb 0.6–1.2m high, glabrous; culms erect or ascending, trigonous, 1.8–3mm diam., tufted on short, scaly rhizomes. **Leaves** basal and cauline, erect; leaf-sheaths 2–5cm long; ligules absent; leaf-blades trigonous, 10–40cm long, 3–7mm wide, linear with a red to yellowish-brown apex. **Flowers** 3–6 bisexual or male in 1–3 slightly flattened spikelets 3–5mm long, 1.5–2mm wide, ovate, in 3–6 moderately dense clusters 2–7cm long, 1.5–3cm wide, on many erect branches 1–3cm long, the central ones shorter than laterals, subtended by leaf-like bracts 1–3cm long; floral bracts membranous, rusty-brown, 2.5–3.7mm long, 2–3mm wide, ovate with apical mucro; perianth bristles 6; stamens 2–3; ovary bearing trigonous style. **Fruit** a short-stalked brown nut 1–1.6mm long, 1–1.4mm wide, compressed-obovoid with transverse wrinkles and rectangular cells.

Distribution: Anglestem beakrush is native to subtropical and tropical north America; in the Hawaiian Islands it is known on Kaua'i, O'ahu, Maui and Hawai'i. First collected on Hawai'i in 1972, it has rapidly spread into wetlands, from 20 to 1220m elevation. Introduced aggressive-invasive; FACW.

Rhynchospora chinensis Nees & Meyen ssp. *spiciformis* (Hillebr.) T.Koyama
Kuolohia, spiked beakrush   CYPERACEAE

Description: Perennial herb 10–30cm high, glabrous; culms erect, rigid, 0.5–1.5mm diam., densely tufted, arising from very short rhizomes. **Leaves** basal and a few cauline; leaf-sheaths 5–9cm long, tightly surrounding the stem; leaf-blades flat, 8–25cm long, 2–3mm wide, linear with a scabrous acute apex. **Flowers** 1–2 bisexual, 2–3 males; spikelets broadly lanceolate, 7–8mm long, 2–2.5mm wide, in 2–4 terminal clusters on slender branches 6–15mm long, the central branches shorter than the lateral ones, subtended by leaf-like bracts longer than the inflorescence; floral bracts yellowish-brown, 5–6mm long, ovate; perianth bristles 6, 4–6mm long; stamens 2–3; ovary with conical style base. **Fruit** a sessile glossy, brown nut 2–2.3mm long, 1.5–1.8mm wide, compressed-obovoid with weak transverse wrinkles.

Distribution: *Kuolohia* is native to south and east Asia and the western Pacific islands; in the Hawaiian Islands it is found on Kaua'i, Moloka'i, Maui and Hawai'i in open, wet sites in pastures, wet forests and bogs, from 550 to 1750m elevation. Native non–invasive; OBL.

Note: This species and *Rhynchospora rugosa* are considered by some botanists to be part of a single variable species complex.

Photo: FRW

Rhynchospora spp.

Beakrushes   CYPERACEAE

Rhynchospora radicans (Schltdl. & Cham.) H.Pfeiff. ssp. *microcephala* (Bertero ex Spreng.) W.W.Thomas

Tropical whitetop

Description: Annual or short-lived perennial herb 10–60cm high, glabrous; culms erect or ascending, tufted, teretetrigonous, 1–2mm diam. **Leaves** mostly cauline; leaf-sheath herbaceous, membranous at apex; leaf-blades herbaceous, linear, 5–30cm long, 1.4–5mm wide, flat to slightly rolled margins, veins conspicuous, especially on upper surface, base of margins often with hairs. **Flowers** 2–3 bisexual or 1–2 males in 3–6 spikelets 7–12mm long, 2–4.3mm wide, in terminal, conical to hemispherical clusters 1–1.5cm diam., subtended by 3–5 leaf-like bracts longer than the inflorescence, the lowest bract longest, 4–15cm long, 1.5–4.5mm wide; floral bracts 20–30, reddish-brown, 4.2–5.2mm long, 1.8–3.6mm wide, ovate; perianth bristles absent; stamens 3; ovary with trigonous style-base. **Fruit** a reddish- to orange-brown or white nut 0.9–1.2mm long, 0.8–1.4mm wide, broadly compressed-obovoid with transverse wrinkles; style-base persistent.

Distribution: This subspecies of tropical whitetop is native to the West Indies, Central America and western and northeastern South America; in the Hawaiian Islands it is found on Maui and Hawai'i. First collected on Hawai'i in 1992, it is now spreading through abandoned canefields, from 100 to 180m elevation. Introduced passive-invasive; FACW.

Rhynchospora rugosa (Vahl) Gale ssp. *lavarum* (Gaudich.) T.Koyama
Pu'uko'a, **claybank beakrush**

Description: Perennial herb 20–70cm high, glabrous; culms slender, trigonous, 0.5–0.8mm diam., tufted, without rhizomes. **Leaves** mostly basal; leaf-sheaths 1.5–4cm long; leaf-blades 8–30cm long, 0.8–2.5mm wide, linear. **Flowers** 2–3 bisexual or 1–2 males borne in 2–6 reddish-brown spikelets 4–5mm long, c.2mm wide, in 3–6 terminal clusters on slender branches 0.8–3cm long, the central branches shorter than the lateral ones, subtended by leaf-like bracts, the lower two longer; floral bracts 2.3–3.5mm long, 1.8–2.8mm wide, ovate with acute apex and mucro; perianth bristles 6, 2.5–2.7mm long; stamens 3; ovary with trigonous style base. **Fruit** a reddish-brown nut 1.5mm long, 1–1.1mm wide, obovoid, smooth with very faint transverse wrinkles; style-base persistent.

Distribution: *Pu'uko'a* is native to the American tropics and Hawai'i; in the Hawaiian Islands it is found on Kaua'i, O'ahu, Moloka'i, Maui and Hawai'i, growing primarily in wet forests and bogs, occasionally in mesic forests, 280 to 1620m elevation. Native noninvasive; FACW.

Note: Often confused with *Rhynchospora chinensis* spp. *spiciformis.*

Schoenoplectus californicus (C.A.Mey.) Palla
California bulrush, *kaluhā, 'aka'akai*   CYPERACEAE

Description: Perennial herb 1–4m high, glabrous; culms erect, green, 1–2cm diam., terete below and trigonous towards top, smooth or weakly rough on edges, arising from a stout creeping rhizome 1–2cm diam. **Leaves** basal; leaf-sheath splitting into coarse fibers; leaf-blades mostly absent. **Flowers** many, bisexual, borne on 1–4 spikelets 5–10mm long, 2.5–3mm diam., ovoid-elliptic, terminating compound umbels consisting of 25–150 spikes 2–20cm long, subtended by 2–3 involucral bracts, the lowest one erect, 1–8cm long with rough margins; floral bracts reddish-brown-flecked, 2.5–2.8mm long, 1.7–2mm wide, ovate with membranous margins and rounded apex with 0.3mm long mucro; perianth 2–4 dark reddish-brown feathery bristles; stamens 2. **Fruit** a dark brown nut 1.8–2.2mm long, 1.2–1.4mm wide, compressed-obovoid, smooth.

Distribution: California bulrush is native to coastal areas of the tropical and subtropical Americas, now distributed worldwide in brackish to freshwater marshes and shores; in the Hawaiian Islands it is found on seven main islands (not Kaho'olawe). First collected on Moloka'i in 1912, it is now common in salt and freshwater wetlands, from sea level to 1220m elevation. Introduced or native? aggressive-invasive; OBL.

Note: Some botanists consider *Schoenoplectus* as a section in the genus *Scirpus* viz., *S. californicus* (C.A.Mey.) Steud.

Schoenoplectus juncoides (Roxb.) Palla
Kaluhā, rock bulrush   CYPERACEAE

Description: Annual or short-lived perennial herb 20–70cm high, glabrous; culms erect, pale green or yellowish-green, 1–4mm diam., terete or 5–6-angled, smooth, densely tufted on a short rhizome. **Leaves** basal; leaf-sheath 2–20cm long, oblique, disintegrating into coarse fibers; leaf-blades mostly absent. **Flowers** many, bisexual, borne on 2–10 sessile spikelets 6–18mm long, 3–8mm wide, ovoid to oblong, yellowish-brown, subtended by a single involucral bract 5–15cm long, erect; floral bracts membranous, pale brown, 2.8–4mm long, 1.8–2.5mm wide, weakly 3-veined and pointed apex; perianth of 4–6 pale brown bristles; stamens 2. **Fruit** a glossy, dark brown nut 1.8–2.3mm long, 1.5–2.1mm wide, broadly compressed-obovoid, smooth to transversely wrinkled.

Distribution: *Kaluhā* is native to wet sites in Eurasia and Asia; in the Hawaiian Islands it is found on Kaua'i and Hawai'i in and around bogs and ponds and in wet forests, from 180 to 1370m elevation. Native non-invasive; OBL.

Note: Some botanists consider *Schoenoplectus* a section in the genus *Scirpus*, viz., *S. juncoides* Roxb. *Schoenoplectus rockii* Kükenth. is a younger synonym.

This species is similar in appearance to *Cyperus laevigatus*, but can readily be distinguished by the presence of perianth bristles (absent in *Cyperus*).

Schoenoplectus mucronatus (L.) Palla
Bog bulrush

CYPERACEAE

Description: Perennial herb 0.4–1m high, glabrous; culms erect, stout, stiff, green or grayish-green, (2–)3–8mm diam., trigonous, smooth, tufted on short rhizomes. **Leaves** basal, erect; leaf-sheath 1–10cm long, oblique, brown to pale green, not disintegrating into coarse fibers; leaf-blades absent. **Flowers** many, bisexual on 4–25 sessile spikelets 7–20mm long, 4–6mm wide, ovate, brownish, a single erect involucral bract 1–10cm long, 3-angled, becoming re-flexed with age; floral bracts tightly overlapping, orange-brown to pale yellow, 2.7–3.5mm long, 2–2.5mm wide, ovate, many-veined with obtuse apex and mucro; perianth of 6 stout brown bristles; stamens 2. **Fruit** a glossy, dark to blackish-brown nut 1.7–2.2mm long, 1.4–2mm wide, broadly trigonous to compressed-obovoid, faintly transversely wrinkled, beak 0.2mm long.

Distribution: Bog bulrush is native to tropical Africa, southern Europe to southeast Asia and Australia, now widespread; in the Hawaiian Islands it is found on Hawai'i, where it was first recorded in 1986 from taro patches. It is now becoming widespread in wetlands, from near sea level to 730m elevation. Introduced passive-invasive; OBL.

Note: Some botanists consider *Schoenoplectus* a section in the genus *Scirpus*, viz., *S. mucronatus* L.

Schoenoplectus tabernaemontani (C.C.Gmel.) Palla
'Aka'akai, giant bulrush

CYPERACEAE

Description: Perennial herb 0.7–3m high, glabrous; culms erect, dull bluish-green, 5–10mm diam., terete, smooth, arising in a row along stout, creeping rhizomes. **Leaves** basal; leaf-sheath 10–40cm long; oblique, disintegrating into coarse fibers; blades absent or 1–10cm long. **Flowers** many, bisexual, in spikelets 6–15mm long, 3–4mm wide, ovoid, rusty-brown, solitary or 2–3 together, subtended by a 2–3 involucral bracts 1–3cm long, 1 erect, others scale-like; floral bracts membranous, rusty brown, 2.5–3.2mm long, 1.8–2.2mm wide, ovate to elliptic, weakly 3-veined with a pointed apex; perianth of 2–5 pale brown bristles with backward-pointing hairs; stamens 2–3. **Fruit** a glossy, gray-ish-brown nut 1.8–2mm long, 1.5–2.1mm wide, compressed-obovoid, smooth or transversely wrinkled.

Distribution: *'Aka'akai* is widespread in tropical and temperate regions of the world; in the Hawaiian Islands it is found on Ni'ihau, Kaua'i, O'ahu, Moloka'i and Hawai'i, in fresh and saltwater marshes, from sea level to 1220m elevation. Native passive-invasive; OBL.

Note: Some botanists place *Schoenoplectus* in the genus *Scirpus.* Until recently in the islands this species was known as *Schoenoplectus lacustris* (L.) Palla ssp. *validus* (Vahl) T.Koyama, and in the past as *Scirpus validus* Vahl or *S. lacustris* L. ssp. *validus* (Vahl) T.Koyama.

243

SECTION 7 — GRASSES
Herbs with two floral bracts and hollow terete stems

Due to a continuous availability of water and soil nutrition most grasses in wetlands grow to the upper or larger end of their natural size range. As a consequence the leaves and stems tend to be highly variable in length and provide very few conclusive features for identification. Determination of species and even genera revolves around the structure of the spikelet. Non-flowering individuals are difficult if not impossible to identify in the field. Every effort should be made to locate the flowering stem and remainders of the spikelets if the plants are past flowering.

The complete floret (flower) consists of an ovary, three stamens and two lodicules (tepals). Below the floret there are normally two floral bracts. The bract closest to the stem and subtending the floret is the palea. Below the palea is a second floral bract positioned away from the stem, the lemma. Below this there are usually two bracts without florets, called glumes. In this treatment floral bracts with stamens only are male unisexual florets; with ovary only—female unisexual; with stamens and ovary—bisexual (perfect); and lacking florets or empty bracts—sterile (some floras refer to both empty and male florets as sterile and only the female as fertile). Any bracts can be armed with an awn, a long spine-like mucro extended from a vein. A group of florets on a floret stem (rachilla) make up a spikelet. The fruit of a grass is a nut that in most floras is called a caryopsis or grain.

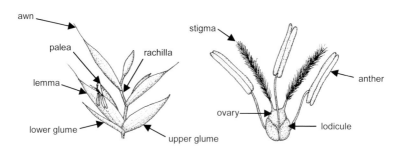

<u>Key to the grasses of Hawaii's wetlands</u>

1   Spikelets 1 to many-flowered, if 2-flowered then both bisexual or the upper male or sterile 2

     Spikelets 2-flowered, the lower floret male or sterile, the upper bisexual 12

2(1) Spikelets with 2 or more bisexual florets 3

     Spikelets with 1 bisexual floret with or without additional sterile florets 5

3(2) Inflorescence composed of separate racemes bearing many spikelets ....
.... *Leptochloa fusca*
Inflorescence an open, contracted or spike-like panicle 4

4(3) Panicle feathery (plumose), large, on robust stems; lemma with a thickened base
(callus) and feathery hairs .... *Arundo donax*
Panicle not feathery, small; lemma callus without hairs .... *Distichlis spicata*

5(2) Glumes absent; spikelets unisexual, the male in lower parts of panicle ....
.... *Zizania latifolia*
Glumes present; spikelets bisexual 6

6(5) Spikelets shedding florets above the more or less persistent glumes ....
.... *Sporobolus virginicus*
Spikelets falling entire at maturity 7

7(6) Inflorescence of several to many digitately radiating spikes 8
Inflorescence a single erect terminal spike 10

8(7) Spikelets strictly 1-flowered without sterile bracts above ..... *Cynodon dactylon*
Spikelets with 2–3 florets, 1 bisexual below 1–2 sterile   9

9(8) Spikelets with 3 florets, 2 sterile above 1 bisexual .... *Chloris barbata*
Spikelets with 2 florets, 1 sterile above 1 bisexual .... *Chloris radiata*

10(7) Glumes and lemmas awnless .... *Polypogon viridis*
Glumes awned; lemmas awned or awnless 11

11(10) Glumes 2-lobed; awns (4–)5–10mm long .... *Polypogon monspeliensis*
Glumes acute or rounded, rarely 2-lobed; awns 1.5–3(–5)mm long ....
.... *Polypogon interruptus*

12(1) Glumes thicker than lemma of upper floret; upper floret lemma membranous;
glumes of lower floret as long as the spikelet or almost so
...............................*Coix lachryma-jobi*
Glumes thinner than lemma of upper floret; upper floret lemma stiff; glumes of
lower floret often shorter than spikelet 13

13(12) Spikelets subtended by 1 or more bristles or spines 14
Spikelets not subtended by bristles 16

14(13) Panicle spike-like, terete; base of spikelets swollen on one side (gibbous) ....
.... *Sacciolepis indica*
Panicle open or contracted, not spike-like; base of spikelets not swollen 15

15(14) Bristles persistent on branches, not falling with the spikelets .*Setaria palmifolia*
Bristles forming an involucre, falling with the spikelets *Pennisetum purpureum*

16(13) Spikelets arranged on open, more or less spreading panicles 17

Spikelets arranged on 1-sided spikes or spike-like racemes; the spikes or racemes digitate or scattered 18

17(16) Lowest glume 1–1.5mm long, 3–5-veined; upper glume 5-veined; second floret lemma with transverse ridges .... ***Panicum maximum***

Lowest glume 0.6–0.8mm long, obscurely veined; upper glume 7–9-veined; second floret lemma smooth or glossy .... ***Panicum repens***

18(16) Spikelets with awns or short bristles present on glumes, lemmas or both, or if awnless, then the spikelets conspicuous hispid 19

Spikelets awnless or with a minute bristle less than 1 mm long 22

19(18) Leaf blades linear; racemes dense; spikelets ovoid to ellipsoid 20

Leaf blades lanceolate to ovate; racemes loose to moderately dense; spikelets lanceolate to narrowly ellipsoidal 21

20(19) Racemes less 1–2cm long; glumes and lemmas apices pointed .... ***Echinochloa colona***

Racemes 1.5–10cm long; glumes and lemmas with awns to 5cm long .... ***Echinochloa crus-galli***

21(19) Lowest raceme less than 4mm apart, 2–4cm long .... ***Oplismenus hirtellus***

Lowest raceme 4–12mm apart, 3–11cm long .... ***Oplismenus compositus***

22(18) Glume of lowest floret present, less than 1 mm long .... ***Urochloa mutica***

Glume of lowest floret absent 23

23(22) Spikelets biconvex, attached in 2 rows, elliptic to narrowly obovate, closely appressed to the rachis .... ***Axonopus fissifolius***

Spikelets plano-convex, attached singly or in pairs in 2 rows along the flattened rachis, suborbicular to broadly ovate, placed edgewise to the rachis 24

24(23) Upper glume with a row of fine hairs on the margin 25

Upper glume without a row of fine hairs on the margin 26

25(24) Stolons long; racemes 2; spikelets 1.5–1.8mm long .... ***Paspalum conjugatum***

Stolons absent; racemes 12–18; spikelets 2.2–2.7mm long .... ***Paspalum urvillei***

26(24) Stolons long; racemes 2(–5); spikelets elliptic-ovate, 2.5–4.5mm long; lower lemma 3–7-veined .... ***Paspalum vaginatum***

Stolons absent; racemes 4–6; spikelets orbicular, 2–2.5mm long; lower lemma 3-veined .... ***Paspalum scrobiculatum***

Arundo donax L.
Spanish reed

POACEAE

Description: Perennial herb 1–8m high, glabrous; culms erect or arching, 1–4cm diam., hollow, branched or unbranched, borne on short, thick, scaly rhizomes. **Leaves** cauline, ascending; leaf-sheaths longer than the internodes; ligules 1–1.5mm long, membranous, fringed with short hairs; leaf-blades 45–60cm long, 4–6cm wide, thick, leathery with fine lines and scabrous margins. **Flowers** 3–5 in densely clustered spikelets 10–17mm long, borne on stiff, ascending branches 40–70cm long, forming a dense, ovate, plumose panicle; lower glume 10–13mm long, 3- or 5-veined; upper glume 9–12mm long; lemmas 2, 10–12mm long with white silky hairs and midvein extending to a 2–3mm long awn; palea 4–5mm long; stamens 3. **Fruit** an elongate nut 1–1.5mm long.

Distribution: Spanish reed is native to Europe and north Africa, but is now commonly found in warm temperate and tropical areas of the world; in the Hawaiian Islands it is found on Kauaʻi, Oʻahu, Maui and Hawaiʻi. Established in Hawaiʻi prior to 1871, it is cultivated in gardens and is naturalized in coastal wet areas. Introduced passive-invasive; FAC.

Note: This is the reed of the Christian Bible, used for 5000 years in musical instruments, including more recent inventions such as the pipe organ, clarinet, oboe, bassoon and saxophone. The culm also is used for walking sticks, fishing rods and as a source of cellulose for manufacturing rayon and paper. The species, especially a form with variegated green-and-white leaves, is cultivated as an ornamental.

Photo: F&KS

247

Axonopus fissifolius (Raddi) Kuhlm.
Narrow-leaved carpetgrass

POACEAE

Description: Perennial herb 20–60cm high, glabrous; culms erect, 1–2mm diam., unbranched, dense, tufted. **Leaves** cauline, erect; leaf-sheaths flattened with hairs on the edges; ligules a fringed membrane 0.3–0.5mm long; leaf-blades linear, flat or folded, 4–15cm long, 3–5mm wide, a few short, blunt hairs at the base, apex rounded. **Flowers** 2 (sterile below bisexual) in spikelets 2.3–2.8mm long, arranged in 2 rows borne on 2–7 slender, trigonous branches 3.5–5cm long, on 1–2 terminal culms up to 16cm long; lower glume absent; upper glume, lemma and palea equal in length, 2-veined; stamens 3. **Fruit** a nut 1.4–1.8mm long, compressed-ellipsoid.

Distribution: Narrow-leaved carpetgrass is native to the tropical and subtropical Americas and widely naturalized; in the Hawaiian Islands it is found on six main islands (not Niʻihau and Kahoʻolawe). First collected on Oʻahu in 1913, it is now common in wet pastures, disturbed wet forests and bogs, from 160 to 1220m elevation. Introduced aggressive-invasive; FAC.

Note: The species is used as a pasture grass and occasionally as a lawn grass. A second species naturalized in Hawaiʻi, *Axonopus compressus* (Sw.) P.Beauv., is similar in appearance and occupies the same environmental niche, but is less common. It can be distinguished from the former by a spikelet with a rounded apex.

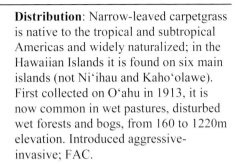

Chloris barbata (L.) Sw.
Swollen fingergrass

POACEAE

Description: Annual herb 30–70cm high, glabrous; culms erect or sometimes decumbent, 1–2mm diam., smooth, rooting at the base, mostly flat and purple or pink. **Leaves** cauline, ascending; leaf-sheaths 2–6cm long, somewhat flattened, usually hairy at throat; ligules membranous, 0.5mm long; leaf-blades flat, up to 12cm long, 1–5mm wide, decreasing in size toward upper part of stem, rough on the edges and often with long hairs near the base of the blade. **Flowers** 3 (1 bisexual below 2 sterile), overlapping in 2 rows in spikelets 2–2.5mm long, in 5–22 flexuous, ascending to spreading, feathery, purple, finger-like spikes 4–8cm long; lower glume 1–1.5mm long; upper glume 2–2.5mm long; lemma 2–2.5mm long, obovate with awn 0.5–1cm long; palea 2–2.5mm long; distal sterile lemma 0.8–1mm long with awn 2–5mm long; stamens 3. **Fruit** a brown nut 1–1.2mm long, trigonous-ellipsoid.

Distribution: Swollen fingergrass is native to Central and South America and the West Indies and now widely naturalized; in the Hawaiian Islands it is found on Kure, Midway and all eight main islands. First collected on Oʻahu in 1902, it now occurs mostly in dry disturbed areas and occasionally in wetlands, from sea level to 600m elevation. Introduced passive-invasive, FAC.

Note: Previously known in Hawaiʻi by the younger name *Chloris inflata* Link. In recent time a Hawaiian name has been given to this species, *mauʻu lei.*

Chloris radiata (L.) Sw.
Radiate fingergrass   POACEAE

Description: Annual herb 25–60cm high, glabrous; culms decumbent at base, upper part erect, 1–2mm diam., often branched at base. **Leaves** cauline, ascending; leaf-sheaths flattened, 4–7cm long with membranous edge; ligules 0.5–1mm long, ragged; leaf-blades up to 15cm long, 3–6mm wide, upper surface rough to the touch, usually with long hairs, marginal veins thick, apex rounded. **Flowers** 2 (1 bisexual below rudiment of 1 sterile) in narrow spikelets 2–3mm long, apex long-acute with one conspicuous, rough green vein and a slender awn 7–10mm long, on lax, erect or ascending spikes 3–7cm long, hairy at base, in 1–2 whorls; lower glume 1.2–2mm long; upper glume 2–2.5mm long; lemma 2–2.5mm long, obovate with 2-lobed apex and awn 0.7–1cm long; palea 2–2.5mm long; distal sterile glume 0.5–1mm long with awn 2–4mm long; stamens. **Fruit** a reddish-brown nut 1.5–2mm long, trigonous-ellipsoid.

Distribution: Radiate fingergrass is native to the tropical Americas; in the Hawaiian Islands it is found on six main islands (not Niʻihau and Kahoʻolawe). First collected on Oʻahu in 1895, it mostly occurs in disturbed mesic sites and wetlands, from sea level to 170m elevation. Introduced passive-invasive; FAC.

Coix lachryma-jobi L.
Job's tears, *pū'ohe'ohe*   POACEAE

Description: Annual herb 1–3m high, glabrous; culms erect, robust, 3–6mm diam., much-branched, tufted. **Leaves** cauline, ascending; leaf-sheaths loose, marked with fine parallel lines; ligules a ragged membrane, finely hairy along the top edge, 1.5–2mm long; leaf-blades 10–50cm long, 2–5cm wide, flat, narrowly lanceolate with a strong midvein and acute apex. **Flowers** 1 female surrounded by a bony, shiny, bluish-grey to white glume 5–15mm long, globose with 2 males above, in 3–20 spikelets, on racemes 3–5cm long borne on stout pe-duncles from upper leaves; glumes of male florets 7–9mm long (as long as spikelet), lemma 3-veined; palea 2-veined; stamens 3; female floret lemma 6–8mm long and palea scale-like. **Fruit** a nut 2.5–5mm long, subglobose.

Distribution: Job's tears is native to southeast Asia, now worldwide; in the Hawaiian Islands it is found on Kaua'i, O'ahu, Moloka'i, Maui and Hawai'i. Probably well established before 1871, it is common along streams, ditches and seeps, also in mesic forests, from sea level to 610m elevation. Introduced passive-invasive; FACW.

Note: The fruit are strung as beads in lei and seed necklaces.

Cynodon dactylon (L.) Pers.
Bermuda grass   POACEAE

Description: Perennial herb 5–30cm high, 20–80cm long, mostly glabrous; culms prostrate to ascending, 0.5–1mm diam., many-branched with stolons and rhizomes forming dense mats. **Leaves** cauline, ascending, lax; leaf-sheaths open with dry, membranous margins; ligules membranous, 0.2–0.5mm long, fringed with few long hairs; leaf-blades 1–12cm long, 1.5–4mm wide, flat, sometimes hairy above with scabrous margins and acute apex. **Flowers** 1 bi-sexual in sessile spikelets 2–2.8mm long in rows on 2 sides of 3–6 slender, ascending, trigonous spikes 3–5cm long, radial on a slender, 10–25cm long stem; lower glume 0.7–1.5mm long, falcate, 1-veined; upper glume 1.2–2mm long, lanceolate, 1-veined with a short awn; lemma 1.8–2.5mm long, ovate, 3-veined; palea 1–2mm long; stamens 3. **Fruit** a nut 2.2–2.7mm long, compressed-ellipsoid.

Distribution: Bermuda grass is possibly native to tropical Africa, but now culti-vated and naturalized worldwide; in the Hawaiian Islands it is found on Kure, Midway, Pearl and Hermes, Laysan, French Frigate Shoals and seven main islands (not Niʻihau). Deliberately intro-duced to Hawaiʻi in 1835, it is now com-mon on roadsides and in wetter areas such as seeps, from sea level to 2270m elevation. Introduced aggressive-invasive; FAC.

Note: Also widely known as couch grass. Occasionally cultivated as a lawn grass or for erosion control; a large form is grown for fodder.

Distichlis spicata (L.) Greene
Salt grass   POACEAE

Description: Perennial herb 10–50cm high, mostly glabrous; culms erect, 1–2mm diam., from creeping, scaly, mat-forming rhizomes. **Leaves** cauline, ascending; leaf-sheaths 1–2cm long; ligules a fringed membrane; leaf-blades 2–10cm long, 1–6mm wide, flat becoming rolled, scabrous above. **Flowers** 6–15 unisexual on different plants, in few strongly flattened spikelets 0.7–1.5cm long, borne on a short, narrow, dense panicle 3–8cm long; lower glume 2.2–3.6mm long; upper glume 2.4–4.8mm long; lemma and palea 3–6mm long; stamens 3. **Fruit** a pale brown nut 1–1.5mm long, ellipsoid.

Distribution: Salt grass is native to tropical and temperate North America; in the Hawaiian Islands it is found on O'ahu and Maui. First collected on O'ahu in 1977, it is becoming common in salt marshes from sea level to 10m elevation. Introduced aggressive-invasive; FACW.

Note: The local colonies appear to be female, thus can reproduce only by vegetative means.

Echinochloa colona (L.) Link
Jungle rice
POACEAE

Description: Annual herb 20–60cm high, mostly glabrous; culms decumbent to ascending, 1–3mm diam., bent at base, swollen nodes reddish-purple, tufted, rooting at lower nodes. **Leaves** cauline, weakly ascending; leaf-sheaths 3–7cm long, keeled; ligules absent; leaf-blades 4–30cm long, 3–8mm wide, linear, flat with slightly wavy, scabrous margins and acute apex. **Flowers** 2 (sterile or male below female) in spikelets 1.5–3mm long, crowded in 4 rows on 4–15 trigonous racemes 1–2cm long, hairy, borne on a central culm 5–15cm long; lower glume 1.2–1.5mm long, ovate, 3-veined; upper glume and lemmas 2.5–3mm long, ovate, 5–7-veined with a pointed apex; palea 2.5–3mm long, hyaline; stamens 3. **Fruit** a nut 1.7–2mm long, ovoid.

Distribution: Jungle rice is native to the tropics of Africa and Asia, now world-wide; in the Hawaiian Islands it is found on all eight main islands. First collected on Oʻahu in 1835, it is now common in seasonally wet, disturbed areas, from sea level to 280m elevation. Introduced agressive-invasive; FACW.

Echinochloa crus-galli (L.) P.Beauv.
Barnyard grass

POACEAE

Description: Annual herb 0.2–2m high, mostly glabrous; culms stout, decumbent to ascending, 2–3mm diam., bent at base, swollen nodes reddish-purple, tufted, rooting at lower nodes. **Leaves** cauline, ascending; leaf-sheaths slightly keeled; ligules absent; leaf-blades 5–30cm long, 6–20mm wide, linear, flat with scabrous margins. **Flowers** 2 (sterile or male below female) in spikelets 2.8–3.5mm long, paired, crowded, usually arranged in 2–4 rows on 5–20 trigonous racemes 1.5–10cm long, hairy, borne on a central culm 5–27cm long; lower glume 1.2–1.6mm long, ovate, 3-veined with short mucro; upper glume 2.5–3.2mm long, ovate, 5-veined with an awn 0.7–1.5mm long; lemma 2.5–4mm long with an awn 0.1–5cm long; upper floret lemma and palea stiff, 2–3mm long, glossy; stamens 3. **Fruit** a brown nut 1.4–2mm long, ovoid.

Distribution: Barnyard grass is common in warm areas of the world; in the Hawaiian Islands it is found on Midway and six main islands (not Niʻihau and Kahoʻolawe). First documented from Oʻahu in 1846, it is common in wet or seasonally wet sites, such as ditches, streams and cultivated fields, from sea level to 520m elevation. Introduced aggressive-invasive; FACW.

Note: Synonyms include *Echinochloa stagnina* (Retz.) P.Beauv. and *E. walteri* (Pursh) A.Heller.

Leptochloa fusca (L.) Kunth ssp. *uninervia* (J.Presl) N.Snow
Sprangletop
POACEAE

Description: Annual herb 0.2–1.1m high, scabrous; culms erect or ascending, branching above base, tufted. **Leaves** cauline, ascending; leaf-sheaths leathery, slightly rough, loosely clasping stem with 2 ear-like tabs at apex; ligules 1.5–2mm long, membranous with frayed margins; leaf-blades linear, 3–50cm long, 2–7mm wide, flat or rolled, scabrous. **Flowers** 5–11 in erect spikelets 5–10mm long, in 2 rows along underside of branches, overlapping about one third their length, on many erect to ascending lateral branches, arranged along a central stem 10–35cm long, oblong or ovate; glumes ovate or oblong, 1-veined, rough with short apex and mucro; lower glume 1–2.6mm long; upper glume 1.8–2.8mm long; lemma pale green, 2–3.6mm long, 3-veined with membranous margins and appressed hairs; palea 2–2.5mm long, 2-veined; stamens 1–3. **Fruit** a pale brown nut 1–1.2mm long, obovate.

Distribution: Sprangletop is native to the tropical Americas; in the Hawaiian Islands it is found on Midway, Kaua'i, O'ahu, Moloka'i, Lāna'i and Hawai'i. First recorded from O'ahu in 1967, it is now widespread in disturbed wet areas, such as ditches and shallow standing water, from sea level to 580m elevation. Introduced aggressive-invasive; FACW.

Note: *Leptochloa fusca* is similar in appearance to *Eragrostis curvula* (Schrad.) Nees, but that species usually grows in drier areas and has long hairs at the base of its sheaths.

Oplismenus spp.
Basket grasses
POACEAE

Oplismenus compositus (L.) P.Beauv.

Diagnosis: This species differs from *O. hirtellus* (see below) by having spikelet pairs on the lowest raceme 4–12mm apart and 3–11cm long.

Distribution: This basket grass is native to tropical Asia, Africa and the Americas; in the Hawaiian Islands it is found on Kaua'i, O'ahu, Moloka'i, Maui and Hawai'i in mesic valleys and forests, from 245 to 500m elevation. Introduced passive-invasive; FACU.

Oplismenus hirtellus (L.) P.Beauv.

Description: Perennial herb 10–20cm long, soft-hairy; culms decumbent, weak, 20–40cm long, rooting adventitiously at nodes. **Leaves** cauline, lateral; leaf-sheaths 3–6mm long, loosely clasping; ligules membranous with hairs 0.6–0.8mm long; leaf-blades thin, 5–13cm long, 8–20mm wide, lanceolate to ovate. **Flowers** 2 (sterile or male below bisexual) in spikelets 0.5–4mm apart on 5–12 ascending, trigonous racemes 2–4cm long; lower glume 2–3.5mm long, 5–7-veined with awn 5–10mm long; upper glume 2–3.5mm long, 5-veined with awn 1–2mm long; lemma 3–4mm long, 5–7-veined with a short awn; upper floret lemma glossy, stiff, 2.5–3mm long, 5-9-veined; palea (when present) hyaline, 3–3.5mm long; stamens 3. **Fruit** a nut 2–2.5mm long, terete.

Distribution: Basket grass is native to tropical America, now distributed worldwide; in the Hawaiian Islands it is found on six main islands (not Ni'ihau and Kaho'olawe). First documented from Hawai'i in 1819, it is common in mesic and wet forests, from 10 to 920m elevation. Introduced passive-invasive; FAC.

Note: A cultivated ornamental used in hanging baskets, especially the form with variegated leaves.

O. hirtellus

O. hirtellus

Panicum maximum Jacq.

Guinea grass POACEAE

Description: Perennial herb 0.7–4.5m high, hirsute; culms somewhat flattened, seldom branched, usually with long hairs on their swollen joints. **Leaves** cauline, ascending; leaf-sheaths with ligules membranous, 1–3mm long; leaf-blades 15–90cm long, 0.6–3cm wide, flat, usually hairy behind the ligule. **Flowers** 2 (male below bisexual) in elliptic-obovoid spikelets 2.7–3.5mm long, borne on diffusely branched, obovoid panicles 9–60cm long, the lowest branches whorled, 10–40cm long; lower glume 1–1.5mm long, 3–5-veined, ob-tuse; upper glume 5-veined, acute; upper lemma 2–5mm long, 5–7-veined and with minute, transverse ridges; palea equal in length to lemma; stamens 3. **Fruit** a pale yellow nut 2.2–2.5mm long, ellipsoid.

Distribution: Guinea grass is native to Africa, but this important forage grass is now naturalized through the tropics; in the Hawaiian Islands it is found on Midway and all eight main islands. It was introduced to Hawai'i prior to 1871 and is now widespread in wet to drier habitats, from sea level to 850m elevation. Introduced aggressive-invasive; FAC.

Note: In some parts of the world this species is used for fodder.

Panicum repens L.
Torpedo grass, quack grass

POACEAE

Description: Perennial herb 0.1–1.3m high, usually glabrous; culms 2–3mm diam., unbranched, rhizomatous, covered with bladeless sheathes. **Leaves** cauline, ascending; leaf sheath 3–8cm long; ligules membranous with 0.4–1mm long hairs; leaf-blades stiff, 4–30cm long, 0.2–0.8cm wide, linear, flat or folded. **Flowers** 2 (male below bisexual) in white, turgid spikelets 2.5–3mm long, oblong to narrowly elliptic, borne on stiffly ascending branches 3–22cm long; lower glume thin, 0.6–0.8mm long, with no visible veins and obtuse apex; upper glume, lower lemma and palea 7–9-veined; second floret lemma 1.7–2.2mm long, smooth and glossy with acute apex; stamens 3. **Fruit** a pale yellow nut 1.2–1.5mm long, narrow ovoid.

Distribution: Torpedo grass, of unknown origin, is a ubiquitous weed in moist soils of temperate and tropical regions; in the Hawaiian Islands it is found on Oʻahu, Lānaʻi, Maui and Hawaiʻi. First collected on Hawaiʻi in 1916, it is now common in wet disturbed areas, along ditches and roadsides in cane fields, from 30 to 1100m elevation. Introduced aggressive-invasive; FAC.

Note: In some parts of the world torpedo grass is used for soil stabilization.

Paspalum conjugatum P.J.Bergius
Sour grass, Hilo grass
POACEAE

Description: Perennial herb 0.3–1m high, mostly glabrous; culms erect, 0.8–1mm diam., unbranched or branched, arising from leafy wiry stolons. **Leaves** cauline, ascending; leaf-sheaths 2–6cm long, flattened; ligules membranous, 0.5–1mm long with 1–2mm long hairs; leaf-blades thin, 6–20cm long, 5–15mm wide, flat with scabrous margins and acute apex. **Flowers** 2 (sterile below bisexual) in flattened, yellowish-green spikelets 1.5–1.8mm long, ovate with acute apex, overlapping in 1 row per side of 2 widely spreading scabrous racemes 6–10cm long; lower glume absent; upper glume glabrous except for long, lax hairs along the edges, 2- or 4-veined, lemma glabrous, membranous with 2 green sub-marginal veins; upper floret lemma leathery, 1.5–1.8mm long; palea 1.2–1.4mm long, ovate, 2-veined; stamens 3. **Fruit** a nut 1–1.2mm long, strongly compressed-ovoid.

Distribution: Sour grass is native to the tropical Americas, now distributed worldwide; in the Hawaiian Islands, where it is known as Hilo grass, it is found on six main islands (not Ni'ihau and Kaho'olawe). First noticed in the Hilo District on Hawai'i in 1840, it is now common in moist to wet, disturbed areas along roadsides, trails and in open fields, from 10 to 950m elevation. Introduced aggressive-invasive; FAC.

Paspalum scrobiculatum L.
Ditch millet, *mau'u laiki*

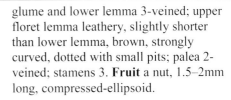

Description: Perennial herb 0.6–1.2m high, mostly glabrous; culms stout, erect, 1–6mm diam., bulbous at base, tufted. **Leaves** mostly basal, erect; leaf-sheaths 7–14cm long, often purple at base; ligules membranous, 1–1.5mm long with dense hairs 1–2mm long; leaf-blades 12–40cm long, 3–15mm wide, linear, flat with midvein visible on underside, scabrous margins and acute apex. **Flowers** 2 (sterile below bisexual), in single or overlapping pairs of spikelets 2–2.5mm long, 1.5mm wide, broadly elliptic, on 4–6 widely spaced alternate, ascending branches 2–4cm long, borne on a 4–9cm long stalk; lower glume absent; upper glume and lower lemma 3-veined; upper floret lemma leathery, slightly shorter than lower lemma, brown, strongly curved, dotted with small pits; palea 2-veined; stamens 3. **Fruit** a nut, 1.5–2mm long, compressed-ellipsoid.

Distribution: Ditch millet is native to tropical Asia, now worldwide; in the Hawaiian Islands it is found on Kaua'i, O'ahu, Moloka'i, Maui and Hawai'i. It is common on slopes with poor thin soil and in swampy sites, from sea level to 1070m elevation. Introduced or ?native passive-invasive; FAC.

Note: In Hawai'i ditch millet has been known by the younger name *Paspalum orbiculare* G.Forst. It is used as fodder for livestock in some parts of the world.

Paspalum urvillei Steud.
Vasey grass

POACEAE

Description: Perennial herb 0.7–2.5m high, mostly glabrous; culms erect, stout, 2–8mm diam., tufted, branched from lower nodes. **Leaves** cauline, ascending; leaf-sheaths keeled, glabrous or with long hairs at the throat and along the margins, loose, often with small flaps at throat; ligules 3–5mm long, trigonous; leaf-blades firm, 20–60cm long, 3–25mm wide, flat, dense cover of long hairs at base, margins scabrous. **Flowers** 2 (sterile below bisexual) in overlapping, ovate paired spikelets 2.2–2.7mm long,

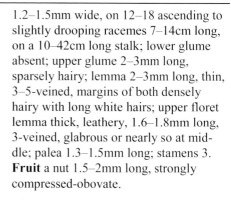

1.2–1.5mm wide, on 12–18 ascending to slightly drooping racemes 7–14cm long, on a 10–42cm long stalk; lower glume absent; upper glume 2–3mm long, sparsely hairy; lemma 2–3mm long, thin, 3–5-veined, margins of both densely hairy with long white hairs; upper floret lemma thick, leathery, 1.6–1.8mm long, 3-veined, glabrous or nearly so at middle; palea 1.3–1.5mm long; stamens 3. **Fruit** a nut 1.5–2mm long, strongly compressed-obovate.

Distribution: Vasey grass in native to the tropical and warm temperate Americas, now widespread worldwide; in the Hawaiian Islands it is found on Midway and six main islands (not Niʻihau and Kahoʻolawe). First collected on Lānaʻi in 1914, it is common in disturbed moist to wet areas such as along ditches, roadsides, fields and pastures, 20 to 1280m elevation. Introduced passive-invasive; FAC.

Paspalum vaginatum Sw.
Saltwater couch, seashore paspalum

POACEAE

Description: Perennial herb 10–60cm high, 25–50cm long, glabrous; culms 3–4mm diam., slightly flattened, sometimes branching, wiry to stout, somewhat fleshy, stolons forming a dense mat. **Leaves** opposite, ascending; leaf-sheaths short, loose, mostly overlapping, often flattened with small projections at apex; ligules 0.5–2mm long, membranous with a line of soft white hairs up to 5mm long behind it; leaf-blades stiff, 2.5–22cm long, 3–8mm wide, base abruptly constricted, rolled with an acute apex. **Flowers** 2 (sterile below bisexual) in overlapping, oblong, single spikelets 2.5–4.5mm long, 1.2–1.5mm wide, on 2 (–5) ascending, opposite branches 1.5–7.5cm long, 1–2mm wide; lower glume absent or minute; upper glume and lemma 4–5mm long, thin, 3–7-veined, glabrous; upper floret lemma and palea 3–5-veined, glabrous except for apex with a few short, stiff hairs; stamens 3. **Fruit** a nut 2.5–3mm long, compressed-narrowly obovate.

Distribution: Saltwater couch is native to Africa and the Americas, now widely distributed in warm temperate to tropical sea coasts and brackish marshes worldwide; in the Hawaiian Islands it is found on Kaua'i, O'ahu Moloka'i, Maui and Hawai'i. First collected on O'ahu in 1936, it occurs in coastal sites in shallow brackish water and on brackish sands, often forming pure stands at sea level. Introduced aggressive-invasive; FACW.

Note: In some parts of the world the species is used for stabilization of coastal areas. Another species, *Paspalum distichum* L., has been widely confused with *P. vaginatum* in Hawai'i.

Pennisetum purpureum Schumach.
Elephant grass, napier grass   POACEAE

Description: Perennial herb 1–4m high, mostly glabrous; culms erect, 1–2.5cm diam., often bent, sparingly branched, tufted, rooting at base. **Leaves** cauline, ascending; leaf-sheaths 15–25cm long; ligules 1–3mm long, membranous with long stiff hairs; leaf-blades 0.3–1.2m long, 2–4cm wide, midrib prominent on underside and scabrous margins. **Flowers** 2 (male below bisexual) in clusters of 1–5 spikelets 4–7mm long, subtended by many scabrous, golden-brown bristles 10–15mm long, forming a terete, densely hairy spike 20–30cm long, 1–2cm diam., on 1–7 ascending branches; lower glume absent or a small rounded scale 0–0.7mm long; upper glume 1.5–2.6mm long, ovate, 1-veined; lower lemma 4–5mm long, 3-veined with acute apex; upper floret lemma and palea 5–7mm long, 5–7-veined, glossy; stamens 3. **Fruit** a nut 1.5–2mm long, obovoid, falling with spikelet clusters and associated bristles.

Distribution: Elephant grass is native to tropical Africa, now worldwide; in the Hawaiian Islands it is found on six main islands (not Niʻihau and Kahoʻolawe). First collected on Lānaʻi in 1922, now common in mesic to wet disturbed areas, along roadsides and fields, from 10 to 1220m elevation. Introduced aggressive-invasive; FAC.

Note: In some parts of the world the species is used for fodder and paper.

Polypogon interruptus Kunth
Ditch rabbit's-foot grass

POACEAE

Description: Annual herb 30–80cm high, glabrous; culms erect or decumbent, branched, bent and rooting at base, tufted. **Leaves** basal and cauline; leaf-sheath smooth to scabrous, open with overlapping margins; ligules 3–7mm long, bilobed; leaf-blades to 20cm long, 2–6mm wide. **Flowers** 1 in stalked spikelets, borne on a compact interrupted spike 2–9 cm long, 5–12mm diam; glumes 1.7–2.5mm long, ovate, minutely bifid with an awn 1.5–3(–5)mm long; lemma 1–1.5mm long, smooth, glossy, narrowly lanceolate with 2–3mm long awn; palea 0.8–1.2mm long; stamens 3. **Fruit** a pale brown nut 0.6–0.8mm long, narrow-ovoid, falling with spikelet.

Distribution: Ditch rabbit's-foot grass is native to warm temperate regions of South America; in the Hawaiian Islands it is found on Kure, Midway, Kaua'i, O'ahu, Maui and Hawai'i. First collected on Maui in 1910, it is now common in wet sites, along ditches, roadsides, streams, by rock seeps, and in wet forests, from sea level to 1980m elevation. Introduced passive-invasive; FACW.

Other *Polypogon* spp.
Beard grass   POACEAE

Polypogon monspeliensis (L.) Desf.
Beard grass
Description: Annual herb 30–90cm
high, scabrous; culms erect or decumbent, branched, bent and rooting at base,
tufted. **Leaves** cauline; leaf-sheath
smooth to scabrous, open with overlapping margins; ligules 3–18mm long,
bilobed; leaf-blades 1.5–32cm long, 1.1–
11mm wide. **Flowers** 1 in stalked spikelets, borne on a compact, continuous or
interrupted spike 0.7–17cm long, 1–
3.5cm wide; glumes 1.5–2.5mm long,
hairy, narrowly elliptic with 2 small
lobes and awn (4–)5–10mm long; lemma
0.7–1.2mm long, smooth, glossy, ovate
with a short awn or absent; palea 0.9–
1.2mm long; stamens 3. **Fruit** a yellow
nut 0.9–1.3mm long, ellipsoid, falling
entire with the pedicel.

Photo: FRW   *P. monspeliensis*

Distribution: Beard grass is native to
southern Europe; in the Hawaiian Islands, it is found on Midway, Kaua'i,
O'ahu, Maui and Hawai'i. First collected
on Hawai'i in 1909, it occurs in mesic to
wet sites, ditches, streams and pastures,
from sea level to 1220m elevation. Introduced passive-invasive, FACW.

Polypogon viridis (Gouan) Breistr.
Water bent
Description: Perennial herb 0.3–1m
high, glabrous; culms slender, erect,
strongly bent and rooting at base, tufted.
Leaves cauline; leaf-sheath smooth,
open; ligules membranous, 2–5mm long,
top flat, somewhat ragged, hairy; leaf-
blades 2–18cm long, 2–12mm wide, flat,
scabrous. **Flowers** 1 in stalked spikelets,
contracted, oblong or ovate, borne on an
interrupted spike 2–14cm long, 0.5–4cm
diam; lower glume 1.6–2mm long, oblong to elliptic, without veins, scabrous,
awnless; upper glume like lower glume
but 1–3-veined; lemma membranous,
0.8–1.5mm long, 5-veined, awnless;
palea 0.6–1.2mm long; stamens 3. **Fruit**
a brown nut 0.8–1mm long, narrow
terete, falling entire with the pedicel.

Distribution: Water bent is found
throughout the tropics, with unknown
origins; in the Hawaiian Islands it is
found on Kaua'i and Hawai'i. First collected on Kaua'i in the mid-1850s, it
occurs along streams, ditches and seep-
age areas, from 160 to 1220m elevation.
Introduced passive-invasive; FAC.

Note: An earlier name for *Polypogon
viridis* is *Agrostis semiverticillata*
(Forssk.) C.Chr.

Sacciolepis indica (L.) Chase
Glenwood grass

POACEAE

Description: Annual or short-lived perennial herb 15–50cm high, glabrous; culms slender, decumbent, 0.5–1mm diam., branched, bent, tufted, rooting at base. **Leaves** mostly basal, erect; leaf-sheaths slightly keeled, shorter than the internodes; ligules 0.1–0.5mm long, membranous; leaf-blades 3–10cm long, 2–4mm wide, narrowly lanceolate, somewhat rolled. **Flowers** 2 (sterile below bisexual) in stalked spikelets 2–3mm long, densely overlapping, forming a terete panicle 1–7cm long, 3–5mm diam., on a 10–23cm long stem; lower glume 1.1–1.5mm long, ovate, 5-veined; upper glume 2.5–2.8mm long, ovate-pouched, 7-veined with a blunt apex; lemma ovate-pouched, 7–9-veined; palea 0.5–1mm long; stamens 3. **Fruit** a nut 0.7–0.8mm long, ellipsoid.

Distribution: Glenwood grass is native to the tropics of Africa and Asia; in the Hawaiian Islands it is found on six main islands (not Niʻihau and Kahoʻolawe). First collected on Maui in 1908, it is now common along trails and open areas in wet forests, from 15 to 1700m elevation. Introduced passive-invasive; FAC.

Setaria palmifolia (J.König) Stapf
Palm grass

POACEAE

Description: Perennial herb 1–2m high, tomentose; culms erect, stout with appressed hairs near the base and at the joints arising from a short rhizome. **Leaves** basal, erect; leaf-sheaths covered with stout hairs swollen at their base; ligules membranous with a ring of hairs; leaf-blades 20–50cm long, 2–9cm wide, narrowly elliptic, folded with a scabrous upper surface, lower surface hairy with a narrowed base, prominent veins and acute apex. **Flowers** 2 (sterile below bisexual) in green spikelets 3–4mm long, lanceolate, glabrous, subtended by a single bristle 5–10mm long, on spikes 2.9–3.9mm long, borne on ascending or spreading primary branches 6–20cm long, forming an open panicle 20–60cm long; lower glume 1.1–2.2mm long, 3-veined, ovate, blunt; upper glume 1.6–2.5mm long, 5- or 7-veined; lower lemma 5-veined, acuminate; upper floret lemma with faint transverse rugose lines, mucronate; stamens 3. **Fruit** a pale brown nut 1.8–2mm long, ovoid, falling as entire spikelets.

Distribution: Palm grass is native to south Asia, now worldwide; in the Hawaiian Islands it is found on Kaua'i, O'ahu, Lāna'i, Maui and Hawai'i. First collected on Hawai'i in 1903, it is common in valleys, wet forests and along streams, from 240 to 1160m elevation. Introduced aggressive-invasive; FAC.

Sporobolus virginicus (L.) Kunth
'Aki'aki, sand couch

POACEAE

Description: Perennial herb 10–50cm high, glabrous; culms erect, 1–2mm diam., many-branched, long-creeping, slender, with rhizomes covered by the overlapping leaf-bases. **Leaves** mostly basal; leaf-sheaths 6–23mm long; ligules a fringe of hairs; leaf-blades stiff, 2–14cm long, 1–5mm wide, linear, flat or rolled with a sharply acute apex. **Flowers** 1 bisexual per spikelet, 2.5mm long, borne on short, tightly appressed, erect branches forming a panicle 2–15cm long, 3–8mm diam.; lower glumes 1.2–2.4mm long, lanceolate, 1-veined; upper glume 2–3.1mm long, ovate, 1-veined with acute apex; lemma and palea papery, 1.9–2.5mm long, ovate, 1-veined with obtuse apex; stamens 3. **Fruit** a nut 0.9–2.5mm long, obovoid.

Distribution: *'Aki'aki* is native to sandy or muddy, usually coastal sites in tropical and subtropical areas of the world; in the Hawaiian Islands it is found on Midway, Laysan and all eight main islands as a common component of the vegetation of coastal dunes and wet coastal sites, from sea level to 15m elevation. Native passive-invasive; FAC.

Note: In Hawai'i the leaves, culms and roots of the plants were used as medicinal remedies. Sand couch is used for erosion control on sand dunes and other unstable coastal areas.

Urochloa mutica (Forssk.) T.Q.Nguyen
California grass, para grass

POACEAE

Description: Perennial herb 1–3m high, up to 6m long, glabrous with hairy nodes; culms decumbent and ascending, 8–15mm diam., branching and rooting from lower nodes. **Leaves** cauline, ascending; leaf-sheaths slightly overlapping, hairy; ligules a densely-fringed membrane 1.5–1.8mm long; leaf-blades flat, 10–25cm long, 7–15mm wide, smooth or with blunt hairs, midrib broad, white near the base, margins thick, purple, rough to the touch. **Flowers** 1–2 in purple sharply acute, ovate spikelets 3.2–3.4mm long, borne on racemes 1–7cm long, velvety-hairy at base, clustered into ascending trigonous terminal panicles 10–20cm long; lower glume 0.8–1.5mm long with 1 vein; upper glume and lemma 4.5–5.5mm long with 5–7 veins; stamens 3. **Fruit** a nut, compressed-ellipsoid, rarely developed in Hawai'i.

Distribution: California or para grass is probably native to tropical Africa, now pantropical; in the Hawaiian Islands it is found on Midway and six main islands (not Ni'ihau and Kaho'olawe). First collected on O'ahu in 1924, it is common in wetlands, along streams, ditches and wet disturbed sites, from sea level to 1100m elevation. Introduced aggressive-invasive; FACW.

Note: Previously widely known as *Brachiaria mutica* (Forssk.) Stapf.

270

Zizania latifolia (Griseb.) Turcz. ex Stapf
Manchurian wild rice
POACEAE

Description: Perennial herb 2–3m high, glabrous; culms erect, robust, cane-like, 0.8–2cm diam., jointed, rhizomatous at base. **Leaves** basal, erect; leaf-sheaths thickened, lower ones with honey-comb pattern; ligules membranous, 2–4cm long, deltoid; leaf-blades 0.3–1.2m long, 1.5–3.5cm wide, linear, upper surface scabrous, smooth below, tapering at base and abruptly acute at apex. **Flowers** 1, unisexual; male spikelets 0.8–1.5cm long on lower branches, female spikelets 1.5–2.5cm long on upper pendulous branches, forming a panicle 30–50cm high, 10–15cm diam.; glumes of male florets minute; lemma linear with awn 1.5–3cm long; stamens 6; glumes of female florets minute; lemma 1.5–2cm long, elliptic-oblong, 5-veined, hairy margins and a scabrous awn 2–8mm long; palea 1–1.3cm long, lanceolate, 3-veined. **Fruit** a nut 5–6mm long, ellipsoid, falling with spikelet.

Distribution: Manchurian wild rice is native to east Asia; in the Hawaiian Islands it is found on Kaua'i, O'ahu and Hawai'i. Probably introduced to Hawai'i by early Chinese immigrants in the 1800s, it is now in wetland margins and along streambanks, from near sea level to 35m elevation. Introduced, passive-invasive; OBL.

Note: Young shoots of *Zizania latifolia*, especially the culms swollen by a smut, were used in Chinese cuisine to give texture to dishes; seeds and young vegetation and inflorescences were eaten.

APPENDICES

Appendix 1 — Soil textural triangle

The American soil textural triangle is based upon the percentage division of an equilateral triangle. The USDA recognizes 12 soil texture classes and four subclasses of sand (coarse sand, sand, fine sand and very fine sand).

The Canadian soil textural triangle uses a right-angle triangle, a schematic sometimes used in the Pacific northwest.

(Courtesy: NRCS Hawai'i)

Appendix 2 — Munsell Soil Color Charts

The Munsell system is the most widely accepted color identification scheme. Color is divided into ten major **hues**, each subdivided into ten divisions. The property of lightness or gray-scale from black to white, is called the **value.** The saturation or intensity of the color is called the **chroma**. The hues, values and chromas are coded, providing a unique identifier for each color. For reading wetland soils, the most important color is chroma (x-axis), which indicates reduction in iron (from grey to bright).

The Munsell charts also include "gley" pages (grey to green to blue), which show obligate wetland soil colors (all iron is reduced).

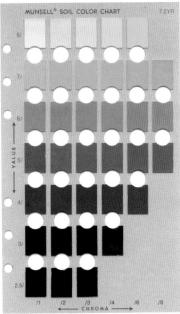

(Courtesy: *Munsell Washable Soil Charts* GretagMacBeth)

273

Appendix 3 — Eh/pH conductivity

Reduction-oxidation (Redox) reactions play a significant role in geochemical processes that occur in water and saturated systems (e.g., wetlands). First, an Eh/pH meter is used to determine electrical conductivity and pH readings of the site. Then the Eh/pH diagram is used to qualitatively fashion redox reactions within variable Eh and pH conditions. Plotting the Eh and pH will demonstrate if there are currently "reducing conditions". The bottom left of the diagram shows the wettest (most reduced) condition and the top right the most aerobic. Hydric conditions are clearly displayed when the iron is reduced and often when manganese is reduced.

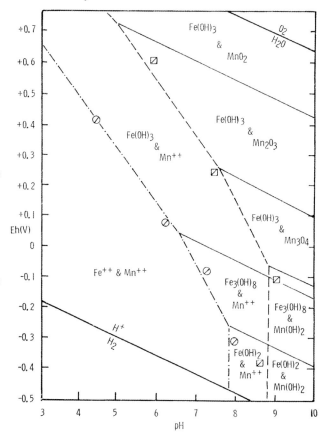

(After Collins & Boul 1970)

274

GLOSSARY

This glossary contains definitions of terms from ecology and botany as they are used in this field guide. The definitions provided may not encompass the complete range of meanings attributed to these terms. The glossary was compiled and interpreted from many sources, including Lesica and Husby (2001), Sohmer *et al.* (1999), and various internet encyclopedias and standard dictionaries.

achene: a type of nut (but commonly misapplied to other types of nuts) — a dry indehiscent fruit developed from a superior ovary containing a single seed (cf. cypsela)

acute: margins forming an angle less than 90 degrees

adventitious roots: a root arising from a mature stem

aerobic: molecular oxygen is present

ahupua'a: traditional unit of land in the Hawaiian Islands, extending from the ocean to the upper mountain slopes

alpha-alpha dipyridyl: chemical used to determine the presence of ferrous iron in soils indicating reduction. For methods see: http://soils.usda.gov/use/hydric/ntchs/tech_notes/note8.html

alternate: arranged singly at each node (cf. opposite, whorled)

amphidromy: a life cycle of fishes where adults live and breed in freshwater streams and newly hatched larvae go out to sea and remain there several months before returning to a stream

aerenchyma: spongy tissue with large air-spaces, particular common in stems and leaves of aquatic plants

anaerobic: molecular oxygen is virtually absent

anchialine: from the Greek meaning "near the sea"; marine or brackish water bodies that, through permeable substrates, have subsurface hydrologic connection to the sea

androecium: male parts of a flower

angiosperms: flowering plants, i.e., having ovules enclosed in an ovary

annual: plants with a lifespan of less than one year (cf. biennial and perennial)

anther: pollen-bearing part of the flower

apical: at or near the top (cf. basal, cauline)

aquic moisture regime: mostly reducing soil moisture regime nearly free of dissolved oxygen due to saturation by ground water or its capillary fringe

attenuate: gradually tapering to a point

atypical situations: areas in which one or more parameters (vegetation, soil and/or hydrology) have been sufficiently altered by recent human activities or natural events to preclude the presence of wetland indicators of the parameter (cf. normal circumstances)

auriculate: like the lobes of an ear

awn: a long-extended stiff point (cf. mucro)

axil: the point between two objects, usually the stem and a leaf

axillary: located in or arising in an axil

basal: arising at or near the base (cf. cauline and apical)

berry: a fleshy indehiscent fruit without a stony layer, containing one or more seeds (cf. drupe, nut)

biennial: a plant that completes its lifecycle in two years

bifid: having two lobes

bilabiate: having two lips or lobes

bisexual: a flower that has fully fertile male and female parts present

blade: flat expanded part of a leaf

bract: scale-like leaves of inflorescences and flowers

bracteole: diminutive of bract

bristle: a stiff hair; the hair-like modified perianth of daisies and sedges; or the hair-like stems forming an involucre beneath the spikelets of some grasses, e.g., *Pennisetum* and *Setaria*

buffer: an upland or riparian area that separates wetlands or other aquatic resources from developed areas or agricultural lands

buttress: the thick flange-like base of some wet-forest trees

caducous: falling off early, deciduous (cf. persistent)

caespitose: growing in dense low tufts

calyx: collective term for the sepals of a flower, particularly used when the sepals are partially fused

cambium: lateral meristem that produce secondary xylem and secondary phloem

campanulate: bell-shaped

capillary fringe: the zone above the water table that draws water up to the root zone; important in determining hydrology requirements in a wetland

capitulum: a head of flowers or fruits

capsule: a dry dehiscent fruit (cf. nut) breaking open along one or several sutures, containing one or more seeds

carpel: the seed-bearing structure of flowers

caryopsis: a type of nut — a dry indehiscent fruit of grasses developed from a superior ovary containing a single seed (= achene, cf. cypsela), also called a grain

cataphyll: a scale-like leaf on a rhizome or stolon

cauline: arising on or pertaining to the stem

channel: a longitudinal groove

chartaceus: thin like paper

chemical reduction: any process by which one compound or ion acts as an electron donor

chroma: the relative purity or saturation of a color; intensity of distinctive hue as related to grayness

ciliate: fringed with fine hairs

cluster: a group, e.g., flowers forming an inflorescence

coccum: the dry dehiscent fruit breaking open along two sutures; equivalent term for legume-like pods not in the Fabaceae

compound: having several similar parts

convex: surfaces bulge outwards

cordate: heart-shaped

coriaceous: thick like leather

corm: a short, vertical, broadly-thickened underground stem

corolla: collective term for all the petals of a flower, generally used when petals are fused together

culm: an aerial stem of a grass or sedges

cyme: an inflorescence with a terminal flower forcing lateral branching

cypsela: a type of nut — a dry indehiscent fruit of daisies developed from a inferior ovary with a single seed (cf. achene)

decumbent: a horizontal stem without adventitious roots, with ends erect or ascending

deepwater aquatic habitat: any open water area that has a mean annual water depth greater than 2m, lacks soil and/or is unvegetated or supports only floating or submerged macrophytes

dehiscent: a fruit breaking open along natural sutures at maturity

deltate: a triangular object with more or less equal sides

deltoid: triangular in 3 dimensions, like a pyramid

dense: crowded together

dentate: toothed

diameter at breast height (DBH): width of a plant stem as measured at 1.5m above the ground surface

dimorphic: having two forms

dioecious: male and female flowers on separate plants (cf. monoecious)

disk floret: tubular flowers of Asteraceae

dissected: deeply divided

distal: towards the unattached end; apical

divided: deeply cut

dominance: a descriptor of vegetation that is related to the standing crop of a species in an area, usually measured by height, aerial cover or basal area (for trees)

dominant species: a plant species that exerts a controlling influence on or defines the character of a community

drupe: an indehiscent fruit that is fleshy outside and stony inside (cf. berry and nut)

duration (inundation/soil saturation): length of time during which water stands at or above the soil surface (inundation) or during which the soil is saturated; a period during the growing season

ellipsoid: elliptic in long-section and circular in cross-section

elliptic: a compressed circle more than twice as long as broad

endemic: confined to a specific geographical region

entire: with a smooth margin

Fe/Mn concretions: firm to extremely firm, irregularly shaped bodies of iron and manganese that have sharp to diffuse boundaries; when broken in half, concretions having concentric layers

Fe/Mn nodules: firm to extremely firm irregularly shaped bodies of iron and manganese that have sharp to diffuse boundaries; when broken in half, nodules do not have visibly organized internal structure

fertile: able to reproduce sexually

filament: stem of stamen supporting an anther

filiform: very slender

fleshy: succulent

flooded: a condition in which the soil surface is temporarily covered with flowing water from any source, such as streams overflowing their banks, runoff from adjacent or surrounding slopes, inflow from high tides or any combination of sources

floret: a small flower in a cluster

flower: specialized group of leaves including the reproductive organs

flowering plant: plants with ovules enclosed in a carpel and seeds in a fruit

frequently flooded or ponded: a frequency class in which flooding or ponding is likely to occur often under usual weather conditions (more than 50 percent chance in any year or more than 50 times in 100 years)

fruit: structure that develops from an ovary and associated stems

gametophyte: the part of the lifecycle that produces the gametes (sperm and egg cells)

glabrous: without hairs

glandular: with secretory hairs

gleyed: a soil condition resulting from prolonged soil saturation that is evident by the presence of bluish or greenish colors through the soil mass or in mottles (spots or streaks) among other colors; gleying occurs under reducing soil conditions as a result of soil saturation, by which iron is reduced predominantly to the ferrous state

gleyed matrix: soils with combinations of hue, value and chroma and the soils that are not glauconitic; in some places the gleyed matrix may change color upon exposure to air (reduced matrix)

globose: spherical

glume: small pair of bracts at the base of a spikelet in grasses (and often applied to sedges)

gynoecium: the female parts of a flower

habit: stature or general appearance of a plant

habitat: the environment occupied by individuals of a particular species, population or community

hair: unicellular or multicellular epidermal outgrowths

head: compact group of florets; capitulum

herb: plants that do not develop secondary wood, usually dying back to the ground at the end of each growing season

histic epipedon: a thick (20–60cm) organic soil horizon that is saturated with water at some period of the year unless artificially drained and that is at or near the surface of a mineral soil

histosols: soils that have organic material in more than half of the upper 80cm or any thickness when overlying rock or fragmental materials having interstices filled with organic soil materials. See USDA-NRCS Soil Taxonomy (1999) for complete definition

horizon: a layer, approximately parallel to the surface of the soil, distinguishable from adjacent layers by a distinctive set of properties produced by soil forming processes.

See USDA-NRCS, Soil Taxonomy (1999) for complete definition

hydric soil definition (NRCS 1994): a soil that formed under conditions of saturation, flooding or ponding long enough during the growing season to develop anaerobic conditions in the upper part

hydrogen sulfide odor: odor of H_2S similar to rotten eggs

hydrology: the science dealing with the properties, distribution and circulation of water

hydromorphic: features in the soil caused or formed by water

hydrophyte: any macrophyte that grows in water or on a substrate that is at least periodically deficient in oxygen as a result of excessive water content; plants typically found in wet habitats

hypertrophied lenticels: an oversized pore on the stem of woody plants through which gases are exchanged

hypocotyl: the part of an embryo between the cotyledons and the root; particularly enlarges in some mangroves

indehiscent: a fruit not breaking open along natural sutures at maturity

indicator: an event, entity or condition that typically characterizes a prescribed environment or situation; indicators determine or aid in determining whether or not certain stated circumstances exist

indicator status: one of the categories (e.g., OBL) that describes the estimated probability of a plant species occurring in wetlands

inferior ovary: the perianth and stamens are attached to the wall and top of the ovary

inflorescence: cluster of flowers on stems

internode: the part of the stem between two adjacent nodes

introduced: has been transferred to a place that an organism did not previously exist

inundation: water from any source temporarily or permanently covering a land surface

involucre: ring of bracts surrounding florets

jointed: a point of natural separation

keel: angled central fold of a leaf, bract, scale, petal, etc

labellum: modified filament of gingers; also a modified and enlarged petal of orchids

lanceolate: shaped like a spearhead

lateral: on the side

lax: loose, well separated, not densely packed

leaf: generally a broad flat photosynthetic organ of a plant

leaflet: subdivision of a leaf when divided to the midvein or rachis

legume: the dry dehiscent fruit breaking open along two sutures; species of Fabaceae

lemma: the bract below and opposite the palea in grasses

lenticular: lens-shaped in cross-section, used for biconvex fruits, e.g., lentils

ligule: extension of leaf-sheath at the departure of a leaf-blade

linear: object with parallel sides

lip: lobes of corolla or calyx

lobe: a protrusion from margin

margin: edge

matrix: the dominant soil volume that is continuous in appearance and envelopes microsites

membranous: thin like a membrane

mericarp: a drupe-like fruit that divided into its two carpels for dispersal; also the parts of a schizocarp

mesic: moist

micro-hummocks: small grassy mounds less than 1 meter tall, caused by cattle grazing

midvein: central vein of a leaf

mitigation: compensation of wetland loss or degradation through restoration, enhancement, creation or preservation

monoecious: male and female flowers borne on the same plant (cf. dioecious)

mottles: spots or blotches of different color or shades of color interspersed within the dominant color in a soil layer, usually resulting from the presence of periodic reducing soil conditions (now called redoximorphic features)

muck: an organic soil in which virtually all of the organic material is decomposed, not allowing for identification of plant forms (cf. peat)

mucro: a short stiff point

mucronate: having a mucro

native: the place where an organism occurs naturally

naturalized: introduced by human intervention and now part of the environment

node: point on a stem where leaves and branches arise

nonwetland: an area that has sufficiently dry conditions such that indicators of hydrophytic vegetation, hydric soils and/or wetland hydrology are lacking; any area that is neither a wetland, a deepwater aquatic habitat nor other special aquatic site

normal circumstances: situations in which the vegetation, soils and/or hydrology have not been substantially altered by human's activities (cf. atypical situations)

nut: a dry indehiscent fruit (cf. capsule)

ob-: a prefix for the reverse direction

oblong: rectangular, narrower than wide

obovate: egg-shaped in outline, attached at its narrow end

obovoid: egg-shaped, attached at its narrow end

obtuse: forming an angle greater than 90 degrees

opposite: two objects arising at the same node

orbicular: circular in outline

organic soil material: soil material that is saturated with water for long periods or artificially drained and, excluding live roots, has an organic carbon content of 18 percent or more with 60 percent or more clay, or 12 percent or more organic carbon with 0 percent clay

orographic rainfall: rain occurring as moist air is forced to rise up mountain slopes

ovary: the part of a carpel bearing the ovules

ovate: egg-shaped in outline, attached by the wide end

ovoid: egg-shaped attached by the wide end

oxidation-reduction process: a complex of biochemical reactions in soil that influ-ences the valence state of component elements and their ions; prolonged soil saturation during the growing season elicits anaerobic conditions that shift the overall process to a reducing condition

palea: the bract subtending the flower of a grass (cf. lemma)

paleoecology: a multidisciplinary science that uses the evidence from sediments, fossils and historical sources to reconstruct past environments

palmate: parts radiating from a common point

panicle: an inflorescence with flowers borne on secondary branches

pappus: the calyx of daisies

passive restoration: the use of natural processes, sequences and timing after the removal or reduction of adverse stresses without other specific remedial actions

peat: a fibrous organic soil material that has virtually all of the organic material allowing for identification of plant forms (cf. muck)

ped: a unit of soil structure (e.g., aggregate, crumb, prism, block or granule) formed by natural processes

pedicel: the stem of a single flower

peduncle: the stem of an inflorescence or single flower below the pedicel of the flower

peltate: attached from the middle

perennial: lifespan of more than two years

perfect: complete, fertile flower, having female and male parts

performance standards: criteria for mitigation/restoration projects that include descriptions of the classification scheme (e.g. ensuring proper flow, water chemistry, geomorphology, substrate, and type of wetland). Performance standards can also include additional requirements, such as specific duration or depth of water for certain plant or animal species

perianth: collective term for the petal, sepals and tepals, or their derivatives when indistinguishable

persistent: remaining attached

petal: one of the inner whorl of the perianth

petiole: the axis attaching the leaf-blade to the stem

phloem: the cells produced to the outside of the vascular cambium that carry the photosynthetic products (sugars) around the plant

phyllode: a vertically expanded petiole with the appearance of the leaf-blade

pinna: a leaflet or subdivision of a leaf to the midvein or rachis

pistil: the female parts of a flower, collectively all the carpels (ovaries, styles and stigmas)

pit: stony layer within the fleshy outer layer of drupes

plicate: folded, as in the longitudinal folds of fan palms

pneumatophore: specialized erect roots of mangroves

pod: a dry fruit produced by one carpel that breaks open along one margin, e.g., peanut

polymorphic: having several different forms

ponding: standing water in a closed depression that is removed only by percolation, evaporation or transpiration

prevalent vegetation: the plant community or communities that occur in an area during a given period, characterized by the dominant macrophytic species that comprise the plant community

prop root: roots arising from an above-ground stem supporting the plant

prostrate: flat on the ground, not rooting at the nodes

proximal: close to the end that is attached (cf. distal)

punctuate: with small depressions

pyramidal: pyramid-shaped

raceme: an unbranched inflorescence with flowers on pedicels (cf. spike)

rachilla: stem of a spikelet in grass-like plants

rachis: axis of a divided leaf or inflorescence

ray floret: the strap-shaped flowers of daisies

receptacle: stem that supports the flower parts; the platform for the cluster of flowers in daisies

redox concentrations: bodies of apparent accumulation of Fe/Mn oxides; redox concentrations include soft masses, pore linings, nodules and concretions; nodules and concretions are excluded from the concept of redox concentrations unless otherwise specified by specific indicators

redox depletions: bodies of low chroma (2 or less) having value 4 or more where Fe/Mn oxides have been stripped or where both iron and manganese oxides and clay have been stripped; redox deletions contrast distinctly or prominently with the matrix

redoximorphic features: features formed by the processes of reduction, translocation or oxidation of Fe and Mn oxides; formerly called mottles

reduction: when the redox potential (Eh) is below the ferric/ferrous iron threshold as adjusted for pH; the point in hydric soils when the transformation of ferric iron (Fe+++) to ferrous iron (Fe++) occurs

relict features: soil morphological features that do not reflect recent hydrologic conditions of saturation and anaerobic conditions

reniform: kidney-shaped

reticulate: forming a network

rhizome: underground stems (cf. roots) of flowering plants and all stems in ferns

root: underground axis of a plant bearing water-absorbing rootlets

rosette: circular cluster of leaves

routine wetland determination: a type of wetland determination in which office data and/or relatively simple, rapidly applied onsite methods are employed to determine whether or not an area is a wetland

runner: a horizontal stem or stolon rooting at the nodes

saturated soil conditions: all easily drained voids (pores) between soil particles in the root zone are temporarily or permanently filled with water

scabrous: prickly rough with stiff hairs

scale: small, more or less triangular leaf subtending a branch, inflorescence or flower; also trichome, the specialized structure of hairs in ferns

schizocarp: a drupe-like fruit that divides into two or more an indehiscent carpels for dispersal

seed: the fertilized ovule of a fruit

sepal: one of the outer whorl of the perianth

serrate: a dentate margin with stiff forward-pointing teeth

sessile: not borne on a pedicel, peduncle, petiole, gynophore, etc

sheath: a tube that surrounds another part of the plant

shrub: a woody plant that has multiple stems at or near ground level; plants with DBH less than 8cm and greater than 1m (pg. 20)

silique: a capsule that divides into two carpels exposing a central column of seeds

simple: not divided

sinuate: wavy

smooth: a surface without projections

solitary: single

spadix: a dense spike of flowers of some monocotyledons

spathe: a large showy bract that encloses the spadix or other inflorescences of some monocotyledons

spathulate: shaped somewhat like a spoon or spatula

species: a population of organisms that are capable of producing fertile offspring

spike: an unbranched inflorescence with sessile flowers (cf. raceme), or the stem bearing spikelets

spikelet: ultimate branch of an inflorescence bearing flowers

sporophyte: the part of the lifecycle that produces the spores

spreading: widely separated to horizontal

stalk: stem

stamen: the male part of a plant, composed of a filament and an anther

stellate: star-shaped, often used to describe radiating branched hairs

stem: the basic supporting axis of leaves or their derivatives

sterile: not bearing fertile anthers and/or ovaries

stipule: a part of the leaf-base, usually in pairs on many plants

stolon: specialized horizontal above-ground stems rooting at the nodes

style: the stem between the ovary and the stigmas

subtended: an object joining immediately below another

superior ovary: the perianth and stamens are attached below the ovary

synonym: another name for the same species

taxon: a species, genus or any other systematic group of organisms

tepal: collective term used for petals and sepals when they are indistinguishable

terete: a solid figure, circular in cross-section with parallel sides (e.g., stems, culms, leaves and fruit)

tomentose: non-specific term for various types of hairiness

tree: a woody plant with one main stem at ground level

trichome: general term for hair-like epidermal outgrowths, but often restricted to multicellular hairs forming scales, e.g., in ferns

trifid: having three limbs or parts

trigonous: a solid figure, 3-sided in cross-section, sometimes sharply 3-angled; in this treatment used for stems, culms and fruits with three ribs

tuber: swollen part of a rhizome

tubular: a hollow tube, generally referring to the leaf-base, leaf-sheath or perianth, when united into a tube

typically adapted: normally or commonly suited to a set of environmental conditions due to some feature of its morphology, physiology or reproduction

umbel: an inflorescence or part thereof, with all the branches arising from a common point

unisexual: a flower that has only fertile male or female parts present

upland: a non-wetland at all elevations

utricle: a bladder

vascular: the vessels of a plant; the xylem and phloem

vein: strands of vascular bundles in a structure, e.g., leaf

venation: the arrangement of veins

vine: a terrestrial plant with long stems that are not self-supporting

viviparous: germinating on the parent plant

water budget: the assessment of all water inputs and outputs to a hydrologic system

weed: a plant colonizing or growing in a place where it is not wanted

whorl: a group of three or more leaves or branches arising at the same level (node) on a stem

wing: a flat structure; the lateral petals in some Fabaceae

wood: the secondary xylem of trees and shrubs; the cells produce to the inside of the vascular cambium; most of the fibrous cells in the stems of woody plants

xylem: the supporting cells that carry water in vascular plants

REFERENCES AND SELECTED READING

Baron, J.S., Poff, N.L, Angermeier, P.L., Dahm, C.N., Gleick, P.H., Hairston, N.G. Jr., Jackson, R.B., Johnston, C.A., Richter, B.D. and Steinman, A.D., 2003. Sustaining healthy freshwater ecosystems. *Issues in Ecology* **10**: 1–16.

Brinson, M.M., 1993. *A hydrogeomorphic classification for wetlands*. Wetlands Research Program Technical Report WRP-DE-4. 79p.

Brummitt, R.K. and Powell, C.E. (eds.), 1992. *Authors of plant names*. Royal Botanic Gardens, Kew, United Kingdom. 732p.

Burney, D.A., 2004. Paleoecological research and management recommendations for the Kawaihau wetland restoration, Kaua'i, Hawai'i, Department of Biological Sciences, Fordham University. Prepared in consultation with staff of the Natural Resources Conservation Service (USDA) for the Bette Midler Family Trust. p.28.

Burney, D.A., James, H.F., Burney, L.P., Olson, S.L., Kikuchi, W., Wagner, W.L., Burney, M., McCloskey, D., Kikuchi, D., Grady, F.V., Gage, R. II, and Nishek, R., 2001. Fossil evidence for a diverse biota from Kauai and its transformation since human arrival. *Ecological Monographs* **7**: 615–641.

Choi, D., Jacobs, B., Kronmal, D. and McCandless, J., 2006. *Washington's wetlands*. Washington Department of Ecology, 88-24. 14p. http://courses.washington.edu/hypertxt/cgi-bin/students.washington.edu/dlk2/english281/wetlands/final/splash.htm

Chun, M. N. (translator & ed.), 1994. *Native Hawaiian medicines*. First People's Productions, Honolulu, HI. 276p.

Collins, J.F. and Boul, S.W., 1970. Effects of fluctuations in the Eh/pH environment on iron and /or manganese equilibria. *Soil Science* **110**: 111–18

Committee on Mitigating Wetland Losses, Board on Environmental Studies and Toxicology, Water Science and Technology Board, 2001. *Compensating for wetland losses under the Clean Water Act*. National Research Council of the National Academy of Sciences. 348p.

Correll, D.S. and Correll H.B., 1975. *Aquatic and wetland plants of southwestern United States*. Stanford Univ. Press, Stanford, CA. 1777p.

Cowardin, L.M., Carter, V., Golet, F.C. and LaRoe, E.T., 1979. *Classification of wetlands and deepwater habitats of the United States*. Publ. No. FWS/OBS-79/31, U.S. Fish and Wildlife Service, Washington, DC. 103p.

Crago, L.M., Puttock, C.F. and James, S.A., 2005. *Riparian plant restoration: a management tool for restoration in Hawai'i*. CD Version 2.0. Hawai'i Department of Health and Bishop Museum, Honolulu, HI. http://hbs.bishopmuseum.org/botany/riparian/ (11 May 2005).

Cronk, J.K. and Fennessy, M.S., 2001. *Wetland plants: biology and ecology*. Lewis Publishers, Boca Raton, FL. 462p.

CTAHR, 1997. *Taro, mauka to makai: a taro production and business guide for Hawaii growers*. College of Tropical Agriculture and Human Resources, Honolulu, HI. 108p.

Dahl, T.E., 1990. *Wetlands losses in the United States 1780s to 1980s*. U.S. Department of the Interior, Fish and Wildlife Service, Washington, D.C. Jamestown, ND: Northern Prairie

Wildlife Research Center. http://www.npwrc.usgs.gov/resources/othrdata/wetloss/
wetloss.htm (16 July 1997).

eflora *Flora of China.* http://www.eflors.org/flora_page.aspx?flora_id=2

eflora *Flora of North America.* http://www.eflors.org/flora_page.aspx?flora_id=1

Elliott, M.E. and Hall, E.M., 1977. *Wetlands and wetland vegetation of Hawaii.* US Army
Corps of Engineers, Pacific Ocean Division, Fort Shafter, HI. 344p.

Engilis, A. Jr., Pyle, R.L. and David, R.E., 2004. Status and occurrence of migratory birds in
the Hawaiian Islands: Part 1 — Anseriformes: Anatidae (waterfowl). *Bishop Museum Occasional Papers* **81**: 1–28.

Englund, R.A., 2002. The loss of native biodiversity and continuing nonindigenous species
introductions in freshwater, estuarine, and wetland communities of Pearl Harbor, Oahu,
Hawaiian Islands. *Estuaries* **25**: 418–430.

Environmental Defense, 1999. *Mitigation banking as an endangered species conservation tool.*
http://www.envronmentaldefense.org/documents/146_mb.pdf

Erickson, T.E. and Shade, P., 2005. Kīhei wetlands: going going, almost gone. In: Abstracts.
2005 Hawai'i Conservation Conference. Hawai'i Conservation Alliance. p.124

GretagMacbeth, 2006. *Munsell Washable Soil Charts.* http://gretagmacbethstore.com

Herbarium Pacificum Staff, 1998. New Hawaiian plant records for 1997. *Bishop Museum Occasional Papers* **56**: 8–15.

Howarth, F. and Polhemus, D.A., 1992. A review of the Hawaiian stream insect fauna. In *New
Directions in Research, Management and Conservation of Hawaiian Freshwater Stream
Ecosystems.* Proc. 1990 Symp. on Freshwater Stream Biology and Fisheries Management.
Hawai'i Department of Land and Natural Resources, Honolulu. pp. 40–50.

Imada, C., Staples, G.W. and Herbst, D.R., 2000. New Hawaiian plant records for 1999. *Bishop
Museum Occasional Papers* **63**: 9–16.

Integrated Taxonomic Information Scheme (USDA - ITIS). http://www.itis.usda.gov

Interstate Technology and Regulatory Council, 2005. Characterization, design, construction,
and monitoring of mitigation wetlands. WTLND-2. Washington, D.C.: Interstate Technology and Regulatory Council, Mitigation Wetlands Team. http://www.irtcweb.org

King, D.M. and Price, E.W., 2004. *Developing defensible wetland mitigation ratios: a compan-
ion to the "five-step wetland mitigation ratio calculator".* University of Maryland, Center
for Environmental Science, MD. 43p.

Kosaka, E., 1990. Technical Review of Draft Report, Wetland Losses in the United States,
1780's to 1980's). U.S. Fish and Wildlife Service. (Correspondence to T. Dahl March 29,
1990)

Lesica, P. and Husby, P. 2001. Field guide to Montana's wetland vascular plants. A non-
technical key to the genera with keys to the species of sedges and rushes. Montana Wetlands Trust, MT. 92p.

Mitsch, W.J and Gosselink, J.G., 2000. *Wetlands.* 3rd edn. John Wiley & Sons, New York,
NY. p.936.

Mohlenbrock, R.H., 1989. *Midwest wetland flora: Field office illustrated guide to plant spe-*

cies. Midwest National Technical Center Lincoln, NE. USDA NRCS PLANTS Database / USDA-SCS. http://www.plants.nrcs.usda.gov

National Employment Development Center (NRCS), 2005. *Wetland restoration and enhancement.* Phase 1 – Preclass Assignment, February 2005.

Nishida, G.M., (ed.), 2002. Hawaiian Terrestrial Arthropod Checklist. 4th edn. *Bishop Museum Technical Report* No. 22. iv + 313p.

Palmer, D.D., 2003. *Hawai'i's ferns and fern allies.* University of Hawai'i Press, Honolulu, HI. ix + 234p.

Polhemus, D.A. and Asquith, A., 1996. *Hawaiian damselflies: a field identification guide.* Bishop Museum Press, Honolulu, HI. x + 122p.

Polhemus, D.A., Maciolek, J. and Ford, J., 1992. An ecosystem classification of inland waters for the tropical Pacific islands. *Micronesica* **25**: 155–173.

Poole, A. and Gill, F. (eds), 2002. *The Birds of North America.* Academy of Natural Sciences, Philadelphia. See also http//:bna.birds.cornell.edu/BNA/

Puttock, C.F. and Imada, C., 2004. Wetland Status List for Hawaiian Plants. Final report for U.S. Fish and Wildlife Service, Honolulu.

Pyle, R.L., 2002. Checklist of Hawaiian birds — 2002. *Elepaio* **63**: 137–148. http://www.hawaiiaudubon.com/checklist/checklist2002.pdf (updated 31 March 1005)

Reed, P.B. Jr., 1988. *National list of plant species that occur in wetlands. 1988 national summary.* U.S. Fish and Wildlife Service Biological Report **88**: 1–244.

Richardson, J.L. and Vepraskas, M.J. (eds.), 2000. *Wetland soils: genesis, hydrology, landscapes and classification.* Taylor & Francis. 440p.

Scholl, M., Gingerich, S., Loope, L. and Giambelluca, T., 2004. Quantifying the importance of fog drip to ecosystem hydrology and water resources in tropical montane cloud forests on East Maui, Hawaii. Venture Capital Project Final Report. USGS. http://water.usgs.gov/nrp/proj.bib/hawaii/maui_fog.htm

Smith, C.W. and Kelley, T.E., 1997. The relationship between water table depth, saturation levels, redox potential, hydric soil indicators, and vegetation in three typical Hawaiian bottomland setting. USDA NRCS Hawai'i (7/29/07 conducted under COE Hawai'i District contract) 33p.

Smith, R.D., Ammann, A., Bartlodus, C. and Brinson. M.M., 1995. An approach for assessing wetland functions using hydrogeomorphic classification, reference wetlands, and functional indices. Wetland Research Program Technical Report WRP-DE-9. U.S. Army Corp of Engineers Waterways Experiment Station. Vicksburg, MS. 90p. http://el.erdc.usace.army.mil/wetlands/pdfs/wrpde9.pdf

Society for Ecological Restoration International Science and Policy Working Group, 2004. *The SER international primer of ecological restoration.* Society for Ecological Restoration International, Tucson, AZ. http://www.ser.org. 13p.

Society of Wetland Scientists, 2004. *Wetland mitigation banking.* 3p. http://sws.gor/wetlandconcerns/banking/html.

Spjut, R.W., 1994. A systematic treatment of fruit types. *Memoirs of the New York Botanical Garden* **70**: 1–182.

Spjut, R.W., 2003. *A systematic treatment of fruit types.* http://worldbotanical.com/ fruit_types.htm (updated: Feb. 2006)

Staples, G.W. and Herbst, D.R., 2005. *A tropical garden flora: plants cultivated in the Hawaiian Islands and other tropical places.* Bishop Museum Press, Honolulu, HI. xxiv + 908p.

Stemmermann, R.L., 1981. *A guide to Pacific wetland plants.* US Army Corps of Engineers, Honolulu, HI. 118p.

Strong, M.T. and Wagner, W.L., 1997. New and noteworthy Cyperaceae from the Hawaiian Islands. *Bishop Museum Occasional Papers* **48**: 37–50.

Tiner, R.W., 1999. *Wetland indicators: a guide to wetland identification, delineation, classification, and mapping.* Lewis Publishers, Boca Raton, FL. 392p.

Tobe, J.D., Burks, K.C., Cantrell, R.W., Garland, M.A., Sweeley, M.E., Hall, D.W., Wallace, P., Anglin, G., Nelson, G., Cooper, J.R., Bickner, D., Gilbert, K., Aymond, N., Greenwood, K. and Raymond, N., 1998. *Florida wetland plants: an identification manual.* Florida Dept. Environmental Protection, Tallahassee, FL. 598p.

US Army Corps of Engineers, 1987. *U.S. Army Corps of Engineers wetlands delineation manual.* Technical Report Y-87-1. U.S. Army Corps of Engineers, Vicksburg, MS. http:// www.wetlands.com/regs/tlpge02e.htm (update: 26 May 1999)

USDA NRCS, 1972-1973. *Hawaii soil surveys geographic.* Fort Worth. hppt://.soils.usda.gov

USDA NRCS, 1999. *Soil taxonomy. A basic system of soil classification in the USA for making and interpreting soil surveys.* USDA NRCS Handbook No. 436, 2nd edn. http:// soils.usda.gov/technical/classification/taxonomy

USDA NRCS, 2003. *Field indicators of hydric soils in the United States, guide for identifying and delineating hydric soils.* Version 5.01. 40p.

USDA NRCS, 2006. *The PLANTS Database.* http://plants.usda.gov (February 2006)

USEPA, 1980. Guidelines for specification of disposal sites for dredged or fill material. *Federal Register* **45**: 85336–85357.

USEPA, 2006. *Wetlands: status and trends.* http://www.epa.gov/owow/wetlands/vital/ status.html (22 Feb. 2006)

Wagner, W.L., Herbst, D.R. and Sohmer, S.H., 1999. *Manual of the flowering plants of Hawai'i.* 2nd edn. University of Hawai'i Press and Bishop Museum Press, Honolulu, HI. xviii + 1919p.

Williams, F.X., 1936. Biological studies in Hawaiian water-loving insects. Part I. Coleoptera or beetles. Part II. Odonata or dragonflies. *Proceedings of the Hawaiian Entomological Society* **9**: 235-349.

Williams, F.X., 1939. Biological studies in Hawaiian water-loving insects. Part III. Diptera or flies. B. Asteiidae, Syrphidae, and Dolichopodidae. *Proceedings of the Hawaiian Entomological Society* **10**: 281-312.

Yamamoto, M.N. and Tagawa, A.W., 2000. *Hawai'i's native and exotic freshwater animals.* Mutual Publishing, Honolulu, HI. 200p.

Zedler, J.B. (ed.), 2000. *Handbook for restoring tidal wetlands.* CRC Press, Boca Raton, FL. 464p.

INDEX

This index includes all scientific and vernacular names used in the field guide. Page numbers with **boldface** designate the main entry for each plant species. The index also includes some key words relating to the ecology, mitigation and restoration of wetlands.

291

Where to find Wetlands in Hawai'i

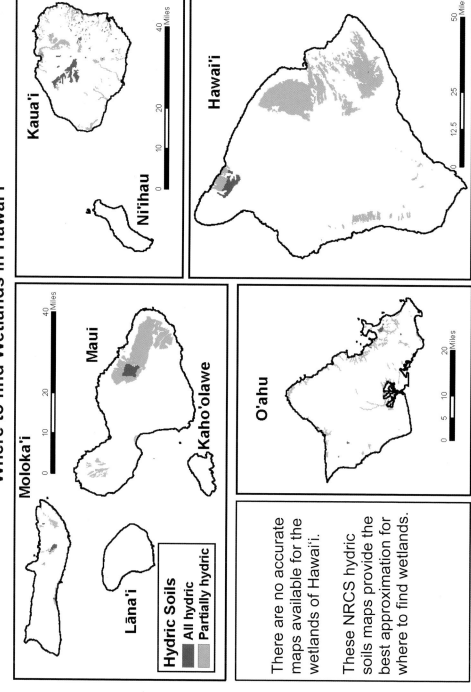

Kaua'i

Ni'ihau

Hawai'i

Moloka'i

Maui

Kaho'olawe

Lāna'i

O'ahu

Hydric Soils
- All hydric
- Partially hydric

There are no accurate maps available for the wetlands of Hawai'i.

These NRCS hydric soils maps provide the best approximation for where to find wetlands.